"Patrick Schreiner deftly integrates exegesis, biblical theology, and systematics in a work that brilliantly rescues the transfiguration from its undeserved obscurity and second-class status in both biblical studies and dogmatic theology alike. Here is a contribution to Christology that is as edifying as it is scholarly. I can only describe what he has achieved by using the same term the disciples might have used to describe Jesus's shining face: glorious!"

—**Kevin J. Vanhoozer**, Trinity Evangelical Divinity School

"Christ's transfiguration is a relatively brief scene in the Synoptics, and yet it offers a breadth of theological and exegetical potential. In this book, Patrick Schreiner helps to unlock this potential by drawing out the transfiguration's canonical, christological, and churchly significance. The result is a primer that is sure to benefit many."

—**Brandon D. Smith**, Oklahoma Baptist University; co-founder, Center for Baptist Renewal

"Jesus's transfiguration is a fountain of rich theology and a wellspring of joyous hope for contemplation. In *The Transfiguration of Christ*, Patrick Schreiner excavates treasures of glory, blessing the church with a sure guide to this momentous and oft-neglected event in the life of our Lord. His book will lead you to the summit of revelation to behold the eternal light of the Triune God in the face of Jesus Christ and the unveiling of God's infinite love for his people. Read it, and long for the beatific vision."

—**L. Michael Morales**, Greenville Presbyterian Theological Seminary

"The transfiguration: The Bible proclaims it. The church celebrates it. The Son reveals himself through it. Why, then, would we neglect it? In this fine contribution, Patrick Schreiner encourages us to gaze anew upon Jesus's glory on the mountain—his future glory as one of us and his preexistent glory as one of a kind with the Father. If you've ignored the transfiguration, you'll do so no longer. If you've loved the transfiguration, you'll come to love it still more."

—**Michael Kibbe**, Great Northern University

The Transfiguration of Christ

The Transfiguration of Christ

AN EXEGETICAL AND THEOLOGICAL READING

Patrick Schreiner

Baker Academic
a division of Baker Publishing Group
Grand Rapids, Michigan

Published by Baker Academic
a division of Baker Publishing Group
Grand Rapids, Michigan
www.bakeracademic.com

Printed in the United States of America

Library of Congress Cataloging-in-Publication Data
Names: Schreiner, Patrick, author.
Title: The transfiguration of Christ : an exegetical and theological reading / Patrick Schreiner.
Description: Grand Rapids, Michigan : Baker Academic, a division of Baker Publishing Group,
    [2024] | Includes bibliographical references and index.
Identifiers: LCCN 2023025962 | ISBN 9781540965967 (paperback) | ISBN 9781540967527
    (casebound) | ISBN 9781493445424 (ebook) | ISBN 9781493445431 (pdf)
Subjects: LCSH: Jesus Christ—Transfiguration. | Bible. New Testament—Criticism, interpretation,
    etc. | Spiritual formation—Christianity.
Classification: LCC BT410 .S37 2024 | DDC 232.9/56—dc23/eng/20230710
LC record available at https://lccn.loc.gov/2023025962

Baker Publishing Group publications use paper produced from sustainable forestry practices and post-consumer waste whenever possible.

24   25   26   27   28   29   30   7   6   5   4   3   2

To my Mom,
who always shines with Christ's light
and will one day shine even brighter
when she sees him face to face.

Come now—if you trust me—as I spread out before you a spiritual banquet of words: let us ascend with the Word today, as he goes up the high mountain of the Transfiguration.

—St. Andrew of Crete

Let us climb the mountain, and join in contemplation, and let us be changed along with him, and radiate light along with him.

—Leo the Wise

Come, let's go up to the mountain of the Lord.

—Isaiah 2:3

Contents

Abbreviations

Bible Versions

CSB   Christian Standard Bible
ESV   English Standard Version
KJV   King James Version
LXX   Septuagint

Secondary Sources

AnBib   Analecta Biblica
AJT   *American Journal of Theology*
ANF   *Ante-Nicene Fathers*
BECNT   Baker Exegetical Commentary on the New Testament
Bib   *Biblica*
BibInt   *Biblical Interpretation*
BibSac   *Bibliotheca Sacra*
BTB   *Biblical Theology Bulletin*
CBQ   *Catholic Biblical Quarterly*
CCSL   Corpus Christianorum: Series Latina
CTQ   *Concordia Theological Quarterly*
EQ   *Evangelical Quarterly*
ET   *Expository Times*
FC   Fathers of the Church
HTR   *Harvard Theological Review*
ICC   International Critical Commentary
JBL   *Journal of Biblical Literature*
JETS   *Journal of the Evangelical Theological Society*
JSNT   *Journal for the Study of the New Testament*
JTI   *Journal of Theological Interpretation*
JTS   *Journal of Theological Studies*
LCL   Loeb Classical Library

LNTS	Library of New Testament Studies
MT	*Modern Theology*
NAC	New American Commentary
NICNT	New International Commentary on the New Testament
NPNF	*Nicene and Post-Nicene Fathers*
NovT	*Novum Testamentum*
NTS	*New Testament Studies*
PG	Patrologia Graeca [= *Patrologiae Cursus Completus:* Series Graeca]
PL	Patrologia Latina [= *Patrologiae Cursus Completus:* Series Latina]
PNTC	Pillar New Testament Commentary
ProEccl	*Pro Ecclesia*
RB	*Revue biblique*
ResQ	*Restoration Quarterly*
RTP	*Revue de théologie et de philosophie*
SJT	*Scottish Journal of Theology*
SNTSMS	Society for New Testament Studies Monograph Series
TNTC	Tyndale New Testament Commentaries
TrinJ	*Trinity Journal*
TZ	*Theologische Zeitschrift*
WSA	Works of Saint Augustine
WTJ	*Westminster Theological Journal*
WUNT	Wissenschaftliche Untersuchungen zum Neuen Testament
ZECNT	Zondervan Exegetical Commentary on the New Testament
ZNW	*Zeitschrift für die neutestamentliche Wissenschaft*
ZTK	*Zeitschrift für Theologie und Kirche*
ZWT	*Zeitschrift für wissenschaftliche Theologie*

Preface

The principle of transfiguration says nothing, no one and no situation, is "untransfigurable."

—Desmond Tutu[1]

The words "transfigure" and "transform" are not used interchangeably in our English Bibles, and therefore we distinguish them in our Christian vocabulary. "Transfigure" refers to what happened to Jesus on the mountain, while "transform" is employed for the spiritual change Christians undergo in Christ. However, the Greek term behind both is the same: *metamorphoō*.

We do employ the Greek word in English but not so much in the religious sense. The sciences have taken it over. When we hear the word, we probably think of the organic development in insects and other animals.[2] From a scientific perspective, metamorphosis is the process of transformation from an immature form to an adult form. A butterfly "morphs" from an egg to a caterpillar to a chrysalis to a butterfly. "Metamorphosis" refers to physical change.

However, in the ancient world, the term had a resilient religious dimension. Two Roman writers even composed works with the term in their titles.[3] It was

---

1. Desmond Tutu, *God Has a Dream: A Vision of Hope for Our Time* (New York: Doubleday, 2004), 3.

2. The word "transfiguration" might make modern people think of the classes Harry, Ron, and Hermione attended at Hogwarts with Professor McGonagall.

3. Ovid, *Metamorphoses*, trans. David Raeburn (London: Penguin Classics, 2004); Apuleius, *The Golden Ass: The Transformations of Lucius*, trans. Robert Graves (New York: Farrar, Straus and Giroux, 2009). Ovid's work is a lengthy poem concerning the history of the world up to the death of Julius Caesar, wherein he describes Caesar's deification. Lucius Apuleius's work is

used of gods who temporarily assumed human or animal form and of humans who were changed into animals or gods.

In this book I will attempt to recover this religious use. For Christians, "metamorphosis" refers both to the physical unveiling of Jesus on the mountain (Matt. 17:2; Mark 9:2) and to the change that progressively occurs in Christians (Rom. 12:2; 2 Cor. 3:18) as we behold "God's glory in the face of Jesus Christ" (2 Cor. 4:6) and eventually "see him as he is" (1 John 3:2).

The relationship between Jesus's metamorphosis and our own metamorphosis is essential. In Jesus's metamorphosis we see "how the divine can penetrate the human without destroying it." In our metamorphosis we see "how the human can be conformed to the divine without ceasing to be human."[4]

As you begin this journey up the mountain with me, I want to note the structure of this book, as it may vex some. Those who come to this book for biblical theology might be irritated by the dogmatic sections, and those who come for the dogmatic parts might be confused by the spiritual formation sections.

Apart from authorial incompetence—perhaps a justified accusation!—one possible source of this discomfort may be our tendency to read the Scriptures one-dimensionally. We are taught to read in one mode and are tempted to think that our way is superior to those of our fellow travelers. To put this in the words of Paul, we tend to think we are the interpretive all-seeing eye that says to the foot, "We have no need for you!" But this is not how most Christians have read the Bible over the centuries. It is a lamentable development.

The body of this book (chapters 2, 3, and 4) is written to intentionally confront this one-dimensional reading. In it, I place side by side three subjects that are sometimes divorced.

First, I will develop a theological grammar for how to speak about different aspects of the transfiguration. There are dogmatic rules for exegesis—hermeneutical, trinitarian, and christological—that enlighten rather than suppress interpretation. Presuppositions rooted in the Scriptures and in Christian tradition are our friends, not our foes. I am increasingly convinced that one cannot understand the depth of the transfiguration without the aid of dogmatic categories.

In fact, we might say the transfiguration functions as a "revealing test of an exegete's presuppositions and methodology."[5] As G. B. Caird writes, "The

---

a novel about a man being turned into a donkey before being returned to a human form by the Egyptian goddess Isis.

4. Hywel R. Jones, *Transfiguration and Transformation* (Edinburgh: Banner of Truth, 2021), xvi.

5. W. L. Liefeld, "Theological Motifs in the Transfiguration Narrative," in *New Dimensions in New Testament Study*, ed. R. N. Longenecker and M. C. Tenney (Grand Rapids: Zondervan, 1974), 163.

transfiguration is at once the commentator's paradise and his despair."[6] Classical doctrines of the Trinity and Christology function as "a well-stocked keychain that can open exegetical doors" that otherwise have remained shut in accordance with modern exegetical conventions.[7]

R. B. Jamieson and Tyler Wittman are right to distinguish between extrinsic and intrinsic rules for exegesis. Extrinsic rules are imposed from without, while intrinsic rules are derived from the material itself. My grammar will intentionally be intrinsic, being derived from Scripture and therefore regulating our reading of Scripture.[8] Hermeneutical, trinitarian, and christological grammars are resources that help enable better exegesis rather than projections forced onto texts.

Second, I will trace the themes of the transfiguration through the storyline of Scripture. Jesus's transfiguration on the mountaintop draws together various biblical narratives into one vibrant image. It is a verbal icon that fuses storylines like an intertextual tapestry. Key events like Adam's glory in the garden, Israel's exodus from Egypt, Moses's visions, and Elijah's ministry foreshadow the transfiguration. These events need to be connected to render a full picture of the meaning.

If systematic theology draws a circle around Scripture, then biblical theology draws a line through it.[9] Or using another metaphor, Michael Horton compares the different approaches to different kinds of maps. If systematic theology is more like a street map, in that it points out the logical connections between various doctrines spread throughout Scripture, then biblical theology is a topographical map that traces the terrain, development, and evolution.[10]

The transfiguration needs to be viewed in terms of both its connection to the major thoroughfares of Scripture and its topography—in relation to both doctrines and the storyline. Jesus's transformation is part of the Bible's story; we would be imprudent to neglect the events that prefigured it. But we will also fall short, and risk unassumingly adopting unorthodox beliefs, if we turn a blind eye to orthodox trinitarian and christological doctrines, which give us guardrails for thinking about Jesus's transformation and which help us articulate what Peter could not (Matt. 17:4; Mark 9:5–6; Luke 9:33).

Finally, I will end chapters 2, 3, and 4 with brief reflections on our own transfiguration or *metamorphōsis*. Jesus's transfiguration is not an impractical or

---

6. George B. Caird, "Expository Problems: The Transfiguration," *ET* 67, no. 10 (1956): 291.

7. R. B. Jamieson and Tyler R. Wittman, *Biblical Reasoning: Trinitarian and Christological Rules for Exegesis* (Grand Rapids: Baker Academic, 2022), xxii.

8. Jamieson and Wittman, *Biblical Reasoning*, xxi–xxii.

9. Geerhardus Vos, *Biblical Theology: Old and New Testaments* (Edinburgh: Banner of Truth, 1975), 15–16.

10. Michael Horton, *The Christian Faith: A Systematic Theology for Pilgrims on the Way* (Grand Rapids: Zondervan Academic, 2011), 29.

ethereal event. It calls for participation, for action. Shining atop the mountain is our future, for "we will all be changed" (1 Cor. 15:51). The transfigured Christ is the hope of the church.

Too often we do the work of biblical and systematic theology and think our task is done. But in doing this, we have only started our journey. The most important undertaking is to ask how this forms us into the image of Christ, how we can progress in sanctification, and how we become "partakers of the divine nature" (2 Pet. 1:4 ESV).

The stages of spiritual formation have been labeled by some throughout church history as *purgation, illumination,* and *union.*[11] These stages move us from separation from God to a transfigural relationship with God and fit particularly well with the transfiguration narrative. If we do not meditate on how we are transfigured, then we really have missed the point. The transfiguration is "a pledge of the perfectibility of the human person."[12]

———

I began thinking more earnestly about the transfiguration on spring break in March of 2022. Our family traveled to Washington and Oregon for some speaking engagements. There I read my first book on the subject, *Light on the Mountain,* edited and translated by Brian Daley. It remains to me the best book on the transfiguration and the place I would recommend everyone start. In fact, the richness of the patristic commentary in this work is such that a preacher could skip all modern commentaries in sermon preparation and simply read those homilies. They without a doubt display the superiority of precritical exegesis. I only hope this book follows in their footsteps.

In Washington we were allowed to stay at the Bachman-Turner Overdrive mansion in Lynden. (Bachman-Turner Overdrive is famous for the songs "Takin' Care of Business" and "You Ain't Seen Nothing Yet.") My five-year-old, Canaan, will sometimes ask when we can stay at a mansion with a pool inside the house again. I will fondly remember reading homilies and then jumping in the pool with the kids.

I turned in the first draft of this book in February of 2023, during my sabbatical from Midwestern Baptist Theological Seminary. Thank you to all who read the manuscript and helped to improve it. Quinn Mosier and Tom Schreiner were the first to see the document, and they pointed out places where my argument wasn't clear, where I had over-argued, and where I had uncritically adapted

---

11. These stages are attributed to Pseudo-Dionysius, Thomas Aquinas, and St. John of the Cross.

12. Dale M. Coulter, "The Taboric Light," *First Things* (blog), August 15, 2014, https://www.firstthings.com/blogs/firstthoughts/2014/08/the-taboric-light.

Eastern Orthodox terminology. Quinn also helped me with the bibliography. Mike Kibbe kindly sent me many of his resources on the transfiguration, including those by John Gatta, and provided significant feedback.

Sam Parkison read an early version and was an interlocutor on the beatific vision. Kevin Vanhoozer, who was working on his own book on how the transfiguration informs hermeneutics, offered helpful feedback. Chad Ashby helped me improve my writing mechanics and made exegetical recommendations. He took the fluff out of much of the manuscript, reducing the word count by close to twenty-thousand words. Bryan Dyer encouraged me to shorten the book and to make sure I wasn't trying to do too much. I put the finishing touches on the manuscript during my stay at Tyndale House in Cambridge, England, in June 2023.

Most of my early readers recommended that I abandon the term "allegory" in favor of "spiritual reading." They are probably right, but this was a difficult step for me to make because "allegory" was the term of the early church. Vanhoozer said the term is likely beyond redemption. Yet all can be saved.

The soundtrack for this book includes Steffany Gretzinger, Jensen McRae, Novo Amor, Bonny Light Horseman, and the Wanderlust playlist.

My gratitude also goes to Thou Mayest and Rochester, two downtown Kansas City coffee shops where I wrote significant portions of this book. Their atmospheres were perfect for writing. I fine-tuned the book in my new home office during my sabbatical.

I'm also appreciative of Midwestern Baptist Theological Seminary, President Jason Allen, and Provost Jason Duesing for granting me a sabbatical in 2022–23 to work on this book and other projects. In a turbulent time in higher education, their constant support, generosity, and outlook for the good of God's people is unique. They make decisions for the long-term good rather than having only temporary goals. This perspective ought to be emulated by other institutions.

Introduction

A Two-Level Christology

Now, Father, glorify me in your presence with that glory I had
with you before the world existed.

–John 17:5

I t is a truth universally acknowledged that the Western church has overlooked
the transfiguration.

However, the Eastern tradition has consistently put the transfiguration front
and center. The Feast of the Transfiguration (August 6) continues to loom large
on the church calendar. In the Western tradition, this day passes by unsung,
unhonored, unacknowledged.[1] Consider: How many sermons have you heard
on the transfiguration? How many songs do you know that sing about the transfiguration? The transfiguration is a curiosity in want of practical significance.

The lack of work done on the transfiguration became apparent when I started
research for this book. I went to my school's library and perused the "Jesus"
section. Books abounded on the historical Jesus, his birth, his death, and his
resurrection. Only three books on Jesus's transfiguration sat on the shelves. N. T.
Wright's 741-page work on Jesus mentions the transfiguration only once, and

1. In the Anglican tradition, the Feast of the Transfiguration disappeared from the 1549 Book
of Common Prayer and then reappeared on the calendar in 1662 without any other provisions.
From 1474 until at least 1969, the Feast was observed in the Roman Catholic Church on the Second
Sunday of Lent. In some modern calendars the transfiguration is now commemorated on the last
Sunday in the season of Epiphany—the Sunday immediately before Ash Wednesday. This last
date is an appropriate time to celebrate the transfiguration because this event marked a transition
in Jesus's ministry when he "set his face to go to Jerusalem" (Luke 9:51 ESV).

somewhat apologetically in passing.[2] It is difficult to find any significant comment on it in the standard systematic theologies. Maybe some modern scholars have shunned it because they are suspicious of the supernatural.

Maybe scholars have also neglected it because we don't know what to do with it. We have become like Peter, befuddled (Mark 9:6). It seems like an unimpressive magic trick: a shining person who does the disciples little practical good. Jesus's other miracles make sense—feeding people, healing them, and raising the dead—but the transfiguration is confusing. One author begins his book by stating, "It has not been found easy to give a satisfying interpretation of the transfiguration story."[3] Another mentions how many get lost in the maze of scholarly speculations.[4]

If I were to ask you what difference it would make if Jesus had not died on the cross or been raised from the dead, the answer would come quite quickly. But what if Jesus had not been transfigured? An answer to that question is not so forthcoming. This is not to assert that the transfiguration deserves the same prominence as the cross or the resurrection, but it does reveal how little attention we give it. Would the story of Jesus be any different if the transfiguration hadn't happened? Or to put it another way, would your reading of the Scriptures change at all if you "Thomas Jeffersoned" the transfiguration out of the Bible?[5]

I'm afraid these questions are harder to answer. This might be because we don't think the transfiguration is central to the gospel or reveals anything unique about Jesus's identity. We assume that the salvation of humankind could have been accomplished without it and that other texts resource our Christology. Because of this, the transfiguration has had little impact on our reading of the Scriptures.

However, the transfiguration is one of those events we can never seem to plumb the depths of. The simplicity of the story conceals it profundities. It leaves its fingerprints on every major doctrine: the Trinity, Christology, anthropology, soteriology, and eschatology. The light of the transfiguration refracts over all these core beliefs.

The transfiguration is a revelatory tour de force. It brings the past into unison with the present. The one who said "Let there be light" is now shrouded

---

2. N. T. Wright, *Jesus and the Victory of God* (London: SPCK, 1996), 650. Larry Hurtado's *Lord Jesus Christ* (Grand Rapids: Eerdmans, 2005) is similar (263, 333).

3. G. H. Boobyer, *St. Mark and the Transfiguration Story* (Edinburgh: T&T Clark, 1942), viii.

4. Allison Trites, *The Transfiguration of Christ: A Hinge of Holy History* (Hantsport, Nova Scotia: Lancelot, 1994), 11.

5. Thomas Jefferson is famous for having produced an edition of the Gospel records with the miraculous events edited out.

in light. It is a microcosm of the gospel.[6] It reveals the great mystery of Christianity, the uniqueness of Jesus. As one scholar states, in the transfiguration "the diverse elements in the theology of the New Testament meet."[7] However, both systematic and biblical theologians have still largely ignored this event in their writings.

This book is an attempt to raise the profile of the transfiguration in the Western tradition. I will do so by examining this event from three main perspectives: (1) the glorious setting, (2) the glorious signs, and (3) the glorious saying.

As one can see, the concept of *glory* is key. The English name for the event is "the transfiguration," in reference to the Greek term *metamorphoō* and the Latin *transfiguratus*. However, the significance of the event may be better expressed by its German name: *die Verklärung*—the glorification.[8] Though only Luke employs the word "glory" in his transfiguration account, both Matthew's and Mark's accounts radiate with glory. In addition, when Peter retells the event in his second epistle, he says that Jesus "received *honor* and *glory* from God the Father when the voice came to him from the Majestic *Glory*" (2 Pet. 1:17).[9] Glory is an important concept for the transfiguration, maybe even *the* fundamental concept.

In this introduction I will offer a brief refresher on the transfiguration and then examine the *what* and the *why*: What happened in the transfiguration? And why did the transfiguration occur?

A Refresher on the Transfiguration

"The transfiguration" refers to Jesus's trip up on the mountain with three of his disciples where his figure was transformed: his face shone, his clothes turned bright white, Moses and Elijah appeared alongside him, and a voice came from heaven declaring that Jesus is God's beloved Son.

This event is recounted in full in Matthew 17:1–8, Mark 9:2–8, and Luke 9:28–36 and briefly in 2 Peter 1:17–18. The word "transfigured" (*metamorphoō*) occurs only four times in the New Testament (Matt. 17:2; Mark 9:2; Rom. 12:2; and 2 Cor. 3:18).

6. As in the subtitle of Allison Trites, "The Transfiguration of Jesus: The Gospel in Microcosm," *EQ* 51, no. 2 (1979): 67–79.

7. Arthur Michael Ramsey, *The Glory of God and the Transfiguration of Christ* (Eugene, OR: Wipf & Stock, 2009), 144.

8. Ramsey, *Glory of God*, 101.

9. I will be using the CSB as my standard English translation and will have a note if I deviate or provide my own translation. It is my favorite translation, and my dad was one of the editors, so he forced me to like it.

The transfiguration takes place at the conclusion of Jesus's Galilean ministry, just before Jesus heads toward Jerusalem. It occurs a week after Peter confessed that Jesus is the Messiah, and it fulfills the prophecy that "there are some standing here who will not taste death until they see the kingdom of God come in power" (Mark 9:1; see also Matt. 16:28; Luke 9:27).

The Synoptic Gospels' accounts of what took place on the mount are extraordinarily parallel. While there are differences in the resurrection and crucifixion stories, in stories about Jesus's healings, and in his teachings, the transfiguration seems to have been largely "tamper-proof" in the memories of Jesus's followers. In other words, it had a big impact on them—a bigger impact than it has had on us.

The Synoptic accounts agree on all the essential details: Jesus goes up the mountain and takes with him Peter, James, and John. A glorious transformation of his physical appearance takes place. Moses and Elijah appear next to Jesus, and they engage in conversation. Peter responds by saying it is good they are there and offers to build three tents. A cloud overshadows them, and a voice from the cloud says, "This is my beloved Son; listen to him!" (Mark 9:2; see also Matt. 19:5; Luke 9:35). After this, the disciples see only Jesus. As they come down the mountain, Jesus charges them to tell no one what they have seen until he has been raised from the dead.

While the storytelling is remarkably consistent, minor differences exist in the stories that fill out the picture. I will discuss these differences as the book proceeds. But here this question arises: How are we to understand the meaning (the what) and significance (the why) of this event?

The What: Jesus's Double Sonship

My basic assertion in this book is this: *The transfiguration reveals Jesus's double sonship.*[10] In the transfiguration, both *the future glory of the earthly and suffering messianic Son* and *the preexistent glory of the heavenly and eternally begotten Son* are revealed.

Understood this way, this mountaintop revelation might be the clearest narrative picture we have of the two natures of Christ in one person—possibly a key resource for the early church in articulating Jesus's ontology.[11]

---

10. The rest of the book will further explain this language of "double sonship." See especially the christological grammar in chap. 4. I'm affirming not two Sons but two natures in one person. Additionally, the argument for double sonship is found not in a solitary detail but in the coalition of setting, signs, and sayings.

11. The author of Hebrews affirms that Jesus is the "radiance of God's glory" (Heb. 1:3), and the Nicene Creed confesses that Jesus is "Light from Light."

The transfiguration is both forward looking and backward looking, both anticipation and retrospection, both expectation and recognition. Jesus's proleptic and preexistent glory are inseparable. In fact, they can't be divorced. Jesus could only be the faithful Messiah and receive glory from the Father because this glory was already his. The future glory of the messianic Son is grounded in his eternally begotten nature.

This argument might seem uncontroversial to confessional Christians.[12] When I recounted my thesis to one student, the student replied, "Are you carving new ground? Or do most people already think that?" That's a fair question. In response, I say that one major consideration should be kept mind: this book contradicts the predominant modern scholarly view that the Synoptic Gospels don't support Jesus's preexistence and that the transfiguration is *only* a preview of the messianic glory to come.[13] Such a view reserves high Christology for John's Gospel on the presumption that it was written much later when the church was still developing its beliefs.

I'm afraid that confessing Christians have also imported these misunderstandings about Christology into their readings of the transfiguration. Scholars only see Jesus's earthly mission in the transfiguration; people in the church only see Jesus's divinity. Neither connect the two. I will contend that both have insufficiently scrutinized the transfiguration.

James Dunn is representative of the modern scholarly view when he asserts that in the transfiguration there is "no thought of pre-existence."[14] Dunn supports this argument with three points:

First, the Gospels saw the episode as foreshadowing Jesus's resurrection and exaltation.

Second, Jesus's transformation and the cloud recalls the glorification of Moses.

Third, the dazzling white garments are typical of heavenly beings, including the glorified saints.

Dunn concludes, "There is certainly nothing like a clear allusion to pre-existent glory here, and probably no implication of incarnation at all."[15]

12. F. W. Beare (*The Earliest Records of Jesus* [Nashville: Abingdon, 1962], 141) is right when he says there is probably no other passage in the Gospels that has received such divergent interpretations as the story of the transfiguration.

13. This view finds its presuppositions about the early church in the work of Walter Bauer and the Bauer thesis, which claims there were competing views of orthodoxy in the early church. See Bauer, *Orthodoxy and Heresy in Earliest Christianity* (Mifflintown, PA: Sigler, 1996).

14. James Dunn, *Christology in the Making: A New Testament Inquiry into the Origins of the Doctrine of the Incarnation* (Philadelphia: Westminster, 1980), 47. Boobyer (*St. Mark and the Transfiguration Story*, 66) affirms that the story is more likely anticipation than retrospection.

15. Dunn, *Christology in the Making*, 48.

Dunn is not alone. Mark Stein notes that people view the transfiguration as either a sign of the preincarnate glory of Christ *or* a proleptic glimpse of the glory of the Son of Man in his future coming. Stein concludes, "Nothing in the account suggests that Jesus possessed before the transfiguration a hidden glory that was veiled up to this point."[16] John Paul Heil argues that the transfiguration describes Jesus's "external, proleptic, and temporary transformation by God into a heavenly being while still on earth."[17] More pointedly, he states that the transfiguration *does not* support interpretations that speak in terms of an unveiling, disclosure, or revelation of a glory that Jesus already possesses. Later he says it is not "an internal self-transformation but an external transformation effected by God."[18]

The same comments are standard for the transfiguration account in 2 Peter 1:16–18. Peter H. Davids emphasizes the reception aspect of the transfiguration when he writes, "For 2 Peter the point of the Transfiguration is not that the divinity or glory of Jesus was revealed, but that 'he received honor and glory from God the Father.'"[19]

Even those arguing for early high Christology have not fully considered the implications of the transfiguration. Larry Hurtado, who recognizes an early "devotional pattern" toward Jesus, underplays preexistence as the basis for worship.[20]

16. Mark Stein, *Mark*, BECNT (Grand Rapids: Baker Academic, 2008), 417. David E. Garland (*Luke*, ZECNT [Grand Rapids: Zondervan Academic, 2011], 384) is similar to Stein when he states that the transfiguration is a preview of Jesus's eternal glory. R. T. France (*The Gospel of Matthew*, NICNT [Grand Rapids: Eerdmans, 2007], 641–51) mainly speaks of how Jesus is the new Moses.

17. John Paul Heil, *The Transfiguration of Jesus: Narrative Meaning and Function of Mark 9:2–8, Matt 17:1–8 and Luke 9:28–36*, AnBib 144 (Rome: Pontifical Biblical Institute, 2000), 76.

18. Heil, *Transfiguration of Jesus*, 92. J. R. Daniel Kirk (*A Man Attested by God: The Human Jesus of the Synoptic Gospels* [Grand Rapids: Eerdmans, 2016], 191–99) argues Jesus is an idealized and glorified human figure who is not endowed with his native glory but instead reflects the glory of his father. Dilbert Burkett ("The Transfiguration of Jesus (Mark 9:2–8): Epiphany or Apotheosis?," *JBL* 138, no. 2 [2019]: 413–32) claims that the transfiguration in Mark is an apotheosis, not an epiphany: Mark's Jesus is not a god who becomes man but a man who becomes God.

19. Peter H. Davids, *The Letters of 2 Peter and Jude*, PNTC (Grand Rapids: Eerdmans, 2006), 202. Michael Green (*2 Peter and Jude: An Introduction and Commentary*, TNTC [Downers Grove, IL: IVP Academic, 2009], 104–5) makes a similar assessment when he writes, "Notice how Jesus is said to receive honour and glory from God the Father. What a contrast to the supposed Hellenistic *theios anēr* (divine man). It shows how far off the mark Ernst Käsemann was in supposing that 2 Peter saw the transfiguration as an epiphany of Jesus' hidden divinity. In line with primitive Christian understanding, Jesus is given divine glory because he is appointed to the task of carrying out God's salvation and judgment." Thomas Schreiner (*1, 2 Peter, Jude*, NAC 37 [Nashville: B&H, 2003], 314) is unique in affirming that "the word 'majesty' (*megaleiotēs*) in this context points to the deity of Jesus Christ ([2 Pet.] 1:1; of God—Luke 9:43; Jer 40:9 LXX; 1 Esdr 4:40), though the term 'majesty' does not necessarily signify deity (1 Esdr 4:40)."

20. Larry W. Hurtado, *One God, One Lord: Early Christian Devotion and Ancient Jewish Monotheism* (New York: T&T Clark, 2015).

Rather, he says that Jesus was worshiped because of what he became: the risen, exalted, and glorified Christ.[21] In essence, Hurtado and others say there was no worship of Jesus of Nazareth during his earthly life. The apostle Paul might make statements about Jesus's preexistence and the worship of Jesus, but the Synoptics are uncommunicative on this front.

This book asserts that they are wrong—or at least half-wrong. The transfiguration is both an indication of what is to come *and* an unveiling of what was—a preview of future glory *and* a sign of preexistence. It's both/and. The two parts are in fact logically related, and they are also ordered.[22] Jesus's transfiguration is grounded in his nature. I don't think we can truly understand the transfiguration unless we understand both of these realities.[23] Typically, we focus on either Jesus's earthly mission or his divine nature to the exclusion of the other: the transfiguration is either about Jesus being divine (as the early church confessed) or about his future glorified body (as modern commentators argue).[24] However, the transfiguration is about both. Jesus is a cosmic figure *and* the historical Jesus of Nazareth.

The transfiguration thus concerns how Jesus is both man and God, where God's work *ad intra* and *ad extra* meet. It tells us who the Son *is* and who he *will be*. It speaks of the Son in terms of his ontology and his mission. We must distinguish without dividing the Son's divinity and his humanity. Some biblical

21. Hurtado defends his case by saying that he does not deny preexistence but examines the historical impetus and basis for Jesus-devotion (Larry W. Hurtado, "The Origins of Jesus-Devotion: A Response to Crispin Fletcher-Louis," *Tyndale Bulletin* 61, no. 1 [2010]: 5; see also Crispin Fletcher-Louis, *Jesus Monotheism*, vol. 1, *Christological Origins: The Emerging Consensus and Beyond* [Eugene, OR: Cascade Books, 2015], 65–88). Richard Bauckham (*Jesus and the God of Israel: God Crucified and Other Studies on the New Testament's Christology of Divine Identity* [Grand Rapids: Eerdmans, 2008]) does believe the Synoptics accord to Jesus divine identity during his earthly life, but he is also less interested in the incarnation and puts the focus on the risen and exalted Christ.

22. Some might rightly wonder if a "future glory" necessarily implies a "past glory" since angels have glory, humanity will be transformed, and so will the earth. However, the future glory of created realities stems from participation in the glory of God. It is from being united with or related to God that these other creatures derive their glory.

23. The apocryphal Acts of John and Acts of Peter both interpret the transfiguration as a theophany.

24. Some modern commentators speak of both Jesus's eternal glory and his future glory. D. A. Carson ("Matthew," in *The Expositor's Bible Commentary*, vol. 9, *Matthew and Mark*, rev. ed. [Grand Rapids: Zondervan, 2010], 437) says the disciples saw a glimpse of Jesus's preincarnate glory *and* anticipated his coming exaltation. James R. Edwards (*The Gospel according to Mark*, PNTC [Grand Rapids: Eerdmans, 2001], 261–71) affirms that the disciples see Jesus's true nature in the transfiguration but proceeds to affirm that it is mainly an *anticipation* of Jesus's future glory. John Chrysostom (*Homily 21* [PG 63:700]) is representative of the early church when he says that, in the transfiguration, Jesus "opened out a little of the godhead and showed them the indwelling God."

texts speak more about Jesus's nature before time (theologize); other texts speak about Jesus's work in salvation history (economize). In the transfiguration texts, the Father's voice affirms the double sonship of Jesus. Jesus's appearance in human flesh and divine personhood mode are hypostatically linked in the transfiguration. Jesus's *humanity* is transfigured, and his *deity* is revealed. The light on the mount discloses what he always was *and* what he was to become. The eternal God did not lay aside his deity when he became man. The humanity of Christ didn't suppress his deity, and his deity didn't suppress his humanity. It freed it, liberated it, enhanced it.

A verse in John's Gospel expresses the argument of this book in short: "Now, Father, glorify me in your presence with the glory I had with you before the world existed" (John 17:5). Jesus affirms his own double glory in this verse, his light before time and in time. Jesus asks to be glorified (in the future) with the glory he has always possessed (from the past and in the present).

This is precisely what takes place in the transfiguration: the Father glorifies the Son with the same glory the Son always possessed.[25] Inasmuch as he was God, Jesus displayed his inherent glory. Inasmuch as he was man, Jesus received glory from the Father.

The Why: Hope by Revelation

The transfiguration reveals the double sonship of Jesus, but for what purpose? Why didn't Jesus show the disciples his future glory earlier? Why did he choose to show it to only three of them? And how does the event fit into Jesus's progressive revelation through his actions and miracles? These questions all pertain to the narrative placement of the transfiguration.

The transfiguration must be interpreted in the context of the immediate narrative, the gospel story, and the Scriptures as a whole. What we usually fail to recognize is that it also needs to be interpreted in the cosmic story of God's internal life. The context of this event goes beyond Matthew, Mark, Luke, and even the Scriptures as whole. It must also go back to before time.

Let's first begin with the immediate context of the Synoptics. Thankfully, all the Synoptics have largely the same framework for this scene. The setting of the transfiguration can be outlined in the following way.

---

25. One can also look at the transfiguration through the prophet-priest-king lens: As the prophet, Jesus speaks with a voice that must be heeded. As the priest, Jesus radiates with light as the true mediator who is about to perform an offering. As the king, he not only radiates majestic glory but gives gifts of glory.

Pericope	Matthew	Mark	Luke
Peter's confession	16:13–20	8:27–30	9:18–21
passion prediction	16:21–23	8:31–33	9:22
"Take up your cross"	16:24–28	8:34–9:1	9:23–27
The transfiguration	**17:1–8**	**9:2–8**	**9:28–36**
the coming of Elijah	17:9–13	9:9–13	
failed healing	17:14–20	9:14–29	9:37–43a
passion prediction	17:22–23	9:30–32	9:43b–45
paying taxes	17:24–27		
"Who is the greatest?"	18:1–5	9:33–37	9:46–48

Four realities should be observed. First, *the transfiguration confirms Peter's confession but also goes beyond it.* All the Synoptics place the transfiguration in the orbit of Peter's confession at Caesarea Philippi. The reason is that the transfiguration confirms Peter's confession that Jesus is the Messiah of Israel, but it also uncovers more.[26]

The narrative moves from Peter confessing Jesus as the Messiah to Jesus referring to himself as the Son of Man and finally to the Father declaring him to be the Son of God. The Father's voice presses deepest into Jesus's identity. Jesus is more than Israel's Messiah; he is the one true God of Israel. He is the Son whom the Father made a pact with before time.

In this sense, the transfiguration is both about the future glory of Jesus and about Jesus's glory that he always possessed. It moves beyond Peter's confession, even though Peter's confession has received much more attention from commentators. Maybe this is why our Christology has not been as precise as it needs to be.

Second, *the transfiguration provides hope and encouragement.* The surrounding narrative is rife with affliction and death. Prophecies of Jesus's impending death and of disorder on the earth bookend the transfiguration narrative. Within the narrative itself, Jesus speaks of his exodus. Before the narrative, after Peter confesses Jesus as the Messiah, Jesus "began to point out to his disciples that it was necessary for him to go to Jerusalem and suffer many things from the elders, chief priests, and scribes, be killed, and be raised the third day" (Matt.

---

26. Only in Matthew does Peter add to Jesus being the Messiah that he is the "Son of the living God" (16:16). Whether this phrase is synonymous with "Messiah" or goes beyond Jesus's messianic status is a matter of debate. My reading is that Peter didn't mean it in the trinitarian sense initially, but when Matthew recorded the words he realized there was a deeper sense of sonship.

16:21; see also Mark 8:31; Luke 9:22). All the disciples hear is that Jesus will suffer and die. After the transfiguration narrative is the account of a convulsing child, a picture of cosmic degradation. As Gatta notes, "The transfiguration is thus a glory bounded by affliction."[27]

The transfiguration is a glimpse of glory so that the disciples won't despair. The story confronts the world's disfigurement as a bright eruption bursts through dark forecasts. It reveals what will happen when death has been swallowed up and there is nothing left except glory. The lines from Tolkien concerning Aragorn, the future king, are applicable to Jesus.

> From the ashes a fire shall be woken,
> A light from the shadows shall spring;
> Renewed shall be blade that was broken,
> The crownless again shall be king.[28]

Jesus arms his disciples against the coming disgrace of his death. The transfiguration's primary aim is to give *paraklēsis* (encouragement, comfort, and hope). As Timothy of Antioch says, in the transfiguration Jesus "did not leave his disciples swimming in the tidal wave of unbelief. Rather, he quickly brought them certainty. . . . [He] revealed to them the divine power of the resurrection."[29] Jesus was so alive in God and to God that death could not overcome him.

The transfiguration is like the Phial of Galadriel given to Frodo to aid him when all other lights go dark: it is the brightest of stars. The reaction of the disciples on the mountain is akin to Frodo's cry in the darkness: "*Aiya Eärendil elenion ancalima!*" (Hail Eärendil, brightest of stars!).[30] Death itself must be taken up into the metamorphic process of light. Light will carry on endlessly, even after death.

Third, *the disciples show that they have not been transformed by their experience, indicating that further metamorphosis is necessary.* The transfiguration is a vision of the future, not its instantiation. Peter makes a fool of himself on the mountain, the other disciples fail at a healing when they come down the mountain, and they argue over who is the greatest as they leave the mountain. Though

---

27. John Gatta, "The Transfiguration of Christ and Cosmos: A Focal Point of Literary Imagination," *Sewanee Theological Review* 49, no. 4 (2006): 489.

28. J. R. R. Tolkien, *The Lord of the Rings*, vol. 1, *The Fellowship of the Ring* (New York: Ballantine Books, 1965), 231.

29. Timothy of Antioch, "Homily on the Cross and Transfiguration," in *Light on the Mountain: Greek Patristic and Byzantine Homilies on the Transfiguration of the Lord*, trans. Brian Daley, Popular Patristics 48 (New York: St. Vladimir's Seminary Press, 2013), 149.

30. J. R. R. Tolkien, *The Lord of the Rings*, vol. 2, *The Two Towers* (1954; repr., New York: HarperCollins, 2012), 720.

the light has come, the darkness still resides. The new era is not here in full; we must press on toward the light.

This reality is emphasized especially in Matthew's account. When Christ's light fades, darkness settles over the world. On the mountain Jesus's face shines like the sun, but when Jesus and the disciples come down the mountain they find a boy who is "moonstruck" (Matt. 17:15).[31] Most translations simply say he has "seizures" or is an "epileptic." However, the Greek word behind it is *selēniazetai*, from *selēnē* (moon). In the ancient world, an epileptic seizure was associated with the transcendent powers of the moon. In the Christian view, Jesus came as the sonlight to heal those struck by the moon's darkness (see 4:24).

This reality is further highlighted as the descent from the mountain is filled will allusions to the rebellion when Moses descended Mount Sinai. In Luke's version he notes that the demon throws the boy down and "shatters" him (Luke 9:39, my trans.). This is the same verb that describes the shattering of the tablets when Moses casts them to the ground (Exod. 32:19). Jesus calls them a perverse generation who have no faith (Matt. 17:17; Mark 9:19; Luke 9:41), a phrase that recalls Israel's disobedience in the wilderness (Exod. 16:28; Num. 14:11, 27).[32]

The purpose of the transfiguration, therefore, is not only to behold the glory of God through Christ the Son but also to be transformed *by beholding*. In beholding Christ, we are conformed to the divine image without ceasing to be human. David Bentley Hart puts it well when he says, "And so the icon [the transfiguration] is at once a revelation of God made man, and all of us made god in Him. In it, we see how the kenosis of the eternal Son—His self-outpouring in the poverty and frailty of infancy, manhood, weariness, sorrow, suffering, and death—is also simultaneously our *plērōsis*—the filling of our nature with the imperishable splendor of divine beauty and limitless life, the light of rebirth and resurrection."[33] Jesus descends to this earth so that we might ascend to God. Jesus, the one full of light, will share his light. The face of God transfigures us.

Finally, *the transfiguration points to God's eternal intra-trinitarian love poured out on humanity*. The context of the transfiguration transcends earthly realities. Jesus's luminosity and the declaration of sonship are heavenly dogmas. Jesus is the eternal Son who has always existed in a relationship of love with the Father and the Spirit. Now the love of the Father, Son, and Spirit is poured

---

31. Thanks to Chad Ashby for pointing this out to me (see 1 Cor. 15:41).

32. Alastair Roberts, "Transfigured Hermeneutics—Transfiguration and Exegesis," *Reformation21* (blog), December 18, 2015, https://www.reformation21.org/blogs/transfigured-hermeneutics-tran.php. This is one article in a six-part series. For the other five, see the bibliography, under the heading "Articles."

33. David Bentley Hart, foreword to *The Uncreated Light*, by Solrunn Nes (Grand Rapids: Eerdmans, 2007), xiv.

out on behalf of humanity. The Son has taken the form of a slave to make his fellow slaves partakers of the divine nature. The Father made an eternal pact with the Son to save humanity. The Son will do so by taking on flesh. The pact precedes the process.

In this way, Jesus's sonship is more about kinship than kingship. Jesus's sonship can't be restricted to his vocation but must be taken up into his relationship with the Father and the Spirit. We know the light of the Father through the Son and in the Spirit.

In summary, the purpose of the transfiguration is to give *hope by revelation*.[34] Jesus's double sonship gives hope to the disciples by showing them that his suffering is not the end of the story, because he is more than Israel's king. He is the one true God of Israel, the eternal beloved Son. Israel's lack of transformation will one day be remedied because they will be united to the one who is light. When he appears, "we will be like him because we will see him as he is. And everyone who has this hope in him purifies himself just as he is pure" (1 John 3:2–3).

Without the transfiguration, Christ's glory is not revealed as light from light. Without the transfiguration, the disciples have no hope considering Christ's impending cross—or their own (Matt. 16:21). Without the transfiguration, we have no hope of being transformed ourselves. The transfiguration guarantees that we will not only be where he is but as he is.

My prayer is that this book will help you behold the glorious Son and that by beholding you also might be transfigured.

34. For pastors, the idea "hope by revelation" could be the central idea for a sermon on the transfiguration. An outline could follow my structure (setting, signs, saying), a spatial progression (up the mountain, on the mountain, down the mountain), or an emphasis on the implied imperatives of each section (ascend, look, listen) or the actions (beholding, listening, being comforted by the Son). It might be titled "Look and Listen," "A Vision of Glory," "Seeing the Light," "Behold: The Light," "Be Transfigured," or "Who Is Jesus?" The main tone of the sermon should be wonder at Christ and encouragement in dark times.

1

The Necessity
of the Transfiguration

Some of the most important recent works upon the theology
and history of the Gospels omit the Transfiguration altogether.

—Arthur Ramsey[1]

The best TV comedy series of all time is *Seinfeld*. If you disagree with me,
I'm sorry that you're wrong.

Seinfeld is the story of four friends in New York City who interact around
the small things that happen during their day. Most of the show consists of
conversations in either Jerry's apartment or the local diner. Despite being a
self-described "show about nothing," Seinfeld almost single-handedly saved
NBC from financial ruin. The show's great success was made more impressive
by the absence of the standard backbone: a plotline that unifies each season.
Every episode basically works on its own. Even individual episodes often lack
unified plotlines.

1. Arthur Michael Ramsey, *The Glory of God and the Transfiguration of Christ* (Eugene, OR:
Wipf & Stock, 2009), 104.

Seinfeld was a hit because in being about nothing, it was also about everything. With no plot, it ended up being about relationships, the quirks of everyday life, the struggle to find meaning, and the way humans interact with one another.

The narrative of the transfiguration can also be confusing. It doesn't fit naturally into the chronology of the Bible or the "way" we are saved, like a discrete episode of *Seinfeld* doesn't fit into an overarching plotline. We may be unsure whether it matters if we skip this particular episode, because the narrative seems to continue after it as if nothing had happened.

However, the detached nature of *Seinfeld* enabled episodes like "The Marine Biologist" and "The Puffy Shirt" to become iconic of the show itself. By transcending normal categories, the transfiguration similarly becomes an icon of Jesus's identity and the gospel message as a whole. It is not only about a Jewish man having a shiny face but about seeing God face to face. It is not only about three frightened fishermen but about the destiny of all humanity. It is not only about dazzlingly white clothes and a bright cloud but about the purpose of the universe.

We have neglected the transfiguration. Now it is time we, like the disciples on the mountain, awake from our sleep (Luke 9:32).

Five Reasons We Neglect the Transfiguration

The transfiguration has fallen on hard times. No longer does this event play a prominent role in our theology or in the story we tell of Jesus. However, we neglect it to our detriment.

The transfiguration seems simple, but there's a hidden complexity under the surface. It ties together some of the most important themes in the Bible, and a thorough meditation on this event will pay dividends in the reading of Scripture and the articulation of doctrine. In this chapter I will outline five reasons we tend to neglect the transfiguration and then five reasons we shouldn't.

We Think It Plays a Minor Role in the Scriptures and the Creeds

The first reason people tend to neglect the transfiguration is that it seems to be a minor note in the biblical storyline and in the historic creeds of the church.

If you polled people on the most important events in Jesus's life, my guess is that forty-nine out of fifty wouldn't mention the transfiguration. If you removed this event from the Bible, it may seem as if it wouldn't make much difference in the Evangelists' stories. Jesus is born in a stable and ends up in the place of the skull. The transfiguration is not essential to our salvation like the life, death, resurrection, or ascension of Jesus is. Moreover, the apocalyptic nature of the event makes it a narrative oddball that we don't know what to do with.

Add to this that while all three Synoptics recount the transfiguration, they don't give it much space. Matthew's account is eight verses (Matt. 17:1–8), Mark's is seven (Mark 9:2–8), and Luke's is nine (Luke 9:28–36). John doesn't include the narrative at all. Paul doesn't speak of it. Outside of the Synoptic Gospels, the event is briefly alluded to once in 2 Peter.

The standard creeds and confessions also don't include the transfiguration when enumerating the key moments of Jesus's life. The Apostles' Creed and Nicene Creed both list Jesus's birth, crucifixion, resurrection, ascension, and future return. There is no mention of his transfiguration.

In summary, we might neglect the transfiguration because it doesn't fit naturally into the storyline of the Scriptures, the narrative itself is quite brief, and the creeds seem to ignore it. This may lead us to wonder, Has the Eastern tradition overhyped this event?

We Are Inattentive to the Goal of Salvation

The second reason the transfiguration is often neglected is that we tend to focus more on *how* we are saved than on *why* we are saved.[2] In the Western tradition, we have sung the praises of the cross and the resurrection. These are the mechanisms by which we are saved. And it is true that the Scriptures put great focus on these glorious events.

But an overemphasis on, for instance, theories of atonement may have had the unintended consequence of distracting us from the *goal* of humanity.[3] The goal is not merely the forgiveness of sins; it is becoming like God by beholding him.

The Christian tradition has called this the beatific vision. The Bible starts and ends with this theme. Adam and Eve enjoyed fellowship with God as they walked in the garden with him. Satan tempted them not with a different goal (being like God) but with a different path (disobeying God). In Revelation, God comes down from heaven to again dwell with his people to the end that they might be transfigured. The goal of the entire biblical storyline is to become like God by seeing the face of God.

---

2. For example, you will find only a small section on the beatific vision in Grudem, and nothing on the topic in Erickson or Berkhof. Wayne A. Grudem, *Systematic Theology: An Introduction to Biblical Doctrine*, 2nd ed. (Grand Rapids: Zondervan Academic, 2020); Millard J. Erickson, *Christian Theology*, 3rd ed. (Grand Rapids: Baker Academic, 2013); Louis Berkhof, *Systematic Theology*, 2nd ed. (Edinburgh: Banner of Truth, 2021).

3. In one sense, the division of the means and goal is oversimplifying things. We also are saved by beholding (2 Cor. 3:7–18; 1 John 3:2).

Tied to this viewpoint is the reality that the Western tradition has a history of making hearing primary; the transfiguration puts emphasis on sight. This might cause some Protestants to squirm. Certainly "faith comes from what is heard" (Rom. 10:17). But in our final state we will experience God with all the senses. The goal of salvation is union with God and seeing him as he is. The transfiguration depicts glorified humanity and what happens as a result of Christ's sacrifice. The devil's aim is to prevent humanity from being "lifted up," like he did in the garden. It would be wise to let the "end" order more of our theology.

We Find It Too Mysterious, Symbolic, and Mystical

The third reason we neglect the transfiguration is because many of us in the West struggle with symbols, mystery, and ambiguity. The transfiguration seems too mystical, esoteric, and escapist. We are more attracted to accounts with clear, direct, and unequivocal meaning. We like clarity, not opacity. We like certainty, not obscurity. However, the transfiguration challenges these tendencies.

The mountain scene is filled with signs and symbols. The transfiguration might be overlooked by Protestants because it is a very "visual" scene. It says that Jesus was transfigured. What does that mean? The text recounts that his face shone like the sun. Why? His clothes become dazzling white. Why does that matter? A bright cloud appears. Moses and Elijah also show up. It sounds like dead people appearing as in a Harry Potter novel.[4]

Add to this that Jesus takes only three disciples up the mountain with him. Why didn't he take more? Also, he tells them not to tell anyone about this until he has been raised from the dead. If it is a revelation scene, why the secrecy? Matthew, Mark, and Luke do little to explain the narrative to us or to offer explicit applications.

Right before the narrative, we have a strange statement from Jesus about the disciples not dying before they see the kingdom of God coming in power. And after the narrative the disciples can't cast out a demon. These are odd events and difficult to interpret.

We simply don't know what to do with the symbols in this story. They baffle our imaginations. Moreover, many Christians sadly lack the biblical literacy to perceive what these symbols evoke from the biblical storyline. That's not to mention that theologians have interpreted these symbols in various ways. It's easy to be disoriented quickly. We like narratives where everything is explained

---

4. If you're counting, which you should be, that is my second Harry Potter reference.

without ambiguity, but the transfiguration is mysterious, mystical, and symbolic. We might not say a lot about the transfiguration because we don't know what to say.

We Are Too Earthly Minded

The fourth reason we might neglect the transfiguration is because we have reemphasized the importance of the physical and earthly—swinging the pendulum away from the spiritual and heavenly.

Abraham Kuyper, N. T. Wright, and others have done important work to demonstrate that the hope of Israel was not a disembodied state but a new creation. The Christian vision is not of human souls soaring on the clouds playing harps but of God ruling on the earth in a very embodied and concrete sense.

At a time when we still have many who think that believing in Jesus is basically about going to heaven when you die, we can be thankful for a more well-rounded picture of the Christian message. However, this renewed earthly mindedness might squeeze out the transfiguration. Elevating the embodied and material can create suspicion toward the ethereal and otherworldly. Since the transfiguration seems to push past Jesus's body and reveal something spiritual, it sits uneasily with those who want to press more into the embodied nature of our faith and get away from the mystical imagery that has occupied Christian thought.

We Are Suspicious of Deification

The final—and maybe most significant—reason the transfiguration is neglected is because the Eastern tradition has associated this event with what they call "deification," or *theosis*. This is a central idea of Eastern Orthodox theology and is viewed as problematic by some Western theologians.[5]

Deification is difficult to define, but we can describe it simply as the glorification of a person into the likeness of a deity. To put it another way, "*Theosis* is the transformation of the soul into union with deity."[6] The Eastern church affirms that Jesus's transfiguration is a preview of our future. As Jesus is

---

5. However, in the premodern tradition, most have affirmed a form of theosis—even the Reformers. See Carl Mosser, "Recovering the Reformation's Ecumenical Vision of Redemption as Deification and Beatific Vision," in *Perichoresis: The Theological Journal of Emanuel University* 18, no. 1 (2020): 3–24; Carl Mosser, "Orthodox-Reformed Dialogue and the Ecumenical Recovery of Theosis," *Ecumenical Review* 73, no. 1 (2021): 131–51.

6. Arthur Michael Ramsey, *The Glory of God and the Transfiguration of Christ* (Eugene, OR: Wipf & Stock, 2009), 138.

transfigured, so we are transfigured into divine beings as we behold the face of God in Jesus Christ.

For some, the concept of deification is troubling. The language doesn't occur in the Scriptures, it seems to blur the line between the Creator and the creature, it occurs through the administration of the sacraments, it can take the focus off God's work and place it on our future, and it underemphasizes the doctrine of justification.

Western Protestants, especially evangelicals, are uniquely uncomfortable with that last point. They stress a view of justification as a change in a person's standing with God that takes places instantaneously. The Eastern Orthodox church, like their Roman Catholic cousins, places more stress on salvation as a process. Because of the close ties of the transfiguration with deification in Eastern theology, we might have a sort of guilt-by-association situation among Western Protestant evangelicals when it comes to the transfiguration. Though no one has said it, it almost seems like some have thought, "If we avoid this text, we won't be tempted by this erroneous view."

Conclusion

The transfiguration is neglected in Western Christianity. Evangelical Protestants especially have tended to gravitate toward events in the Scriptures that push the story forward, to focus on the means rather than the goal of salvation, to capitalize on events that don't include mystery and symbols, to rebuff more heavenly views in favor of earthly texts, and to shy away from texts that have any whiff of the doctrine of deification.

Five Reasons Not to Neglect the Transfiguration

However, the transfiguration is a key moment in the life of Christ. It is a gateway to Jesus's cross, victory, and exaltation. It acts as a balance weight to our theology. Neglecting it can lead to distortions in our theology.

The transfiguration uniquely allies matters that we place in opposition. As Lee notes, it crosses the divide, "bringing together the apocalyptic and epiphanic, spirit and matter, divinity and humanity, glory and suffering, beauty and fear, present and future, the old age and the new, creator and creation."[7] It fuses what we separate. It unites what we tear apart. But the transfiguration also does more. It puts things into proper perspective. It is a revelatory moment, where the curtain is pulled back and we see what truly matters.

7. Dorothy A. Lee, "On the Holy Mountain: The Transfiguration in Scripture and Theology," *Colloquium* 36, no. 2 (2004): 159.

It Combines the Storyline and Dogmatics

The first reason not to neglect the transfiguration is because it uniquely binds biblical and systematic theology together. I argued earlier that we might not know what to do with this narrative, since the Bible and the early creeds seem to give the event only a minor role. However, these characterizations aren't entirely true.

In terms of biblical theology, it is significant that *all* the Synoptics include the narrative, and they tell the story in a very similar way. Additionally, it's not strictly true that John doesn't include the transfiguration. He simply doesn't recount the narrative. The light of the transfiguration permeates John's Gospel; its beams stream into every narrative. As Loisy affirms, John's Gospel affords "a perpetual theophany—a permanent sighting of the appearance of God's glory in Christ, temporarily glimpsed at transfiguration."[8] This can be seen immediately in John's emphasis on Jesus as the light. John affirms that Jesus's life was the "light of men" (1:4), that the apostles observed his glory (1:14), and that the Son has revealed the Father (1:18).

The impact of the transfiguration also ripples beyond the Gospels. In 2 Peter 1:17–18, Peter defends himself against the charge of perpetrating myths and false teaching by pointing to his experience on the mountain. Jesus, he says, "received honor and glory from God the Father when the voice came to him from the Majestic Glory, saying 'This is my Beloved Son, with whom I am well-pleased!'" Peter says the inner three heard this voice from heaven when they were on the holy mountain.

Additionally, while Romans 12 and 2 Corinthians 3 don't explicitly speak of the transfiguration, they certainly allude to it. Paul employs the word *metamorphoō* twice and once connects it to being "transfigured" from glory to glory by beholding the glory of the Lord with unveiled faces (2 Cor. 3:18). Paul also employs light as a key image for God, Christ, and our own formation. Unbelievers are kept from seeing the light of the gospel and the glory of Christ, but God has shone light into the saints' hearts "to give knowledge of God's glory in the face of Jesus Christ" (4:5–6). Paul calls those in Ephesus to walk in the light of the Lord (Eph. 5:8) and to awake and rise up, for "Christ will shine on you" (5:14). In Colossians, Paul speaks of the saints sharing in the "inheritance in the light" (Col. 1:12). In 1 Thessalonians he calls believers "children of light" (1 Thess. 5:5).

The Catholic Epistles speak of the Son as "the radiance of God's glory" (Heb. 1:3), reminiscent of Christ's glimmering face on the mount. Peter affirms that believers have been called out of darkness and into God's "marvelous light"

---

8. Alfred Loisy, quoted in Ramsey, *Glory of God*, 123.

(1 Pet. 2:9). John confesses that "God is light" (1 John 1:5) and associates God's light with the blood of Jesus, which cleanses God's people from sin (1:7). John says we will be like Jesus when we "see him as he is" (3:2).

The transfiguration is also alluded to in almost all Christophanies (appearances of Jesus). One should especially think of Stephen's vision (Acts 6:15; 7:55), Paul's encounter with Jesus on the Damascus Road (9:3; 22:6, 6, 11; 26:13), and John's vision of the heavenly throne (Rev. 1:12–19). In all of these, light plays a prominent role. Importantly, in Revelation, John sees "the Son of Man, dressed in a robe, . . . his face shining like the sun" (1:13), and John falls at his feet. These are all direct echoes of the transfiguration.

It is too simplistic to say the transfiguration is a minor note in the biblical storyline, and I have only covered the New Testament. It was generative for how the earliest Christians spoke about the gospel, Christ, and God himself, as can be seen in the brief survey above.

The transfiguration is also a deep well for systematic theology. The narrative is so beautiful and so demanding because it is a major player in the storyline *and* because it has massive implications for our doctrine of Christ and of God himself. It is one of the only scenes in the whole Bible in which the three persons of the Trinity appear.[9] It may be the clearest picture of Jesus's dual nature. It displays the mystery of the incarnation, reveals that God is light, and showcases the face of God. The transfiguration requires us to possess precise dogmatic categories to properly interpret it.

For this reason, it's not surprising to find that the earliest creeds employ language and imagery from the transfiguration, even if they don't explicitly refer to it. The Nicene Creed confesses that Jesus is the "only begotten Son of God" (*language* sourced from the transfiguration) and "God from God, Light from Light" (*imagery* sourced from the transfiguration). These statements were decisive in defining both trinitarian doctrine and Christology. The transfiguration demands that we don both our dogmatic and our exegetical hats.

The transfiguration thus uniquely binds biblical and systematic theology together. Maybe this is why it has been neglected. The modern division of disciplines leaves systematic theologians out to sea as far as connecting this to the biblical storyline and interpreting the symbols with sensitivity to the Jewish and Greco-Roman cultures. Biblical theologians, on the other hand, don't know how far to press the doctrinal concerns, nor how to do so faithfully.

While the transfiguration uniquely combines the biblical storyline and dogmatics, it also orders them. It reminds us that the place to start is with who God

9. I will argue for the presence of the Spirit in chap. 3.

is, not with his works or with salvation's implications for us. God is God. He doesn't become God by what he does. God's work in redemption is defined by his nature, not the other way around. The Son always was, always is, and always will be glorious. His glory is not dependent on his sacrifice or his revelatory transfiguration. The transfiguration changes nothing about God or about Jesus Christ. It is a starting place where we behold who God is.

It Unites the Means and the Goal of Salvation

The second reason we shouldn't neglect the transfiguration is because it unites the *means* and the *goal* of salvation. The two don't have to be mutually exclusive. It is precisely in the context of Jesus predicting his own death that he provides hope for his disciples by showing them his true glory. Darkness won't defeat this king, because he is light.

The transfiguration reminds us that the cross is the means by which we see the face of God. The Gospels don't allow us to separate the cross from the crown, the gore from the glory, the blood from the brightness. Calvary and Tabor are twin mountains. Yet, at the same time, the transfiguration also forces us to keep things in proper perspective. The means, by definition, are not an end in themselves. We rejoice in the cross for *what* it accomplishes, not only for *how* it accomplishes. The beatific vision, in contrast, is the purpose. The goal is not more important; it would be imprecise to say so. But seeing God in his glory is the goal.

The same can be said of the relationship between hearing and sight. Sight is the goal. We live by faith now, but we long to live by sight (2 Cor. 5:7). The scriptural storyline prioritizes sight over other physical senses.[10] While smell, taste, touch, and hearing are all employed to describe our experience of God (1 John 1:1–4), the most intimate is sight.

Hans Boersma notes that, historically, theologians have privileged the metaphor of vision in the Scriptures.[11] The storyline moves from vision to loss of vision (language) and then to the hope of regaining vision.

Creation	Fall	Redemption	Restoration
Sight	Hearing	Partial Sight	Full Sight

10. Augustine also emphasized the priority of vision: "Let us use for preference the evidence of the eyes; this is the most excellent of the body's senses, and for all its difference in kind has the greatest affinity to mental vision." Augustine, *On the Trinity* 11.1.1 (WSA I/5:304). See also Hans Boersma, *Seeing God: The Beatific Vision in Christian Tradition* (Grand Rapids: Eerdmans, 2018), 248–51.

11. Boersma, *Seeing God*, 3.

According to this framework, hearing serves a mediatory role. Words are limited, and the immediacy of sight makes it better suited for the eschaton. Words take time, but vision is instantaneous.[12] Even though we will sing God's praises for eternity, we will sing his praises because we see him, not the other way around. Sight has a logical priority.

Believers are promised that after death they will see God face to face (Job 19:26–27; Matt. 5:8; John 17:24; 1 Cor. 13:12; 2 Cor 5:7; 1 John 3:2). Stories of God's self-exposure come at key moments in Scripture. Revelation concludes by saying that God's people "will see his face, and his name will be on their foreheads" (Rev. 22:4). The eye takes priority in paradise. Eyes allow for a communion that the ear cannot experience.

The transfiguration reminds us that all our theology should work backward from the goal of "seeing God." This goal puts everything in its proper perspective. It shows us that faith will merge into sight, and sight begins in part even now (1 Cor. 13:12; 2 Cor. 5:7). The transfiguration allows us a present peek at future glory.

It Pairs Mystery and Revelation

The third reason we shouldn't neglect the transfiguration is because it brings together both symbol and word, mystery and revelation. What we tend to oppose, the transfiguration unites. The three disciples experience revelation and hiddenness. They see symbols, and they hear the divine voice. While most think of the transfiguration as a visual scene, it contains both aural and visual elements. The signs and the words clarify one another.

Still, the scene is shrouded in mystery. The shining clothes and face communicate something, but what? The words about Jesus being God's Son are vague: What sort of Son is he? Like in the Old Testament, the story reveals while remaining mysterious. The transfiguration gives a sudden glimpse of who Jesus truly is, but just as quickly, the glimmering Son is enshrouded by a cloud. It is both a revelatory moment and an enigmatic one. The disciples see the Father in Jesus, but invisibility and mystery still reside in the voice, bright light, and cloud.[13]

---

12. The Greek term for contemplation (*theōria*) is derived from the verb "to gaze at, to behold" (*theōreō*).

13. Because the transfiguration contains both light (to see) and a cloud (to cover), it supports both apophatic and cataphatic theology. Apophasis speaks of God in negation, saying what he is not. We behold God in a mystery, and the mystery we behold is unspeakable. The divine is beyond the realm of language and concepts. Cataphatic theology, on the other hand, employs positive terminology to refer to God and refers to what is to be believed about God.

We know who Christ is: he is the eternally begotten Son of God, God from God, light from light, consubstantial with the Father. However, the mind cannot grasp the perfection of God. The infinite God is beyond the full comprehension of finite creatures. John of Damascus appropriately begins his *On the Orthodox Faith* by saying the "divine is ineffable and incomprehensible. . . . As to what he is in essence and nature, that is something beyond our comprehension and knowledge."[14] Paul says, the wisdom and knowledge of God are unsearchable and inscrutable. No one fully knows the mind of the Lord (Rom. 11:33–34).

The transfiguration teaches us to have not only the *confidence* that we can know God in Christ but the *humility* to recognize that God in Christ can never be fully known. When we gaze at the Son, eventually our eyes fail, and we must look down because he is too bright. We use human language to describe God, and our language is not capable of describing him fully. Mystery remains that words can't express; therefore symbols must be used.

It Marries the Heavenly and Earthly

The fourth reason not to neglect the transfiguration is because it marries heaven with earth. We tend to separate the two: either we describe our final state as disembodied and immaterial or we so emphasize our earthy hope that we forget about God being there. However, the transfiguration takes both the heavenly and the earthly and says yes.

The transfiguration is not simply a revelation of Jesus's divinity; it is a revelation of Jesus's divinity *through his humanity*. The Evangelists emphasize Jesus's face and clothes. Peter, James, and John can see God in the face and body of Jesus Christ. God has become knowable by taking on human form. The transfiguration therefore unites both the heavenly and the earthly. Heaven is revealed *through* creation, not by sidestepping it.

Yet the transfiguration also teaches us that heaven is the ultimate reality. All earthly things are a copy, shadow, and pattern of the heavenly things (Heb. 8:5). Earth is the shadowland; heaven is actuality.[15] Heaven is solid; earth is wraithlike. The recent emphasis on the new creation being concrete and earthy carries with it the danger of tipping toward what Michael Allen has called "eschatological naturalism," where earthly things take an unhealthy precedence.[16]

---

14. St. John of Damascus, *On the Orthodox Faith*, trans. Norman Russell (Yonkers: St. Vladimir's Seminary Press, 2022), 59, 64.

15. As C. S. Lewis shows in *The Great Divorce* (New York: HarperOne, 2001), humans are the ghosts that walk on the earth.

16. Michael Allen, *Grounded in Heaven: Recentering Christian Hope and Life on God* (Grand Rapids: Eerdmans, 2018).

However, the transfiguration corrects us. The vertical (heaven) empowers the horizontal (earth). Heaven grounds and gives substance to earthly significance. It frees us to put the things of the earth in the right perspective. The transfiguration reminds us that "true reality" is divine and spiritual, but true reality has also affirmed creation and even been united to it. This union is most clearly seen in the divine Son of God taking on flesh—never to discard it.

It Connects Our Glorious Future with Jesus's Shameful Past

The fifth reason not to neglect the transfiguration is because it highlights how we become "participants" (koinōnoi) in the divine nature (2 Pet. 1:4) without sidelining the cross and our justification.

Again, in Orthodox theology, more mystical and cosmic emphases emerge. The East speaks of this in terms of deification, or theosis. At times, speaking of our ultimate state, it might obscure the way we get there. For the Eastern Orthodox, the transfiguration indeed symbolizes the metaphorphosis of the world by the presence of God.

While I'm not convinced we should use the term "deification," or theosis, the Scripture is abundantly clear that our destiny is to participate in God. Early church writings affirmed that deification was an ontological reality, but it didn't erase the distinction between Creator and creature. Rather metamorphosis occurs attributively in terms of humans participating or sharing in a deity's divinity.[17] The metamorphosis of the believer is rooted in partaking in the divine nature, not in becoming divine essentially. Everything we have and are is borrowed, not existing in and of itself. This means that we remain creatures, God remains the Creator, but we share in his divine nature by being in Christ.

Surprisingly, a good interpretive grasp of the transfiguration protects from over-readings and misapplications of this doctrine. In all the Gospel accounts, the glory belongs essentially and fundamentally to Christ. Moses and Elijah are only changed by proximity to and union with Jesus. Jesus's shining face is essential; Moses's, and ours, is derivative.[18] Moses's visage shines as a reflection;

---

17. Ben Blackwell suggests two major ways to summarize deification in the ancient world: (1) cultically and (2) ontologically. Cultically, deification allows an honored individual to be remembered forever. Ontologically, deification occurs either essentially or attributively. A change of essence would entail becoming a different creature or species, while a change of attributes means that a person participates in a deity's divinity. Since the church fathers greatly emphasized a distinction of essence between the Creator and the created, "attributive ontological deification" is—in Blackwell's terminology—the best way to understand deification in patristic exegesis. Ben C. Blackwell, Christosis: Engaging Paul's Soteriology with His Patristic Interpreters (Grand Rapids: Eerdmans, 2016), 103–10.

18. R. T. France, The Gospel of Matthew, NICNT (Grand Rapids: Eerdmans, 2007), 647.

Jesus's shines because he *is* light. Jesus does not receive anything different, nor is he changed in one very true sense. The transfiguration thus returns us to an emphasis on how we are changed from one degree of glory to another, while it upholds key distinctions.

The transfiguration also prompts us to emphasize both justification and sanctification without confusing them. Evangelical Protestant Westerners have traditionally resisted deification language because it can conflate sanctification and justification. But the transfiguration narrative shows us that participation in the divine nature occurs only if we follow Jesus to the cross. On the cross, Jesus makes those who believe in him right before God. The transfiguration doesn't oppose suffering and glory but holds them together. By suffering, Jesus receives glory; so it is for us (2 Pet. 1:17). As Jesus died, so we must die; as Jesus was raised from the dead, so we will rise from the dead; as Jesus was transfigured, so too will we be transformed when we see him as he is (1 John 3:1–3).

The transfiguration reveals our eternal future. We will come to share more and more in God. We will become more like him. Protestants simply use the term "sanctification" for this, but we sometimes forget the end goal: glorification. The goal is to be changed by beholding the face of God in Jesus Christ. If this reality doesn't loom large in our theology, then our theology will be skewed from the start.

CONCLUSION

Have you ever noticed that no Gospel narrative describes in detail the actual moment of resurrection? When the disciples arrive, Jesus has already been raised, and the tomb is open. The Gospel writers don't depict when Jesus's eyes opened and breath filled his lungs, when the blood rushed again through his body, when he swung his legs over and stood up.

However, the Gospel writers do record a play-by-play of the transfiguration— which should give us pause. While I found only three books on the transfiguration in Midwestern Seminary's library, there are hundreds on the resurrection. Yet the glory of Christ is described in detail in the transfiguration.

The transfiguration marks a vital stage in the revelation of the Son. It points back to his baptism; it also points forward to his suffering and glory. It looks back to the Old Testament but also anticipates the cosmic conclusion of history. It has implications for Christology, anthropology, eschatology, trinitarian theology, biblical theology, and spiritual formation. Ultimately, it shows us who our God is.

The rest of the book will examine this important event in more detail and will follow a simple outline.

In chapter 2, I will look at the *setting* of the transfiguration—examining the timing of, location of, and witnesses to the event.

In chapter 3, I will inspect the *signs* in the transfiguration—Jesus's shining face and white clothes, the bright cloud, and Moses and Elijah's appearance.

In chapter 4, I will examine the *sayings* of the transfiguration—focusing first on Peter's response and then on the declaration and command of the heavenly voice.[19]

In chapter 5, having explored the transfiguration event itself, I will relate it to other events and doctrines to expand our vision.

Come, let us go up the mountain to behold the glorious Son!

---

19. Readers must be prepared to forgive the length of the third and fourth chapters, as there is much to discuss. I tried to subdivide them, but I simply couldn't do so while maintaining the structure of an introductory grammar and a closing reflection on formation.

2

The Glorious Setting

Come, let's go up to the mountain of the Lᴏʀᴅ.

—Isaiah 2:3

Settings are not merely backdrops; they are players in the narrative itself. Some of my favorite movies make the location as much part of the story as the characters or the plot.

Released in 2012, *Mud* tells the story of two fourteen-year-old boys as they meet a fugitive (Mud) who has returned home to find his old girlfriend. Scene after scene is flooded with the murk of the Arkansas Delta. Houseboats populate the screen, and young Delta children turn muddy rudders as they cruise through the sweltering summer heat. Venomous snakes slither into the plot. The movie is as much about the location as the characters.

In a similar way, the power of the transfiguration is found in its setting. The mountain, timing, and three disciples are not mere stage dressing. The backdrop is key to understanding the narrative and its meaning. The simplicity of each element conceals its profundity. Together, they bear testimony to Jesus's double sonship: his identity as both the messianic and divine Son.

But before examining the setting, this chapter will begin by developing a hermeneutical grammar for how to interpret the transfiguration narrative.

A Hermeneutical Grammar

How are we to read the Scriptures? It seems like a simple question, but the subject has been hotly contested throughout church history. Fierce debates remain and divide Christians. The importance of this question is showcased especially in the transfiguration. A plethora of interpretations have been offered over the centuries.

Though the line has not run straight, there has always been an affirmation of the depth, beauty, and diversity to the Scriptures that cannot be discounted. Early interpreters employed the *quadriga* to explore this richness—also known as the fourfold method or the fourfold sense.[1] The fourfold method wasn't solidified until the Middle Ages, but the basic moves seem evident in the Scriptures and in the early church. Essentially, this method asserts that there are multiple senses to the Scripture. Though its usefulness is still disputed, the method has several benefits for interpreters.[2]

First, the four senses provide more specific language than the meaning-application division typical among contemporary Western evangelicals. It is popular to assert that each text of Scripture has one primary meaning that can be applied in various ways. But what is the one meaning of, for example, Acts 2? Is it about mission, the founding of the church, the restoration of Israel, the new covenant, diversity in the early church, the fulfillment of promises, the new creation, Sinai, or temple people? While some hermeneutical methods offer little help beyond the question "What is the meaning?" the fourfold sense provides precise categories to describe the interpretive moves toward these various meanings of Pentecost.

Second, the four senses protect against unwarranted interpretations. No method does this perfectly, but the fourfold method was meant to prevent false interpretations. Sure, it produced some of the most mind-boggling interpretations in the early church, but the modern era has produced its own bizarre readings. The fourfold method has served as a set of guardrails to centuries of Christians seeking to do orthodox textual interpretation.

Finally, the four senses not only serve as a guardrail but are constructive and generative for how we can understand the divine voice found in the pages of the Bible. This method recaptures the beauty of interpretation. It opens rather than stifles the depth of Scripture. Without it, we tend to have one-dimensional readings. Without it, we tend to stop the flow of meaning that captures our imaginations.

---

1. The fourfold "sense" refers to what is found in the Scriptures, while the fourfold "method" flows from those senses and describes how we read the Scriptures. I will use these terms interchangeably.

2. Because this is not a book on hermeneutics, readers might feel I have not done enough work to establish that this truly is a helpful and accurate way of looking at the Scriptures. My aim here is not to defend it against potential objections but to show how it can be useful in interpreting the setting of the transfiguration. I hope to write a book defending the usefulness of the fourfold method in the future.

The fourfold method looks at Scripture through four lenses: the literal (historical), spiritual (typological),[3] tropological (moral), and anagogical (eschatological).

Augustine argued that all the senses are grounded in the literal sense.[4] The *literal sense* of Scripture is typically identified with the historical meaning of the text. In modern parlance, the literal sense is the meaning the author intended to communicate to the original audience. We discover it by analyzing the grammar employed, with respect for the historical background of the writing. The Scriptures are grounded in events that have really transpired in places that really existed involving people who actually lived.

As a test case, consider the word "Jerusalem" in Jesus's lamentation in Matthew 23:37: "Jerusalem, Jerusalem, who kills the prophets and stones those who are sent to her." According to the literal sense, Jerusalem refers to a historical city once inhabited by the Jebusites, captured by David, and made the capital of Israel and later the Southern Kingdom of Judah. This is the initial interpretive move readers must make.

The second sense of Scripture is the *spiritual sense*, or what modern people call the typological sense. This concerns what we should believe. The words on the pages of the Scriptures "not only signify things, but the things themselves signify other things."[5] It can be summarized as the depth within.

Returning to our test case, the spiritual sense of Matthew 23:37 would understand Jerusalem as a cipher for God's people. Jesus's words refer first to the historical city that refuses him, yet Jerusalem spiritually represents all God's people who have killed the prophets—past, present, and future. The literal sense is the foundation while the spiritual sense instructs us what to believe: God's people have always existed and often reject God's servants. We might say that the literal sense listens for the voice of the inspired human author at a punctiliar moment while the spiritual sense listens for the voice of the omnipresent divine author urging us to connect the dots from one part of the canon to the other.

---

3. The spiritual sense has often been called the allegorical sense, but since this is a contested term, I have opted for the term "spiritual" even though that usually covered all three senses following the literal sense. Typically, a spiritual reading simply is the *extended sense of Scripture in accordance with the literal sense* and therefore includes the allegorical, tropological, and anagogical. No matter what one calls this second sense, the important point is that the literal sense is the bedrock. It stands on its own, and the other senses must organically develop from it. The transfiguration can act as an illustration of how this hermeneutic works. The change Jesus undergoes doesn't lead to a different Jesus but reveals more of who he is. Just as Jesus is transfigured but remains human, so we can explore expanded meanings of Scripture without abandoning the literal sense. The literal sense of Scripture, like Jesus's humanity, is never erased.

4. As an example, see Augustine's work *The Literal Meaning of Genesis*. Augustine, *On Genesis*, trans. Edmund Hill (Brooklyn: New City Press, 2004).

5. Hugh of St. Victor (PL 177:375c), quoted in Henri de Lubac, *Medieval Exegesis: The Four Senses of Scripture*, trans. E. M. Macierowski, vol. 2 (Grand Rapids: Eerdmans, 2000), 88.

The third sense is the *tropological sense,* or what could be called the moral sense. It tells us what to do. When Paul quotes the Old Testament, he affirms that "whatever was written in the past was written for our instruction" (Rom. 15:4; see also 1 Cor. 10:6, 11). The Scriptures are not only for historical information but for moral formation.

In Matthew 23:37, we can read Jerusalem as the historical city (literal sense) and as the people of God (spiritual sense). Furthermore, the *tropological sense* leads us to read Jerusalem as the soul. Christ's lament, then, gets personal as an appeal to the human heart not to "kill the prophets" that are sent to us. When Jesus speaks about Jerusalem, it is a call for us to be ready to accept God's Savior. We shouldn't be like historical Jerusalem, which sought to kill him. The historical reference has implications for our own actions. We act either in accord with Jerusalem or in accord with Babylon. Either we rebuff our Savior or we welcome him.

The fourth sense is the *anagogical sense,* which signifies the things to come. If the spiritual sense builds up faith and the tropological sense builds up love, then the anagogical sense builds up hope.[6] Anagogy pushes our minds past the mere present sense and causes us to look to the future.

The *anagogical sense* hears in Matthew 23 a longing for the new Jerusalem. Christ's cry of agony over Jerusalem is a prayer for the new heavens and earth, when his great city will welcome him with open arms. Jesus's cry is laden with the hope that on the last day, he will no longer lament over his people but rejoice over them.

THE FOURFOLD SENSE

Senses	Description	Example: Jerusalem
Literal	What took place	Historical city
Spiritual	What we ought to believe	God's people
Tropological	What we ought to do	Human soul
Anagogical	What we strive for	New Jerusalem

In this example from Matthew 23, we can see how each sense builds on the previous one. History is brought to completion by the spiritual sense, and the spiritual sense is brought to completion by tropology, and tropology is brought to completion by anagogy.[7] The three latter senses are organically related to the literal sense.

---

6. De Lubac, *Medieval Exegesis,* 2:181.
7. De Lubac, *Medieval Exegesis,* 2:201.

This isn't a book on hermeneutics. However, this hermeneutical grammar provides a helpful framework for exploring the transfiguration in all its depth. The transfiguration resists purely literal interpretations. We can't keep these words earthbound; we must follow them to heaven.[8] Therefore, the fourfold method works quite well for understanding the glorious setting of the transfiguration.[9]

While I won't explicitly employ these categories in every chapter, as that would get repetitive, it is this method that I find most helpful in approaching the divine Word. For now, we turn to the fourfold sense of the transfiguration's setting.

Six/Eight Days Later

When I was young, I didn't understand how the timing of Jesus's resurrection amounted to three days. The math didn't seem to add up. Jesus was crucified on Friday afternoon and rose on Sunday morning. That seemed more like a day and a half to me.

As a kid, I didn't realize there were different ways of counting days. Now that I have kids I understand. My third child, ever the little planner, loves to ask questions like, "How many days are there until Saturday?" On a Tuesday evening, I might reply, "Well Julianna, there are three days till Saturday: Wednesday, Thursday, Friday." But then comes her retort: "No Dad, there are five days: Tuesday, Wednesday, Thursday, Friday, Saturday." These are always fun—and frustrating—conversations. I am counting exclusively (excluding Tuesday and Saturday), and she is counting inclusively (including Tuesday and Saturday). We arrive at different numbers because we are counting differently.

The same thing happens in the Scriptures. Some authors count exclusively, some inclusively. That, and when days started, is how Jesus stayed in the grave three days: Friday, Saturday, and Sunday.

The different ways of counting are evident in the time stamp of the transfiguration narrative. Both Matthew and Mark say it was "after six days" that Jesus went up on the mountain with his disciples (Matt. 17:1; Mark 9:2). Luke says it was "about eight days after" (9:28). There is no contradiction here. Matthew and Mark are counting exclusively; Luke is counting inclusively.

---

8. Vanhoozer is right to point out that it is not a mistake to "earth" biblical interpretation, for the gospel is eminently historical. Yet we must not stop there. Kevin J. Vanhoozer, "Ascending the Mountain, Singing the Rock: Biblical Interpretation Earthed, Typed, and Transfigured," MT 28, no. 4 (2012): 781–803.

9. I will withhold a reflection on the tropological (moral) sense of the text until the end of each chapter.

While the different ways of counting are interesting, the real payoff comes when we press into the meaning of these words. The temporal reference speaks with surprising depth to the fulfillment of something.

The Literal Meaning

The literal meaning is that Jesus was transfigured six/eight days after another event. In all the Synoptics, we are told what this event is. Each account of the transfiguration affirms that it occurred after Jesus said the following:

> For the Son of Man is going to come with his angels in the glory of his Father, and then he will reward each according to what he has done. Truly I tell you, there are some standing here who will not taste death until they see the Son of Man coming in his kingdom. (Matt. 16:27–28)

> For whoever is ashamed of me and my words in this adulterous and sinful generation, the Son of Man will also be ashamed of him when he comes in the glory of his Father with the holy angels. Then he said to them, "There are some standing here who will not taste death until they see the kingdom of God come in power." (Mark 8:38–9:1)

> For whoever is ashamed of me and my words, the Son of Man will be ashamed of him when he comes in his glory and that of the Father and the holy angels. Truly I tell you, there are some standing here who will not taste death until they see the kingdom of God. (Luke 9:26–27)

This context is fundamental for understanding the transfiguration. Jesus, in an allusion to Daniel 7:13–14, predicts that some of the disciples will not die until they see the Son of Man coming in his kingdom. The temporal note signifies that the transfiguration *fulfills* Jesus's prediction. The transfiguration is a vision of the Son of Man's glory, victory, and exaltation. This Danielic context guides our interpretation of the transfiguration in three ways.

First, it allows readers to see that the transfiguration is *a preview of the future glory of the human Messiah (in his person)*. The transfiguration is not one-sidedly about Jesus's divinity; it's also about the glory Jesus will receive. Daniel speaks of "the human one" *being given* dominion and glory and a kingdom. The disciples need a preview of this reality because Jesus had just predicted his own suffering. Jesus wasn't going die in a blaze of glory but naked and covered with blood. Thomas Aquinas puts the context of the transfiguration in this way: "Our Lord, after foretelling His Passion to His disciples, had exhorted them to follow the path of His sufferings (Matthew 16:21–24). Now in order that anyone go straight along a road, he must have some knowledge of the end: thus an archer will not shoot the arrow straight unless he first see the target. . . . Above all is this necessary when hard and rough is the road, heavy the going, but delightful the end."[10] Aquinas affirms that the transfiguration is a preview of the Son of Man's future glory. As the human one, he will ride on the clouds and be exalted and glorified.

Second, the Daniel context helps us see that the transfiguration is *a preview of the future kingdom glory (as a place).* Mark says the transfiguration is a preview of "the kingdom of God" coming "in power" (Mark 9:1). The kingdom is God's place, the territory over which he rules. What Jesus said six/eight days earlier helps us see that the transfiguration not only is about Jesus's person but has cosmological consequences. In Daniel's prophecy, the Son of Man is given authority to establish a new kingdom. His glory is to be shared. Thus, the transfiguration is also about the glory of God's coming domain. The bright and shining clothes preview not only his glory but the coming kingdom's glory. That is why Revelation tells us those who conquer will also be dressed in white clothes (Rev. 3:5). God calls his people to buy white clothes from him, and those in the heavens are dressed in white robes (4:4; 7:9–14). The transfiguration previews the transformation of God's people and their home. The transfiguration concerns the metamorphosis of the cosmos.

Third, the time stamp connecting the transfiguration to Daniel suggests the event is *a confirmation of Jesus's present and eternal glory.*[11] Daniel 7 belongs to the corpus of biblical throne visions.[12] However, Daniel also departs from these throne visions by depicting Yahweh in conjunction with another power. For the Son of Man to sit at the right hand of God is to share in the authority and glory of God.

In rabbinic literature, Daniel 7 is commonly associated with what is called "the two powers in heaven" view, which was declared heretical in the second century by some Jews.[13] Certain rabbinic traditions noted a human figure in heaven, and later Jewish theologians speculated on the identity of this figure with guesses ranging from divinized humans to exalted angels. Jesus clarifies

---

10. Thomas Aquinas, *Summa Theologiae*, Pt. III, Q. 45 (trans. Fathers of the English Dominican Province).

11. It is important to affirm Jesus's divinity in the literal sense if one believes that the spiritual sense grows out of the literal sense. However, it is also contested whether "the Son of Man" in Jewish literature has any sense of preexistence.

12. For throne visions, see 1 Kings 22:19; Isa. 6; Ezek. 1; 3:22–24; 10:1; see also 1 Enoch 14:18–23; 60:2; 90:20.

13. Alan F. Segal, *Two Powers in Heaven: Early Rabbinic Reports about Christianity and Gnosticism* (Waco: Baylor University Press, 2012).

that he is this second power, who shares equal power, glory, and dominion with Yahweh.[14]

This reading of Daniel 7 is confirmed at Jesus's trial before the Sanhedrin. When Jesus stands before the high priest, he affirms that he is the Danielic Son of Man (Matt. 26:64; Mark 14:62). Though Jesus claimed to be the Son of Man before, the reference was ambiguous. At the trial he clarifies which Son of Man he is, saying that he shares glory with God. Supporting this suggestion is Jesus's claim to ride on the clouds. Often God or the gods ride on the clouds in the Old Testament (Exod. 14:20; Num. 10:34; Ps. 104:3; Isa. 19:1).[15] The high priest claims that Jesus has uttered blasphemy by making himself one with God (Matt. 26:65; Mark 14:63–64). Israel's leaders think this statement deserves punishment, like those of the kings in the Old Testament who said they would ascend and make themselves like God (Isa. 14:12–14; Ezek. 28:2).

The temporal prelude to the transfiguration is therefore suggestive of Jesus's unique status in relation to Yahweh.[16] Jesus is the messianic Son of Man, but he is more than the messianic Son. He will share Yahweh's throne.

The Spiritual Meaning

The phrase "after six days" can be pressed even deeper. A spiritual meaning (extended meaning) resides in these words as well. The words signify things that signify other things as well. The temporal marker reaches past the immediate context of the Gospel narrative and into the very heart of the Christian Scriptures.

14. A scene in 1 Enoch seems to reflect on the mystery of this figure sharing power and authority with God:
> At that place, I saw the One to whom belongs the time before time. And his head was white like wool, and there was with him another individual, whose face was like that of a human being. His countenance was full of grace like that of one among the holy angels. And I asked the one—from among the angels—who was going with me, and who had revealed to me all the secrets regarding the One who was born of human beings, "Who is this, and from whence is he who is going as the prototype of the Before-Time?" And he answered me and said to me, "This is the Son of Man, to whom belongs righteousness, and with whom righteousness dwells. And he will open all the hidden storerooms; for the Lord of the Spirits has chosen him, and he is destined to be victorious before the Lord of the Spirits in eternal uprightness." (1 Enoch 46:1–3)

15. Though God claims to ride on the clouds, Elijah also goes to heaven in a whirlwind (2 Kings 2:11). See also Greek Apocalypse of Ezra 5:7; Testament of Abraham A 9:8; 10:1; 15:2, 12; B 8:3; 10:2; 12:1, 9.

16. In 1 Enoch, a Messiah figure is called the son of man. This figure has divine attributes, is generated before creation, will judge on the final day, and will sit on the throne of glory (1 Enoch 46:1–4; 48:2–7; 69:26–29). Though it is debated when these texts were written (and we don't have evidence of these texts being used to support Jesus's ontology in early Christianity), if they were written early, then they show a stream of Jewish thought that could fit into the Jewish worldview.

Canonically speaking, the sixth day is the necessary period before a holy day (to cleanse oneself) and a theophany. More specifically, the six-day reference alludes to Moses on Mount Sinai. For six days the cloud rested on Sinai, and then on the seventh day Moses goes up on the mountain: "The glory of the Lord settled on Mount Sinai, and the cloud covered it *for six days*. On the *seventh day* he called to Moses from the cloud. The appearance of the Lord's glory to the Israelites was like a consuming fire on the mountaintop. Moses entered the cloud as he went up the mountain, and he remained on the mountain forty days and forty nights" (Exod. 24:16–18).

This spiritual sense has implications for how we read the transfiguration. First, it reveals that *Jesus is the new and better Moses.* As with Moses, Jesus goes up on a high mountain, a cloud covers the mountain, three individuals are given special privileges, his face shines, a voice speaks from the cloud, witnesses are terrified, and people are comforted. When Jesus comes down the mountain, he only finds rebellion and a faithless generation. This allusion is doubly confirmed by Moses appearing and talking to Jesus on the mountain.[17]

Peter says that Jesus *received* honor and glory from the Father on the mountain (2 Pet. 1:17). Jesus *is transfigured*—a passive verb—he doesn't transfigure himself (Matt. 17:2; Mark 9:2). Jesus is therefore the new prophet in the mold of Moses, who will lead his people on a new exodus (Deut. 18:18–19) and to whom they must listen (18:15).

Additionally, only Luke records the minutes of the meeting between Jesus, Moses, and Elijah. He says that they speak about Jesus's *exodos* (departure, Luke 9:31). Moses must have been particularly interested in this topic, as he was present for the first exodus. Now he understands that his narrative is a small part of a larger tapestry.

Jesus is the new and better mediator between God and humankind, who will plead on behalf of his people and bring true redemption. Jesus is the ultimate prophet who will bring redemption by covering them in blood and interceding for them. Jesus is the new priest. As God gave Moses the plans for the tabernacle on Sinai, so God now reveals his new temple on the mountain in Galilee. To speak of Jesus's transfiguration without reference to Jesus as the new Moses misses the point of the transfiguration.

17. Dale Allison, *The New Moses: A Matthean Typology* (Eugene, OR: Wipf & Stock, 2013); W. D. Davies and Dale Allison, *Matthew 8–18*, ICC (London: T&T Clark International, 1991), 685–86; Patrick Schreiner, *Matthew, Disciple and Scribe: The First Gospel and Its Portrait of Jesus* (Grand Rapids: Baker Academic, 2019), 154–58; Leroy Huizenga, *The New Isaac: Tradition and Intertextuality in the Gospel of Matthew* (Leiden: Brill, 2012), 211. Many church fathers also noted the connections between Moses and Jesus, including Irenaeus and Eusebius. The allusions to Moses are more evident in Matthew than in Mark.

The spiritual meaning of the temporal reference also reveals that *Jesus is greater than Moses*. Too often we think the transfiguration merely paints Jesus as the new Moses, but this is woefully inadequate. On the seventh day Moses went up on Mount Sinai to see God. On the seventh day the disciples went up on the Mount of Transfiguration to do the same.[18] Though connections exist between Moses and Jesus, on the mountain Moses is a spectator of divine majesty much like the disciples. As the disciples behold glory on the mountain, so Moses beholds glory on the mountain. As Moses travels up the mountain to meet with God, so the disciples travel up the mountain to meet with God. On the mountain both the disciples and Moses see a bright light.

Jesus, therefore, is not only the new Moses but the object of what Moses saw on the mountain—Yahweh himself. The period of six days refers to the time before witnessing a theophany; now the disciples see *the* theophany in the face of Jesus. Moses's face only became luminous *after* seeing God. Jesus's face shines *before* the voice from heaven declares that Jesus is the divine Son. Moses's light was borrowed; Jesus's glory was unborrowed. Jesus is not a mirror of divine glory but the manifestation of it. He is light from light, God from God. The "glory of the Lord" that settled on Mount Sinai now settles on the Mount of Transfiguration. When Moses appears, he finally sees in more clarity what he yearned to see so long ago.

In this way, the transfiguration reveals not only what is to come but what is. Jesus is the eternally begotten Son of God, of the same essence as Yahweh. Jesus doesn't only reveal glory that will be given to him; he reveals the glory he has always possessed.[19]

The Anagogical Meaning

The temporal reference also exudes an anagogical (eschatological) meaning, pointing to the new creation.[20] The transfiguration envisions a future metamorphosis of the cosmos by the light of Christ. A globally expansive reconstructive theme emerges from the event.

When interpreters hear that Jesus went up the mountain after six or eight days, they should immediately think of the creation narrative in Genesis. God

---

18. Moses was also enthroned, reflected the glory of God, was brought to heaven after his death, and was divinized.

19. As Kibbe states, "The transfiguration was a creaturely display of Jesus's filial divine perfections: proleptic because he had not yet been raised from the dead, yet fitting because he did possess those perfections even in his pre-resurrection humanity." This comes from an unpublished paper Kibbe sent me in private correspondence.

20. Palamas says that Luke's account (eight days) corresponds to the others (six days) because though there appeared to be six people on the mountain (Peter, James, John, Jesus, Moses, Elijah), there were actually eight if one includes the Father and the Spirit. *The Saving Work of Christ: Sermons by Saint Gregory Palamas*, ed. Christopher Veniamin (Waymart, PA: Mount Thabor, 2008), 41.

created the world in six days, then on the seventh day he rested. The eighth day was known as the first day of the new creation, since it transcended the seven days of creation.[21] The seventh and eighth day imagery therefore symbolizes the reconfiguration of the cosmos.

The church fathers were quick to point this out. John of Damascus writes that in six days God brought out the sum total of things. John takes the "eight" in Luke to signify the coming age.[22] Gregory Palamas likewise says the eighth day represents the coming age, an eternal day not measured in hours, never lengthening or shortening.[23] The transfiguration therefore has eschatological implications in two ways.

First, the transfiguration is *a preview of beholding God's glory*. It is a new creation trailer. Revelation says that the throne of God and the Lamb will be in the new city, and the citizens of that city will see his face. No lamp will be needed, nor even the sun, because the Lord God will give them light (Rev. 22:3–5). This complements and completes the garden story, in which Adam and Eve walk with God and he speaks with them face to face. This is partly realized again with Moses (Exod. 33:11) and in the tabernacle and temple. The longing to see God will finally be satisfied at the end.

The transfiguration previews this seventh-/eighth-day theology by allowing the disciples to see the bright, shining face of Jesus. The only Son reveals God (John 1:18). One day we will all see God's face forever. For now the three disciples see him on the mountain. In this way, Jesus is more than merely their Messiah. He is the one who walked in garden with Adam and Eve, the one Moses saw on Sinai, the one the priests experienced in the temple, and the one all Christians will behold in the new creation.

Second, the creation echo suggests that the transfiguration is not only about the person of Christ but about *God's purpose for creation*. As God's first act in creation was the dissemination of light, so his act of re-creation will also be the diffusion of light. The transfiguration is not only a revelation of glory in a person; it also signals the glory coming for all creation. The groaning creation

21. St. Basil the Great, *On the Holy Spirit* 27.66, trans. David Anderson, Popular Patristics 42 (Crestwood, NY: St. Vladimir's Seminary Press, 2001).

22. John of Damascus, "Oration on the Transfiguration," in *Light on the Mountain: Greek Patristic and Byzantine Homilies on the Transfiguration of the Lord*, trans. Brian Daley, Popular Patristics 48 (New York: St. Vladimir's Seminary Press, 2013), 216.

23. Gregory Palamas, *Saving Work of Christ*, 41, 48. Anastasius of Antioch says the number six corresponds to the present world, but then comes the seventh day, which is representative of the new creation (Anastasius of Antioch, "Homily on the Transfiguration" [Daley, 135]; see also Andrew of Crete, "On the Transfiguration of Christ" [Daley, 187]). Philagathos affirms that the six days represent the creation of the world, after which we will be led up the mountain to the new creation. Philagathos, "Homily 31, on the Saving Transfiguration" (Daley, 280).

will also share in the glory to be revealed (Rom. 8:19). The same light that emanates from Jesus will transfigure the cosmos.

This correlates to Jesus affirming that this is a preview of the kingdom. The transfiguration is an appetizer for how the garden story will be fulfilled. This is why Revelation describes the new Jerusalem's arrival to earth as a scene of radiance: "He . . . showed me the holy city, Jerusalem, coming down out of heaven from God, arrayed with God's glory. Her *radiance* was like a precious jewel, like a jasper stone, clear as crystal" (Rev. 21:10–11). Jesus's glory will be distributed and shared with all of creation (Ps. 8:3–5). His light is unbounded and will illumine all things as his lightnings brighten the world (77:18). Like the tabernacle and temple, the new creation will be vivid because the knowledge of God's glory will cover the earth like the water covers the sea (Hab. 2:14).

The new creation will be filled with white robes, white clouds, white horses, and a white throne—all iridescent with Jesus's white-hot glory. The foundations of the new city are adorned with jewels (Rev. 21:19–20), the twelve gates are twelve pearls, and the main street of the city is pure gold (21:21). The transfiguration has not only personal but cosmological consequences.

Conclusion

Though we tend to skip over the words "after six days" (Matt. 17:1; Mark 9:2) and "about eight days later" (Luke 9:28), they are vital for rightly understanding what is to follow. In them we see that Jesus is the messianic Son—the Son of Man from Daniel 7, who will receive glory and honor, and the new Moses, who ascends the mountain to be the mediator between God and his people. In all this, Jesus is the new mediator who will bring about the glory of the kingdom of God and the new creation.

Yet, the Son of Man in Daniel 7 is also one who shares in the power and glory of Yahweh. Jesus is also more than the new Moses and more than simply a human one. Jesus is what Moses longed to see: God himself. In the new creation, God's people will see the God of Jacob in the face of Jesus, and there will be no need for the sun.

By pointing to Jesus's place as the new mediator and his identity as God himself, the Gospels' time stamp thus testifies to the double sonship of Jesus. Jesus is both the messianic and divine Son.

Up the Mountain

We have looked at the timing of the transfiguration. Now we turn to the location. All three Gospel writers say the transfiguration occurred on a mountain.

Matthew and Mark specify that it was a "high" mountain (Matt. 17:1; Mark 9:2) while Luke simply says that it was a mountain (Luke 9:28). Peter, in his epistle, confirms the location, calling it the "holy" mountain (2 Pet. 1:18).

Interpreters throughout history have found the location to be significant. Anastasius of Sinai says, "The mountain is the place of mysteries, this is the place of the unspeakable, this rock is the rock of hidden things, this summit is the summit of the heavens."[24] Below, we will examine the literal, spiritual, and anagogical meaning of the mountain, which again suggests Jesus's double sonship.

The Literal Meaning

While the Scriptures give no indication of which mountain hosted the transfiguration, since at least the time of Origen the Christian tradition has claimed it was Mount Tabor.[25] This mountain stood between northern and southern Israel.

In fact, it is difficult to find an author in the patristic and medieval ages who does not identity the mountain as Tabor.[26] Language linking the transfiguration to Tabor proliferates. You will find references to "Taboric light," there is a publishing house named "Mount Thabor Publishing," and on Mount Tabor itself is the Church of the Transfiguration. The campus of my first teaching position, Western Seminary, sits under the shadow of another Mount Tabor in Portland, Oregon.

Why do so many authors identify the mountain as Tabor? While some may have simply followed interpretive tradition, the move is not completely unwarranted. The main text the fathers sourced this location from was Psalm 89:12:

> North and south—you created them.
> Tabor and Hermon shout for joy at your name.

The fathers saw Psalm 89:12 as having a deeper meaning: Hermon and Tabor rejoice at the declaration of the name of the beloved Son—revealed at the baptism and transfiguration. Psalm 89:12 foretells *where* Jesus's name was to be publicized. Christian tradition associates Jesus's baptism with Mount Hermon, since Mount Hermon was the source of the Jordan River. At the Jordan River and at

24. Anastasius of Sinai, "Homily on the Transfiguration" (Daley, 165).

25. Daley, introduction to *Light on the Mountain*, 16n4; Origen, *Homily on Psalm 88*, 13 (PG 12:1548). The Taboric tradition may have arisen from the final prepositional phrase in Matt. 17:1, which could be interpreted as modifying the mountain, saying it stands "by itself." Geographically, Mount Tabor does stand out amid a flat plain. However, Mark 9:2 clarifies that the prepositional phrase modifies the disciples (by themselves) by including the adjective *monous*, which matches the antecedent *autous*.

26. Cyril, Jerome, Leonitus, Anastasius of Sinai, St. Andrew of Crete, John of Damascus, Leo the Emperor, Philagathos, Nikephoros, Gregory the Sinaite, and Gregory Palamas all identify the location as Tabor.

Tabor, the Father's voice declared Jesus his beloved Son (Matt. 3:17; 17:5; Mark 1:11; 9:7; Luke 3:22; 9:35). Proclus of Constantinople is representative when he says, "Tabor signifies the mountain where Christ willed to be transfigured and was named Son by the Father's witness. . . . And Hermon is the mountain a little way from the land of the Jordan . . . near to which Jesus will be baptized."[27]

While I'm tempted to follow this interpretation, and I'm quite attracted to the link with Psalm 89:12, Mount Tabor is around fifty-four miles (94 km) from Caesarea Philippi (the last named location in the Gospels before the transfiguration), and at 1,930 feet (588 m), it is not a very high mountain but a mere hill with a gentle slope and a rounded summit.[28] This distance and low altitude compelled A. T. Robertson to state that "the tradition which places the Transfiguration on Mount Tabor is beyond question false."[29] On the other hand, Mount Hermon is immediately north of Caesarea Philippi and is a higher mountain (9,232 feet; 2,814 m).

Historically, it is possible the transfiguration took place on either Hermon or Tabor, but both are impossible to prove. While I'm not convinced the transfiguration occurred on Mount Tabor, it can be useful to follow the tradition by calling it Mount Tabor since the language is so conventional now.

The fact is that no mountain is specifically named in the Gospels or in 2 Peter. Every theory is a guess. I believe the Gospel writers purposively didn't reveal on which mountain Jesus was transfigured. This intentional vagueness allows the mountain to serve as a symbol. By not naming the mountain, the Gospel writers don't limit the symbolism to one locale but extend its significance to touch the various mountains of the Bible. We must therefore follow this interpretive clue and look at mountains as symbols, for in one sense, they are all one.

The Spiritual Meaning

Mountains abound in Scripture. The entire biblical storyline could be summarized by what happens on high places. In the transfiguration these themes cohere and climax. Between Sinai and Golgotha stands Tabor. To neglect the mountain setting is to miss a key clue for how to interpret the transfiguration.

The Bible begins on a mountain. The garden in Genesis is described as a holy mountain of God (Ezek. 28:14). God's new creation project with Noah begins on Mount Ararat (Gen. 8:4). God also meets Abraham on Mount Moriah when he tells him to sacrifice his son Isaac (22:2, 14). On Mount Horeb Moses finds the burning bush (Exod. 3:1). The ground is called holy because God's presence

27. Proclus of Constantinople, "Homily on the Transfiguration of the Savior" (Daley, 95). See also Tertullian, *Against Marcion* 4.22.7 (CCSL 1:602).

28. Rafael Frankel, "Tabor, Mount (Place)," in *The Anchor Yale Bible Dictionary*, vol. 6 (New York: Doubleday, 1992), 304–5.

29. A. T. Robertson, *A Harmony of the Gospels* (New York: Harper & Brothers, 1922), 122.

is revealed there (3:5). God promises that he will bring his people Israel back to worship him "on this mountain" (3:12). This promise is fulfilled just fifteen chapters later when Moses comes again to the mountain of God—Sinai (18:5). On the mountain God meets with Moses in a cloud, in thick smoke and fire (19:18; 24:15; Deut. 4:11; 5:22–23; 9:15). Deuteronomy says that Moses met God face to face on the mountain (Exod. 33:11; Deut. 5:4).[30] Skipping forward a bit, the prophet Elijah also goes to Horeb, the mountain of God, and hears God in "a soft whisper" (1 Kings 19:8–12).[31]

On Zion, Solomon dedicates the newly built temple to the Lord (1 Kings 8). On Zion, God's holy mountain, God installs his king, his Son (Ps. 2:6–7). Isaiah predicts the mountain of the Lord's house will be established as the highest mountain, and all nations will stream to it (Isa. 2:2–3).

In Ezekiel, God brings the prophet to a very high mountain and shows him the future temple (Ezek. 40:2; 43:12). On this mountain the prophet sees a man whose appearance is like bronze (40:3). In Daniel, a stone strikes a statue and becomes a great mountain that fills the whole earth (Dan. 2:35). Micah prophesies, like Isaiah, that in the last days the mountain of the house of the Lord will be established at the top of the mountains, and many nations will stream to it (Mic. 4:1–2).

In summary, mountains often (1) signify progress in the covenantal story and (2) do so through theophanies: revelations of God to humankind. This is

---

30. The pairing of the transfiguration and Sinai is greatly emphasized in the early literature on the transfiguration. Anastasius of Sinai puts it this way:

> There [Sinai] we encountered mist, here the sun; there darkness, here a cloud of light, there the Law of the Decalogue, here the eternal Word who exists before all words; there fleshly riddles, here divine things. There, on the mountain, the tablets were broken because of impious behavior, here hearts are made wise for their salvation. Then water came forth of the rock of unbelief, but now the spring of deathless life bubbles forth. There a staff put forth shoots, here the cross bursts into bloom. There a quail comes down from above to presage punishment, here a dove comes down from above to promise salvation; there the Hebrew Mary plays her cymbal in a mystic sign, here the Lord's Mary brings forth her child in a divine way. There Moses loosed the sandal from his feet, anticipating the end of the Law's worship; here John does not loose it, clearly confirming the bond of union between God the Word and our mortal, skin-covered nature. There Elijah hid from the face of Jezebel; here Elijah gazes on God, face to face. (Anastasius of Sinai, "Homily on the Transfiguration" [Daley, 166]; see also John of Damascus, "Oration on the Transfiguration," [Daley, 210])

31. Proclus says that the high mountain is like where Moses "slew the paschal lamb and sprinkled the doorposts of the Hebrews with its blood; a high mountain, where Elijah cut up a bull in their presence, consuming by fire a sacrifice made in water; a high mountain, where Moses was, who opened and shut the depths of the Red Sea" (Proclus of Constantinople, "Homily on the Transfiguration of the Savior" [Daley, 90]). John of Damascus puts words into Elijah's mouth in connection to his vision on Mount Horeb: "He [Jesus] is the one whom I gazed on long ago, in bodiless form, in the gentle breeze of the Spirit." John of Damascus, "Oration on the Transfiguration" (Daley, 224).

because mountains are places where heaven and earth meet.[32] Both of these are important for our reading of the transfiguration story.

First, the mountain location signifies progress in the covenantal story. All the covenantal figures are linked to mountains: God met with Adam and Eve on the mountain, made a new covenant with Noah on a mountain, and provided a substitute sacrifice for Abraham's only son on a mountain. Moses cut a new covenant with Israel on a mountain. God promised David that one of his sons would sit on God's mountain, and Solomon built God's temple on a mountain. Mountains are central to the progress of God's story. When Jesus arrived, he also ascended mountains. He was tempted on a mountain, taught the Torah on a mountain, fed God's people on a mountain, prophesied on a mountain, was transfigured on a mountain, and died on a mountain.

Thus the mountain location reveals that the transfiguration furthers the covenantal story. Jesus is the new Adam, Abraham, Moses, David, and Solomon. His glory reveals where this story was always headed—the union of heaven and earth. All the other mountain stories prepared for this one and its twin, Golgotha. Jesus is the messianic Son, the new covenantal figure Israel has been waiting for.

Second, mountains are places of theophanies, where God and humankind meet. A mountain is an *axis mundi*, a conduit between earth and heaven, a place of divine revelation. God met with Abraham on a mountain (Gen. 22), revealed himself to Moses in the burning bush on a mountain (Exod. 3:9–10; 19:18–20), and spoke to Elijah on a mountain (1 Kings 19). Mountains are where humans encounter God.

The transfiguration signifies that Jesus is both the one who goes up the mountain (man) *and* the one who comes down to the mountain (God). Anointed figures would ascend, God would descend. As the God-man, Jesus both ascends and descends. He is the ladder the angels ascend and descend on (John 1:51). Several arguments from the text support this, but I will limit my remarks to two.

First, Jesus not only "ascends" but "descends" as indicated by his dazzlingly white clothes. Their transcendent character is underscored when Mark says that these garments are whiter than white (Mark 9:3). Throughout Jewish literature, those who come from heaven are clothed in shining and bright garments.[33] Richard Bauckham notes that their dress is typically "shining like the sun or the stars, gleaming like bronze or precious stones, fiery bright like torches or

---

32. In Orthodox iconography, Christ typically appears with a mandorla (an oval shape) around his head, which sometimes has two circles that overlap, signifying that in Christ heaven and earth meet.

33. 1 Enoch 71:1; 106:10; 2 Enoch 1:5; 37:1; Testament of Levi 8:2; see also Acts 1:10; John 20:12.

lightning, dazzling white like snow or pure wool."[34] Jesus's garments designate him as a heavenly figure.[35]

Second, God's presence on the mountain is confirmed when Peter calls it a "holy mountain" (2 Pet. 1:18). It is holy because God had revealed himself there, just like the ground that Moses stands on in the burning bush scene is called "holy ground" (Exod. 3:5; Acts 7:33). This holiness could be attributed to the mountain because the Father speaks, but the holiness of the mountain is more likely linked to Jesus's luminosity. Moses's bush burned (Exod. 3:2), God's presence in a pillar of fire led Israel (13:21), the tabernacle and temple are called the "holy place" because the fire of God's presence burns there (40:38). The prophet Isaiah sees God on his throne while the seraphim cover their faces. Isaiah rightly asserts, "For the High and Exalted One, who lives forever, whose name is holy says this: 'I live in a high and holy place'" (Isa. 57:15). Peter affirms that the mountain is "holy" because there he beheld the glory of God in the face of Jesus Christ.

In the old covenant, God met with his people in fire, smoke, and darkness. In the new covenant, he now meets with them in light. The revelation on the Mount of Transfiguration surpasses the revelations in the Old Testament. If on Sinai God revealed his name invisibly, then on Mount Tabor he reveals his name visibly.[36] The transfiguration fulfills all theophanies.[37]

Jesus ascends the mountain to reveal that he is God, who will overcome death. The disciples need not fear his death. Jesus is greater than Adam, Moses, and David, for he is the eternally begotten Son, who has life within himself.

The Anagogical Meaning

No exact location for the Mount of Transfiguration is specified in the Scriptures. This causes readers to move both backward *and* forward in the biblical storyline. In this way the unspecified mountain also becomes a preview of the

34. Richard Bauckham, "The Throne of God and the Worship of Jesus," in *The Jewish Roots of Christological Monotheism*, ed. Carey C. Newman, James R. Davila, and Gladys S. Lewis (Leiden: Brill, 1999), 51.

35. Jesus's clothes might simply portray him as an "angel like" figure, and Michael F. Bird (*Jesus among the Gods: Early Christology in the Greco-Roman World* [Waco: Baylor University Press, 2022], 274) is right to note that angel Christology is partly compatible with parts of the New Testament. However, the New Testament also presents Jesus as on the creator side of the creator-creature distinction.

36. For this concept, I am indebted to Anastasius of Sinai, "Homily on the Transfiguration" (Daley, 172).

37. As Mike Bird states, the transfiguration is not a preview of Jesus's resurrection or a preview of the manifestation of Jesus as a Hellenistic deity. "Rather, it is a divine disclosure of Jesus's heavenly identity built largely around the biblical theophany tradition." Michael F. Bird, *Jesus the Eternal Son: Answering Adoptionist Christology* (Grand Rapids: Eerdmans, 2017), 72.

eschatological mountain and the whole of creation. God's transfiguration of the cosmos will be all-encompassing.

The prophets predict a final day when the Lord's mountain will be established. The transfiguration is a preview of that final mountain. Micah's and Isaiah's words are revealing, considering the transfiguration and the command to listen:[38]

> In the last days
> the *mountain* of the LORD's house
> will be established
> at the top of the mountains
> and will be raised above the hills.
> Peoples will stream to it,
> and many nations will come and say,
> "Come, let's go up to the *mountain* of the LORD,
> to the house of the God of Jacob.
> He will *teach us* about his *ways*
> so we may walk in his paths."
> For *instruction* will go out of Zion
> and the word of the LORD from Jerusalem. (Mic. 4:1–2; see also Isa. 2:2–3)

The last-day mountain is both the place of the new temple and the place from which God's law will go forth. There God will teach his people his ways. Based on other texts in the Scriptures, God's teaching comes through his anointed figure—his prophet, priest, and king. The transfiguration account affirms that Jesus is this figure from Psalm 2: he is the Son (king), his garments shine (priest), and he is the one to whom people are called to listen (prophet).

Yet the allusion to the eschatological mountain also implies that Jesus is Israel's destination on the mountain. In the Hebrew Bible, God promises that he will bring his people to his holy mountain (Isa. 56:7) *and* that he will tear the heavens open and come down so that the mountains quake at his presence (64:1). Ezekiel tells of how the Lord will shepherd his people on the mountains of Israel (Ezek. 34:13–14). He also speaks of a vision on a high mountain, where he sees a new temple on the top of a mountain where the Lord's presence resides (Ezek. 40–46). The eschatological mountain is precious because God's presence is there (Rev. 21:3).

When Jesus is transfigured on the mountain in bright clothes and with a bright face, he shows that his body is the new temple and that one day his followers will dwell with him forever and look upon his shining face. Jesus leads

---

38. In chap. 4, I will argue that the command to listen pertains to Jesus's impending death and, in the context of the Synoptics, Jesus tells his disciples to walk in his ways and paths by also taking up their cross (Matt. 16:24; Mark 8:34; Luke 9:23).

them up the mountain as their anointed one, yet he is also the end for which they ascend the mountain.

This anagogical reading of the mountain indicates that the transfiguration scene is a preview of God's future for his people. Jesus remains on earth but also stands at the threshold of heaven. God's people will dwell with God on his mountain as the disciples did in the transfiguration. They will see Jesus's face and be clothed in bright clothes. However, this will only take place through the work of God's servant. The mountain in the transfiguration scene implies that Jesus is both the one to bring them to God and God himself.

Conclusion

The transfiguration plays a role in the progression of the covenantal story that occurred on mountains. The location shows readers that Jesus is the Jewish leader who leads his people up God's mountain. In this sense, the transfiguration reveals Jesus as the messianic Son.

However, the mountain location also reveals that Jesus is not only the one who leads them up the mountain but the one who descends on the mountain. Theophanies occur on mountains. The transfiguration reveals that Jesus is the one all the Old Testament saints saw in the heavenly court.

On the Mount of Transfiguration, the disciples finally see God in light. They see heaven and earth meet. Briefly, they glimpse the face of God. On this mountain, God and humanity dwell together in the person of Christ. The mountain is not an inconsequential location marker; it determines the entire meaning of the transfiguration. However, it does this only in association with the other narrative details.

The Three Witnesses

The final aspect of the setting to examine is the spectators. In all three Gospel accounts, only Peter, James, and John go up on the mountain with Jesus (Matt. 17:1; Mark 9:2; Luke 9:28). This raises several questions: Why only these three? Why these three in particular? Why did Jesus tell them not to speak of this vision until the resurrection? Once again, the fourfold sense serves as a helpful framework for examining this aspect of the transfiguration.

The Literal Meaning

Three disciples—Peter, James, and John—go up on the mountain. The literal meaning is simple. The company that ascends with Jesus is limited and deliberate. At least three reasons stand behind Jesus restricting this revelation to his inner circle.

First, Jesus limited the revelation of his nature because *the other disciples were not ready for this truth*. That there were three witnesses shows us that Jesus was protecting the others, for only those who are called can come into God's presence without being destroyed. Even these three are terrified by the vision (Matt. 17:6; Mark 9:6; Luke 9:34).

Most of the church fathers assert that the other disciples were excluded because they were not able to see the glory of God. Chrysostom affirms that Jesus took these disciples because they were superior in holiness to the others: "Peter clearly showed his superiority in the intensity of his love; John made it clear by being loved intensely; James, from the answer he gave with his brother, 'We can drink this cup.'"[39] Philagathos affirms that the eyes of the uninitiated were not capable of receiving this vision, for only the clean of heart could get a glimpse.[40] Additionally, many of the fathers were appalled by the prospect of Judas witnessing the transfiguration.[41] Thus, Peter, James, and John were brought up the mountain because the other disciples were not ready for—or were disqualified from—this revelation.

Second, Jesus selected these three because *they would also be uniquely involved in his death*.[42] Jesus wanted to arm them against the coming scandal of his death. The transfiguration concerns how Jesus's humility and honor meet. These are the same men Jesus took with him into Gethsemane (Matt. 26:37) and to whom he spoke words of courage.[43] In this sense, the transfiguration displays the glory of the future kingdom to those who would experience the darkness of Jesus's death. Jesus gave the greatest encouragement to those who would experience the greatest sorrow.

Third, Aquinas remarks that the three are there so that *the event may be established by the mouth of two or three witnesses*.[44] Both Peter and John report, or at least allude to, this event in their own writings (John 1:14–18; 2 Pet. 1:17–18).

39. John Chrysostom, "Homily 56 on the Gospel of Matthew" (Daley, 70). Origen says the three were deemed worthy and that Jesus appeared to the children of light who had put off the works of darkness (Daley, 55, 57). Proclus, on the other hand, affirms that Jesus thought of the disciples as one (with the exception of Judas) and brought the three as representatives ("Homily on the Transfiguration" [Daley, 90]).

40. Philagathos, "Homily 31, on the Saving Transfiguration" (Daley, 265).

41. Leontius ("Homily on the Transfiguration" [Daley, 125]) affirms that Jesus didn't take Judas because he was not worthy to gaze on the Lord's glory in such magnitude. Anastasius of Antioch ("Homily on the Transfiguration" [Daley, 135]) likewise says it would not have been proper for Judas to become a visual sharer in these mysteries.

42. Calvin rejects these first two reasons and says three came because it was the number that the Law laid down for proving something. However, this does not explain why *these* three came with Jesus. John Calvin, *Commentary on a Harmony of the Evangelists, Matthew, Mark, and Luke*, trans. William Pringle, vol. 2 (Grand Rapids: Eerdmans, 1949), 309.

43. Philagathos, "Homily 31, on the Saving Transfiguration" (Daley, 268).

44. Thomas Aquinas, *Summa Theologiae*, Pt. III, Q. 45.

They passed down this tradition, which they were called to speak about after the resurrection. Some scholars even propose that these three are called the "three pillars of the church" in Galatians 2:9 because they were the ones "standing" there when the transfiguration occurred (Matt. 16:28).[45] If this is the case, then witnessing Jesus's majesty and glory puts one in a special camp. Divine revelation and a special calling go together in the Scriptures.

To bring these three points together, Jesus brought up the three in the inner circle (1) because they were the most prepared to witness his glory, (2) because they would uniquely be involved in his death, and (3) so that the event would be established by witnesses.

However, there is one more important point. The disciples' response gives us a critical clue for the meaning of the transfiguration. All the Gospel writers affirm that when Jesus is transfigured, the three are "terrified" (Matt. 17:6; Mark 9:6) or "afraid" (Luke 9:34). Matthew even says that when they heard the voice from heaven, the three disciples "fell facedown" (17:6). In Israel's Scriptures this is the posture of those who have seen heavenly beings, such as angels, and it is also the posture of those who have seen God.[46] For example:

Abraham falls facedown before God (Gen. 17:3, 17).

When fire comes from the Lord and consumes the burnt offering, the people of Israel fall on their faces (Lev. 9:24).

Moses and Aaron fall on their faces before the glory of the Lord (Num. 20:6).

Joshua falls facedown before the ark of the Lord (Josh. 7:6).

On Mount Carmel, when the fire of the Lord falls from heaven, all the people fall facedown and claim that the Lord is God (1 Kings 18:39).

When David sees the angel of the Lord, he falls facedown (1 Chron. 21:16).

Ezra falls facedown before the house of God (Ezra 10:1).

Ezekiel falls on his face before the Lord's glory (Ezek. 1:28; 3:23).

Daniel falls facedown before the messenger of God (Dan. 8:17).

John falls down before one whose face shines like the sun (Rev. 1:16–17).

---

45. David Wenham and A. D. A. Moses, "'There Are Some Standing Here . . .': Did They Become the 'Reputed Pillars' of the Jerusalem Church? Some Reflections on Mark 9:1, Galatians 2:9 and the Transfiguration," *NovT* 36 (1994): 146–63.

46. Some might argue that this is a response only to the voice and not to Jesus and his luminosity. Additionally, one may wonder, if they fall in recognition of his divinity, then why are they still worried about the cross? However, it is difficult to separate the voice from the contents of the Father's words. They may have initially fallen not knowing that they were bowing before God but later understood that their actions were telling and therefore worth including in their accounts.

The pattern is clear. When people encounter unapproachable light, they fall to the ground overwhelmed. The posture of the disciples confirms that they are not merely with a new anointed figure but in the very presence of God.

The Spiritual Meaning

The meaning of Peter, James, and John on the mountain with Jesus goes beyond the literal sense. The scene correlates to Aaron, Nadab, and Abihu with Moses on Mount Sinai (Exod. 24:9). On Sinai all of them see the God of Israel. A spiritual reading paints the three disciples as the new priests. Because they too have seen the face of God, they will build God's people as their new covenant priests.[47]

These three disciples on the mount are the only ones given nicknames. Simon was named "Cephas (which means Peter)" (John 1:42). He is "the rock" on which Christ builds his church (Matt. 16:16). Peter was the first to confess Jesus as the Messiah, and he preached the first Christian sermon at Pentecost. Peter would therefore build the church on the chief cornerstone: "As you come to him, a living stone—rejected by people but chosen and honored by God— you yourselves, as living stones, a spiritual house, are being built to be a holy priesthood to offer spiritual sacrifices acceptable to God through Jesus Christ" (1 Pet. 2:4–5).

James and John, the sons of Zebedee, were given the moniker "Boanerges," which means "sons of thunder" or "sons of trembling" (Mark 3:17). This might indicate the quick temper of the brothers, but it also showcases their zeal. James would also build Christ's church as a new priest. Shortly after Jesus's transfiguration, James and John ask to sit on either side of Jesus when he comes in his glory (Mark 10:35–37). In response, Jesus tells them that they must be prepared to "drink the cup" he is about to drink. James was an early martyr, killed by Herod (Acts 12:1–2), and as such, he is a temple sacrifice. His death propels the witnesses of Jesus to the ends of the earth in Acts 13–28. The blood of James is a priestly testimony to the world.

The third witness is John, also a son of thunder. John builds God's temple by witnessing to God's glory. John himself writes of Jesus as light and life and affirms the transformative power of walking in the light (John 12:36). John writes a Gospel in part because he witnessed the light of Jesus on the mountain.

47. John of Damascus says that Jesus took Peter, James, and John with him because Peter was the chief and had received the rudder of the whole church. James was to die for Christ and to drink Christ's cup. John was to be shown the timeless glory of the Son and would then thunder out, "In the beginning was the Word, and the Word was with God, and the Word was God" (John 1:1). John of Damascus, "Oration on the Transfiguration" (Daley, 217).

If Peter is the rock of the church, and James's blood is a temple sacrifice, then John is the priest who comes forth from the temple to bless God's people and tell them that God's favor is upon them. John will again see the face of the Son of Man shining like the sun (Rev. 1:16–17).

Jesus brought Peter, James, and John up the mountain because they would have unique roles in building God's new temple.[48] Peter was the rock, James was the sacrifice, and John blessed future generations by transmitting this message to God's people. While Jesus's transfiguration happened in a moment, those who beheld him were transfigured slowly, "from one degree of glory to another" (2 Cor. 3:18 ESV). This propelled them to be new priests for God's glory.

The Anagogical Meaning

Peter, James, and John are not merely links to the past; they are also harbingers of the future. These three symbolize all those who will one day ascend the mountain of God. Note all the connections between Psalm 24 and the transfiguration:

> Who may *ascend* the mountain of the LORD?
> Who may stand in his *holy place*?
> The one who has clean hands and a pure heart,
> who has not appealed to what is false,
> and who has not sworn deceitfully.
> He will receive *blessing* from the LORD,
> and righteousness from the God of his salvation.
> Such is the generation of those who inquire of him,
> who seek *the face of the God of Jacob*. (Ps. 24:3–6)

The psalmist correlates ascending the mountain of the Lord, his "holy place," with seeing the face of God. Between these, his answer to the question of who may ascend is the one who has clean hands and a pure heart. This is cultic language—the sort of language one would use to describe *new priests*. All God's people are priests who will one day ascend God's mountain (1 Pet. 2:9).

The three disciples are a picture of those with hands, hearts, and tongues cleansed by the glory of the Son. These will ascend the mountain of the Lord in the ultimate sense. They are the ones calling all people: "Come let's go up to

---

48. One of our earliest interpreters affirms this reading. John Chrysostom says, "For 'Peter excelled in the love' he bore to Christ and in the power bestowed on him; John in the privilege of Christ's love for him on account of his virginity, and, again, on account of his being privileged to be an Evangelist; James on account of the privilege of martyrdom." Quoted in Aquinas, *Summa Theologiae*, Pt. III, Q. 45.

the mountain of the LORD" (Mic. 4:2). They answer the question, "Who can live on your holy mountain?" (Ps. 15:1). They say to God on our behalf, "Send your light and your truth; let them lead me. Let them bring me to your holy mountain" (43:3).

Appropriately, when someone ascends God's mountain to behold him, they fall on their face in fear. At the burning bush, Moses hides his face because he is afraid to look at God (Exod. 3:6). When fire comes down from the Lord and consumes the burnt offering, the people fall facedown (Lev. 9:24). Ezra falls facedown before the house of God (Ezra 10:1), and Ezekiel does as well when he sees light and the form of the Lord's glory (Ezek. 1:28; 3:23).[49] When John *again* sees Jesus's face shining like the sun, he doesn't say, "Good to see you in this form again." He suitably drops to his knees (Rev. 1:16–17). Ascending the mountain of God is only for those who have been washed by the blood of Jesus. By being united to Jesus, they are then able to see the face of the God of Jacob.

Conclusion

We tend to read quickly over the particulars of the transfiguration's setting and don't always look into why the three disciples were chosen to accompany Jesus. However, the three disciples are not mere set dressing. These beholders are on the mountain for a reason.

Jesus limits his audience because he chooses those who are ready, and he also protects the other disciples, who are not ready to see his glory. The three disciples are priestly witnesses to future generations, building God's temple and filling it with those who will one day ascend the mountain of the Lord and dwell with him forever. The three witnesses behold the messianic and eternal Son.

Purgation–Spiritual Ascent

We have examined the literal, spiritual, and anagogical senses of the setting. Now it is time to turn to the tropological sense and to see how the setting encourages us to also ascend the mountain of God. These details are meaningful not only for our intellectual understanding of Christ but for our own formation in Christ. We must look at these words through the lens of moral guidance as well (tropology).

The church fathers all affirmed that the transfiguration, while a concrete historical event, was symbolic of our own ascent to God. The setting becomes

---

49. This theme is repeated frequently in the Second Temple Literature (1 Enoch 14:14; 60:3; 71:11; 90:15; 2 Enoch 21:2; 3 Enoch 1:7; Apocalypse of Zephaniah 6:14; Jubilees 15:5; Joseph and Aseneth 15:11; Pseudo-Philo 42:10).

a cipher for what it means to "seek the things above" (Col. 3:1), ascend God's mountain (Exod. 19:3; Ps. 24:3; Isa. 2:3; Mic. 4:2), and reach for the new creation (2 Cor. 5:17). To ascend God's mountain requires casting off that which clings so closely (Heb. 12:1–2) and discarding the deeds of darkness (Rom. 13:12). This has been called the work of purgation—burning the sin from our bodies.

For example, the seventh day theology, according to Origen, indicates we need to overcome worldly things and move from the things that are seen (temporal) to the things unseen (eternal).[50] Anastasius of Antioch further claims that the six days correspond to the course of this present world while the seventh day is like the Sabbath—holy.[51] Gregory the Sinaite sees in the mountain an exhortation: "Let us ascend the spiritual mountain of contemplation, and let us gaze at the view from there, attentively and free from material considerations."[52] In view of the mount, Leo the Wise admonishes us to waste no time on lowly, earth-centered considerations but to lift our eyes to this great vision.[53] John of Damascus ties ascending the mountain to those "who have left the dust to dust, and who have risen up above this lowly body, to be borne up towards the highest, divine region of love, and so to contemplate what lies beyond sight."[54]

The Mount of Transfiguration has thus been associated with transcending the things of the earth and seeking that which is in heaven. We renounce blatant sins and willful disobedience and let our minds and bodies rise to the heavens, to where God resides. We bring our behavior, attitudes, and desires into harmony with Christ.

Purgation is the first step of our spiritual formation.[55] We put our passions and evil inclinations in a state of subjugation to God. To ascend, we must detach from

50. Origen, "Commentary on Matt 12.36–43" (Daley, 55).

51. Anastasius of Antioch, "Homily on the Transfiguration" (Daley, 135).

52. Gregory the Sinaite, "Discourse on the Transfiguration" (Daley, 327).

53. Leo the Wise, "Homily 11" (Daley, 255).

54. John of Damascus, "Oration on the Transfiguration" (Daley, 217–18). Pantoleon says, "Let us climb with great physical effort or with gasping breath, lifting our feet uphill, but rather—equipping ourselves with a leisurely understanding to receive what has been said—let us first of all open the holy books, and then, gazing on the sacred text, we shall grope for the riches hidden within" (Pantoleon, "Sermon on the Most Glorious Transfiguration of Our Lord and God, Jesus Christ" [Daley, 109]). Saint Andrew of Crete says, "Come now—if you trust me—as I spread out before you a spiritual banquet of words: let us ascend with the Word today, as he goes up the high mountain of the Transfiguration. Let us take off the material, shadowy life that we wear, and put on 'the robe woven from above as a single whole,' made beautiful in every part by the rays of spiritual virtue." St. Andrew of Crete, "On the Transfiguration of Christ our Lord, Sermon 7" (Daley, 181).

55. The first stage is actually awakening, which is conversion. Though I will speak of formation in terms of three stages or steps, one should not view these mechanistically. M. Robert Mulholland Jr., *Invitation to a Journey: A Road Map for Spiritual Formation* (Downers Grove, IL: IVP Books, 1993), 79–101.

fleshly passions. This includes Paul's list of what is fleshly: "sexual immorality, moral impurity, promiscuity, idolatry, sorcery, hatreds, strife, jealousy, outbursts of anger, selfish ambitions, dissensions, factions, envy, drunkenness, carousing, and anything similar" (Gal. 5:19–21). These things do not engender wholeness. To seek God, we must seek him where he resides. We must rid ourselves of earthly things. Jesus said, "Blessed are the pure in heart, for they shall see God" (Matt. 5:8).

For most of its history, the church has placed a strong emphasis on renunciation. This lifestyle has fallen on hard times. Some associate it with a sort of monkish existence. However, we need to recover non-legalistic evangelical asceticism. We have certainly lost something when our default lifestyle is simply to satisfy most of our desires. The Scriptures continually push us toward self-denial. We are called to give away our money and time (Luke 12:33–34; Heb. 13:16; James 1:27), control our appetites (Prov. 23:20–31), fast (Matt. 6:16–18), control ourselves (1 Pet. 4:7), abstain from sexual sin (1 Thess. 4:3–4), bear each other's burdens (Gal. 6:2), and seek the good of others instead of our own (1 Cor. 10:24).

John Climacus speaks of the Christian life as a contest where "we must renounce all things, despise all things, deride all things, and shake off all things."[56] In the words of Jesus, we take up our crosses and follow the will of the Father. We give up everything to ascend toward God. We give up lesser goods that we may obtain the highest good. This doesn't mean that we engage in self-loathing or neglect the world, but we do set our minds on things above. To quote a contemporary proverb, "No one has ever become poor by giving." The end is so glorious that it is worth the sacrifice. Maybe our witness has been hindered because Christians have stopped denying themselves and instead embraced self-care.

The first step of spiritual transfiguration is purgation. This is how we begin our journey up the mountain as we cast off all the burdens that weigh us down and prevent us from being transfigured by God's light.

CONCLUSION

The setting of the transfiguration is often disregarded. We are prone to only cursorily note the timing or that it happened on a high mountain. And we don't reflect on why Peter, James, and John are on the mountain with Jesus. However, to dash past these elements of the narrative is to miss key clues for how to interpret it.

The temporal reference serves as a narrative tie to the previous episode, where Jesus says that some of the disciples will see the Son of Man coming in glory. As a result, we recognize that Jesus is the Son of Man from Daniel 7, the new prophet who ascends the mountain and the one who brings in the new creation. In all

---

56. John Climacus, *The Ladder of Divine Ascent*, trans. Archimandrite Lazarus Moore (London: Faber & Faber, 1959), 52.

these ways he is the messianic Son. However, Jesus also shares in the glory and throne of Yahweh. He is the one Moses longed to see, and he is the face of God in the new creation. All these suggest that Jesus is more than an earthly Messiah.

The unspecified mountain is also full of meaning. Mountains signify progress in the covenantal story. However, even more than that, mountains are places where humans encounter God. God's glory shines as Jesus becomes the supreme theophany before his disciples.

The three witnesses impress upon readers the overwhelming glory of the scene. Only three could be with Jesus, as the others could not bear God's glory. They also fall before Jesus, a posture representative of being before God. These three thus represent all God's people, who will ascend God's holy mountain on the last day and see his face.

Certainly on their own, these set pieces don't substantiate the claim for Jesus's double sonship, but they are suggestive. Jesus's preexistent *and* future glory is revealed more and more as the event unfolds. The glorious setting paves the way for the glorious signs.

The Glorious Setting	Meaning
Six or eight days	*Messianic sonship*: the temporal reference reveals that Jesus is the Son of Man from Daniel 7, the new Moses who ascends the mountain, and the one who brings in the new creation.
	Eternal sonship: the temporal note indicates that Jesus is the one who shares the throne with Yahweh, is the one whom Moses longed to look at, and is the face of God in the new creation.
The high mountain	*Messianic sonship*: mountains signify progression in the covenantal story, and Jesus stands as one who inaugurates a new covenant by leading the disciples up the mountain as Israel's anointed one.
	Eternal sonship: it is on mountains that theophanies occur. Jesus is not only their leader but the one they long to behold.
Peter, James, and John	*Messianic sonship*: the three ascend the mountain because only they can behold Jesus's glory, and they will uniquely build the new temple.
	Eternal sonship: the response of the three indicates that this is a meeting with God on his mountain.

3

The Glorious Signs

Then Moses said, "Please, let me see your glory."
—Exodus 33:18

On our fifth wedding anniversary, my wife and I went to Yosemite National Park in California. On our last day we hit the lottery for a permit to hike to the top of Half Dome.

Sitting at the eastern end of Yosemite Valley, Half Dome looks like a dome cut in half with a sheer north face (à la the outdoor brand) and the other sides smooth and round. The fifteen-mile hike up Half Dome is a 4,800-foot rise in elevation and takes ten to twelve hours roundtrip. I remember starting out on the trail in the dark with our headlamps on. Like the disciples, we were ascending a mountain.

When we came to the base of the dome shortly after lunch, the climb up the side of the rock seemed too steep. I'm afraid of heights, and the last leg looks almost vertical. On top of that, we were completely gassed from the hike. I admit, the thought crossed my mind that we had made it far enough. No point in pushing it. The view from where we sat was likely almost as good as at the top.

Then I contemplated it more. I realized I would forever regret it if we didn't finish the climb. So I summoned my courage, strapped on my backpack, and made the final ascent.

The top was glorious. From the peak, we could see the whole of Yosemite Valley. On this particular day, the sun was shining on the folds of evergreen blanketing the canyon. I will never forget the glory of Half Dome. Words can't adequately capture its beauty.

When words fall short, we often stretch toward the inexpressible with metaphors and symbols. Even more than my description atop Half Dome, the Gospel writers realized that words would fail to capture the full glory of the transfiguration. So they employed signs and symbols to describe the indescribable.[1]

In this chapter, we will ascend the mountain with the three disciples and behold three glorious signs: (1) Jesus's shining face and white clothes, (2) the bright cloud, and (3) Moses and Elijah's appearance. Jesus's double sonship is confirmed both by the visible aspects of this scene (this chapter) and by God's audible voice (chapter 4). As we begin, it is important to provide a trinitarian grammar for how to properly think and speak about the revelation on the mountain.

A Trinitarian Grammar

According to all the Evangelists, the transfiguration is a scene of luminosity. Jesus's face shines, and his clothes turn white. Matthew and Luke focus on Jesus's face (Matt. 17:2; Luke 9:29), while Mark centers on his clothes (9:3). Matthew also writes that a "bright" cloud emerged (Matt. 17:5). Luke affirms that Jesus, Moses, and Elijah all appeared in "glory" (Luke 9:31–32). Similarly, Peter writes that Jesus received glory from God on the mountain (2 Pet. 1:17).

To understand the brilliance of the transfiguration, we need a trinitarian grammar, for the transfiguration has a trinitarian texture. Below I will examine (1) how God is light in himself and (2) how God's light shines forth through the Son and Spirit. These two trinitarian truths help us see how the light of the transfiguration points both to Jesus's preexistence and to his mission and thus his double sonship.

To some, it might seem like I have put the cart before the horse. Why are we speaking of who God is before exegeting these symbols? However, dogmatic rules are generative for how to interpret the transfiguration. Modern exegetes have been stymied in their interpretations of the transfiguration's symbols precisely because of our disregard for dogmatics. By canvassing the confessions of the early church, we will be better equipped to understand the glorious signs.

---

1. When I refer to symbols or signs in the transfiguration, I'm not saying that these signs/symbols are unreal. Rather I use the terms "symbols" and "signs" in the way Augustine employs them. He defines *signa* as "things which signify something" and a *signum* as "a thing which causes us to think of something beyond the impression the thing itself impresses upon the senses." Augustine, *On Christian Doctrine* 1.2.2; 2.1.1 (*NPNF*[1] 2:523, 536).

God Is Light in Himself

John confesses that "God is light" (1 John 1:5). He doesn't possess light. Light isn't an attribute of God. He *is* light essentially: "[Light] is the splendor and brilliance that is inseparably associated with all God's attributes."[2] Light, like glory and holiness, is a descriptor that summarizes all God's attributes. To see God's light is to behold his attributes in coherence.

God's glory is often communicated by light. As I noted at the beginning of this book, in German, the word for the transfiguration means "the glorification." This is because "light" and "glory" are closely associated. They are different expressions for the same concept. The transfiguration scene is consistently described with both the imagery of light and the word *doxa*—"glory" (Matt. 16:27; Luke 9:32; 2 Cor. 3:18; 2 Pet. 1:17; John 1:14).

Light and glory are often intertwined in the Scriptures. Isaiah calls Israel to arise and shine, "for your *light* has come, and the *glory* of the LORD shines over you" (Isa. 60:1). Luke likewise calls Jesus "a *light* for revelation to the Gentiles and *glory* to your people Israel" (Luke 2:32). Paul describes his Damascus road experience as one "of *glory* of that *light*" (Acts 22:11). Again, Paul speaks of God shining "in our hearts to give the *light of the knowledge of God's glory in the face of Jesus Christ*" (2 Cor. 4:6).

The transfiguration is a scene of light because *God is light in himself.* Christian orthodoxy confesses God as *a se* (from himself) and simple (not made up of parts). His nature is not composed, and he derives nothing from sources outside of himself. As Bavinck says, God "is whatever he is by his own self or of his own self."[3]

This means God doesn't possess, receive, or reflect light.[4] To say God is light is to affirm an inner luminosity in God with no reference to his creation or creative acts. The radiance of his being is found in his essence. This affirmation, that God is light in himself, leads to several important distinctions for our reading of the transfiguration.

First, this truth reminds us to distinguish between the internal works of God (*ad intra*) and the external works of God (*ad extra*). The transfiguration uniquely reveals both, but most biblical scholars have seen only God's external actions in this narrative. However, who God is in himself is the priority. While we affirm that Jesus receives light in the transfiguration, we also confess that as God the Son, Jesus *is* light and has no need for external illumination.

---

2. Herman Bavinck, *Reformed Dogmatics: Abridged in One Volume*, ed. John Bolt (Grand Rapids: Baker Academic, 2011), 215. I have substituted the word "light" where Bavinck has written "glory."

3. Herman Bavinck, *The Doctrine of God* (Grand Rapids: Eerdmans, 1951), 144.

4. Andrew R. Hay, *God's Shining Forth: A Trinitarian Theology of Divine Light*, Princeton Theological Monograph Series (Eugene, OR: Pickwick, 2017), xviii. The following section is largely indebted to Hay's work on this topic.

Second, the affirmation that God is light in himself calls us to distinguish between created light and uncreated light.[5] When God said "Let there be light" in Genesis 1:3, we see created light—a light that depends on God for its shining. We also see created light in angels, who, though described as having "shining white garments," derive their glory from participation in God's light. In contrast, God's essential light transcends the order of creation and the apprehension of sensible creatures. It does not cease to be or come into being. As Irenaeus affirms, "[God] may most correctly be called Light, but He is nothing like our light."[6] The light of the transfiguration is not simply created light. Tabor communicates the presence of uncreated light in the person of Jesus.

Third, if God is light in himself, then we must correlate the light of the Father, Son, and Spirit. God is light in his triune nature. His light is "the radiant plenitude that he is in himself as Father, Son, and Holy Spirit."[7] Nicene trinitarian theology has argued that all three persons share this light because they are of the same undivided divine essence. It is therefore a "mutual light," a personal property of the Father, Son, and Spirit. God is threefold light. The doctrine of inseparable operations helps here. This doctrine teaches that all three persons of the Holy Trinity are at work in every action. Divine unity *ad intra* entails inseparable actions *ad extra*. The transfiguration reveals God as this threefold light—a light that is christologically centered but trinitarily understood.

God Shines Forth through the Son and in the Spirit

A final distinction must be made between the light of the Father, Son, and Spirit. Not only is God one, but he is one in three persons. While divine unity *ad intra* entails inseparable operations *ad extra*, personal distinctions *ad intra* entail personal actions *ad extra* (also known as appropriation).[8] We must correlate *and* distinguish between the light of the Father, Son, and Spirit. But how? Two historic categories grant us the proper language: eternal relations of origin and missions.

Historically, the Father, Son, and Spirit are distinguished by their *eternal relations of origin*. Pro-Nicene trinitarian theology has affirmed that the three persons of the Trinity share everything except their eternal relations of origin.

---

5. Uncreated light is spiritually nonmaterial and received through spiritual perception. Yet Palamas affirms the disciples saw light on the mountain with their physical eyes and then passed from flesh to spirit. Gregory Palamas, *The Homilies*, ed. Christopher Veniamin (Waymart, PA: Mount Thabor, 2009), 269–70.

6. Irenaeus, *Against Heresies* 2.13.4, in *St. Irenaeus of Lyons: Against the Heresies, Book 2*, trans. Dominic J. Unger, Ancient Christian Writers (Westminster, MD: Newman, 1991), 43.

7. Hay, *God's Shining Forth*, 32.

8. I'm sure I heard this from someone else, but I can't quite remember who. This is my Hebrews footnote—"Someone somewhere says" (see Heb. 2:6; 4:4).

The Father is unbegotten.

The Son is eternally begotten.

The Spirit spirates from the Father.

Because of their relations to one another, there are "proper prepositions" that imply their eternal relations of origin. Everything is from the Father, through the Son, and in the Spirit.

from the Father (*ek patros*)

through the Son (*dia huios*)

in the Holy Spirit (*en pneumati hagiō*)

All originates from the Father, is communicated through the Son, and is in the Holy Spirit. The trinitarian taxonomy orders and shapes the contours of the divine economy.

To apply this principle to our current discussion, all three persons are light. The Father is light in himself, the Son is light in himself, and the Spirit is light himself. The persons are not differentiated by their relations to light but by their relations to one another. But relationally, we can also speak of God's light as being from the Father, through the Son, and in the Spirit.

This is why the Nicene Creed confesses the Son as "Light from Light, true God from true God," Hebrews describes Jesus as "the radiance of God's glory" (Heb. 1:3), and in John Jesus says, "I am the light of the world" (John 8:12). Yet it is also by the Spirit that we see (or are illumined) by this light. Paul prays that we would have the Spirit so that our eyes might be enlightened (Eph. 1:17–18), and Hebrews says those who have been enlightened have shared in the Holy Spirit (Heb. 6:4).

Distinguishing between the light of the Father, Son, and Spirit means distinguishing not only their eternal relations of origin but *the missions of the Son and Spirit*. Modern commentators have deficient exegesis of the transfiguration because they don't reflect on how the mission of the Son and Spirit relates to their eternal procession. The missions of the Son and Spirit are extensions of their eternal relations of origin and relate to God's work *ad extra*. The Son is sent to the earth from the Father, and the Spirit proceeds to the earth from the Father and Son.

This pattern is evident in the Scriptures. As Hay argues, God the Father *elects* from all eternity the gathering of his people as "children of light" (Eph. 5:8).[9] By sending the Son, he rescues his people "from the domain of darkness" and transfers them "into the kingdom of" God the Son (Col. 1:13). This transfer from the domain of darkness is accomplished *through* or *by* the Son, who is the

9. Hay, *God's Shining Forth*, 53.

light of the world. God the Son *accomplishes* this redemption by being "the light of the world" (John 8:12; see also Matt. 4:16).

If the Father elects and the Son accomplishes redemption, then the Spirit *illumines*. God the Holy Spirit calls people out of darkness into the marvelous light of communion with God (John 14:26; 1 Cor. 2:10–13; Eph. 1:17–18).[10] As Gregory of Nazianzus said, "We receive the Son's light through the Father's light in the light of the Spirit."[11] Creatures are able to see the light of the Father *through* the Son *in* the work of the Spirit.

In summary, our trinitarian grammar reminds us that God is light in himself. He shines forth from his own brightness. He does not receive his light from elsewhere, but it flows forth from his plenitude. This means that we must distinguish between God's internal and external works, God's created and uncreated light, and the mutual but distinguished light of the Father, Son, and Spirit. This grammar helps us speak more precisely about Tabor's brightness and, more specifically, (1) Jesus's luminosity, (2) the bright cloud, and (3) the appearance of Moses and Elijah.

Jesus's Shining Face and White Clothes

The transfiguration is a scene of brilliance and glory. Maybe this light is simply electromagnetic waves perceptible to the disciples' optic nerves. However, the storyline of the Scriptures suggests that this light is not *mere* light. This is divine light, uncreated light, light unapproachable, which causes the disciples to fall on their faces.

We will see how the Scriptures support this reading of the transfiguration by first tracing the story of God as light. Then we will narrow the storyline and focus on the theme of God's face and shining clothes. Finally, we will connect both threads to the transfiguration. Jesus's light is both proleptic and preexistent, pointing to his double sonship.

God as Light in the Scriptures

When the apostle John confesses, "God is light" (1 John 1:5), he is not being inventive. He is following the Hebrew tradition, in which God reveals himself as light. Salvation history begins with Adam and Eve walking in God's light. In the garden, we find iridescent gold (Gen. 2:12). Tradition speaks of Adam and

---

10. Hay, *God's Shining Forth*, 53.
11. Gregory of Nazianzus, Oration 31.3 (PG 36:136), in *On God and Christ: The Five Theological Orations and Two Letters to Cledonius*, ed. John Behr, trans. Lionel Wickham and Frederick Williams, Popular Patristics 23 (New York: St. Vladimir's Seminary Press, 2011), 118.

Eve shining and wearing radiant garments.[12] Later, Solomon constructs a new garden, the temple, and overlays it with gold (1 Kings 6:20–28). Ezekiel asserts that the garden was filled with fiery stones (Ezek. 28:13–14). The ubiquity of gold and fiery stones in Eden paints creation as luminous.

However, Adam's fall thrusts humanity into darkness and death. The rest of the Old Testament reiterates this theme. God shines forth his light so that Israel might be a light to the nations, but when they repeat Adam's failure, God snuffs out the light of his temple and sends his people into exile.

One of the first times God is portrayed as light is when he appears to Abraham and makes a covenant with him (Gen. 15:17). At night, God appears to Abraham as a smoking fire pot and a flaming torch. God also appears to Moses in a flame of fire within a bush (Exod. 3:2). God materializes as fire and light in the pillar (13:21). On Mount Sinai, the Lord comes down in fire while smoke and cloud form all around the mountain (19:18).

Israel is allowed to "walk in the light" of God in the tabernacle and temple. The priest entering the tabernacle reenacts Moses's ascent up Sinai. As he enters God's presence, a cloud rests over the tabernacle by day, and fire resides by night (Exod. 40:34, 38). Inside the tabernacle, the priests attend a golden lampstand that it might stay lit perpetually (Exod. 25:31–35; Lev. 24:4). When Solomon first dedicates the gilded temple, fire descends from heaven and consumes the burnt offering, and the glory of the Lord fills the temple (2 Chron. 7:1–3).

God is also portrayed as light in theophanies—visible manifestations of God to figures such as Moses, Isaiah, Daniel, and Ezekiel. Isaiah has a vision of the Lord in brightness (Isa. 6:3, 6). Daniel sees the Ancient of Days, and his throne is flaming fire, its wheels are blazing fire, and a river of fire flows from his presence (Dan. 7:9–10). Habakkuk speaks of God coming in brilliance like light and with rays flashing from his hands (Hab. 3:3–4).[13]

Ezekiel beholds one of the most tragic Old Testament visions as God's light leaves the temple. He sees "fire flashing" and "brilliant light" around the throne (Ezek. 1:4). Fire moves between the creatures before the throne, and lightning envelops the scene (1:13). Ezekiel perceives on the throne a human form gleaming "like amber." "Brilliant light" is "all around him" (1:27–28; see also 8:2). Sadly, Ezekiel sees this glory depart because of Israel's sin (10:4, 18).

---

12. Philo (*Allegorical Interpretation* 1.17–19) even says that when God made the seventh day, he formed it in accordance with divine light and declared it holy. Gregory of Nyssa (*On the Lord's Prayer* 5 [PG 44:1184b]) affirms that in the garden, when humanity had been stripped of their proper radiant garments, they sewed together for themselves garments in an evil way. For more evidence on this theme, see chap. 5.

13. Tertullian (*Against Marcion* 4.22.12–13 [ANF 3:384–85]) and other early interpreters connect Hab. 3:2–4 with the transfiguration.

As a group, the prophets behold God's radiance, frequently call Israel back to the light, and promise a new day of brightness. Isaiah commands Israel to "walk in the LORD's light" (Isa. 2:5). He says that on Mount Zion, "the LORD will create a cloud of smoke by day and a glowing flame of fire by night" (4:5). He predicts that those walking in darkness will see "a great light" (9:2). The prophet also appoints his people to be "a light to the nations" (42:6; 49:6; 51:4). He calls his people in exile to "arise" and "shine." Nations will come to Israel's light and brightness if they follow the Lord (60:1, 3). In the last days, the sun or moon won't be their light; the Lord will be their light (60:19).

The Old Testament ends in darkness. God's people are in exile. The temple no longer holds the former glory. God is light, but his light has been hidden. Israel waits for the true light to come down to the earth.

The Light of the Son in the Transfiguration

In Jesus, the light of God returns. This is true for Jesus's whole life—not only the transfiguration. However, the transfiguration is a capstone, revealing Jesus as God's light. Employing our trinitarian grammar, we can distinguish how God is light (*ad intra*) and how he shines forth his light (*ad extra*). The light from Jesus's face and clothes suggests that Jesus is both the messianic light and the eternal, uncreated, divine light.

Messianic Light: The Mission of the Son

Jesus is the messianic light in reference to his humanity. This is supported in two ways: (1) the portrayal of Jesus's mission and (2) the description of the transfiguration scene itself.

First, the Gospel writers depict Jesus as God's light that came into the world. This relates to the Son's mission on the earth, his incarnation. In Matthew, the magi come to Jesus's light as they see the star shining (Matt. 2:1–2; see also Isa. 60:3). As Jesus begins his ministry, Matthew presents him as "a great light . . . for those living in the land of the shadow of death" in fulfillment of Isaiah's prophecy (Matt. 4:16).[14] At the cross, Jesus bears the darkness, and shadows fill the land at his death (27:45). But the resurrection bursts with light (28:1–3).

In Luke, Zechariah praises God, saying that Jesus's presence will "dawn from on high" and "shine on those who live in darkness" (Luke 1:78–79). The glory of the Lord shines around the shepherds as heavenly hosts announce the good news (2:9). Simeon declares that Jesus is Israel's salvation, "a light for revelation

---

14. Jesus also asserts that his disciples are "the light of the world" as they follow his teaching (Matt. 5:14), and he declares that "the righteous will shine like the sun in their Father's kingdom" (13:43).

to the Gentiles" (2:32). The apostle John is the most explicit with the theme of God as light. Borrowing from Isaiah, he affirms that Jesus is "the light of men" that "shines in the darkness" of the world (John 1:4–5). "The true light" was coming into the world (1:9; see also 3:19; 8:12; 9:5; 12:35–36, 46), and he will give light to all humankind. The light of Jesus relates to his mission of being light *to the world.*

Second, the transfiguration itself is a scene of luminosity, pointing to God's mission on behalf of his creation. Jesus's face shines and his clothes turn white, a bright cloud emerges, Moses and Elijah appear in glory, and the place is called God's holy mountain. The light of the transfiguration points to Jesus as the messianic Son because the Gospels speak of Jesus *being* transfigured in the passive voice (Matt. 17:2; Mark 9:2). This relates to his mission *from the Father.* Jesus, in his human nature, is the recipient of glory from God, as Peter explains (2 Pet. 1:17).

The mission from the Father is also symbolized in the whiteness of his garments.[15] Matthew affirms Jesus's clothes "*became as white* as light" (17:2). Mark asserts that Jesus's clothes "*became . . .* extremely *white* as no launderer on earth could *whiten* them" (Mark 9:3). Luke says, "His clothes *became* dazzlingly *white*" (Luke 9:29). This same symbolism is found in angelic messengers, who are also clothed in white. The two women at Jesus's tomb encounter "a young man dressed in a white robe" (Mark 16:5). When Jesus ascends into heaven, two men in white clothes stand by the disciples (Acts 1:10; John 20:12; 1 Enoch 71:1; 106:10; 2 Enoch 1:5; 37:1). The brilliantly white garments signify that Jesus is God's messenger, the light sent into the world.[16]

We must not miss that Jesus's transfiguration is a sign of his mission and preview of the transformation to come to Jesus's flesh. He *will be* transfigured as he *will be* appointed as messianic head (Acts 2:36; 10:42; Rom. 1:4; Eph. 1:22; Heb. 1:2). In this sense, Jesus *becomes* the light of the world who accomplishes redemption. God's heavenly light has come down to earth in a human person. Jesus has come to his people in their sin and darkness so that they might be brought into the kingdom of light as children of their heavenly Father.

Eternal Light: The Son's Relation of Origin

However, the transfiguration also signifies that Jesus is God's light in a second sense. If we follow the storyline of God appearing as light, then the

15. In Jewish transformation traditions, a change into glorious clothing symbolizes the transformation into angelic form (1 Enoch 62:15; 2 Enoch 22:8; Apocalypse of Zephaniah 8:3).

16. Michael F. Bird (*Jesus among the Gods: Early Christology in the Greco-Roman World* [Waco: Baylor University Press, 2022], 188–254) analyzes Jesus's angel-like appearance in Jewish literature and early Christian exegesis.

transfiguration also suggests that Jesus is the very essence of God, light from light. He is uncreated light.[17] Jesus's light speaks not only to his mission but to his eternal relation of origin. Jesus didn't assume a new substance to himself in his transfiguration. There was a time when the light of the Son was not located in a human body, for the light was first and the body second.[18] Jesus receives light *and* is light. The transfiguration is a new burning-bush moment: the burning fire that once appeared to Moses now pulses from Jesus's being.

While modern commentators will point to Jesus's messianic status in the transfiguration, the earliest Christian commentators were quick to point out Jesus's eternal sonship, his eternal relation of origin, and therefore his eternal light. They follow the apostle John, who prioritizes Jesus as the true light *and then* says that he was coming into the world (John 1:9). Jesus's mission proceeds from his ontology; his ontology precedes his mission.

Origen affirms that Jesus appeared to the disciples "in the form of God in which he existed before."[19]

Pantoleon asserts that this scene is a revelation of Jesus's divinity in their midst, where rays of divinity shine.[20]

Leontius says the transfiguration was necessary because the apostles thought the Lord Christ was simply a man, not God in the flesh.[21]

Anastasius of Sinai pronounces the disciples saw sparks of the divine sunshine, and they were gazing on divine power.[22]

Andrew of Crete says they saw the glory and radiance of Jesus's divinity, more brilliant than lightning.[23]

17. God is also described as having clothing white like snow (Dan. 7:9; 1 Enoch 14:20). For more on the glorious garments of the righteous in heaven, see 4 Ezra 2:39; 1 Enoch 62:15; 2 Enoch 22:8–10. In 1 Enoch 106:5, Lamech has a child who looks like the angels of heaven in that his "eyes are like the rays of the sun, and his face glorious." In 3 Enoch 26:1–4, Metatron describes a prince above him who is full of brightness and light, and his face is like the angels. See also Apocalypse of Zephaniah 6:11; 4 Ezra 7:97; 10:25; 2 Baruch 51:3; Ascension of Isaiah 7:25; Joseph and Aseneth 14:9; Pseudo-Philo 12:1.

18. Gregory Palamas, "The Light of the Transfiguration," *Orthodox Tradition* 31, no. 1 (2014): 55.

19. Origen, "Commentary on Matthew 12:36–43," in *Light on the Mountain: Greek Patristic and Byzantine Homilies on the Transfiguration of the Lord*, trans. Brian Daley, Popular Patristics 48 (New York: St. Vladimir's Seminary Press, 2013), 56.

20. Pantoleon, "Sermon on the Transfiguration of the Lord" (Daley, 108, 110).

21. Leontius, "Homily on the Transfiguration" (Daley, 126). Anastasius of Antioch says that when Jesus took on the form of a servant, he concealed his divine form, but at the transfiguration he "restores the form of the servant to its natural appearance—not putting aside the substance of the servant, but making it radiant with divine characteristics." Anastasius of Antioch, "Homily on the Transfiguration" (Daley, 136).

22. Anastasius of Sinai, "Homily on the Transfiguration" (Daley, 169, 171).

23. Andrew of Crete, "On the Transfiguration of Christ" (Daley, 182).

John of Damascus affirms this light was naturally Jesus's own, the brilliance
of divine glory and of the Godhead.[24]

Leo the Emperor states it was the radiance of Jesus's divinity.[25]

Modern commentators are hamstrung when they come to the transfiguration
because they don't associate the mission of the Son with his eternal procession.
Such an association is too "theological" for them. John Heil is representative
of this view when he asserts that "the depiction of Jesus's transfiguration in all
three versions as an external change, a transformation from the outside of Jesus
effected by God, *does not* support those interpretations that speak in terms of a
'revelation,' or 'disclosure,' or 'unveiling' of an inner, permanent glory or heavenly
status which Jesus already possesses."[26]

However, the messianic light of the Son and the eternal light of the Son
should not be put at odds with each other. The light in the transfiguration is
the eternal light now shown forth in human form. We don't have to pit Jesus's
humanity against his divinity. In fact, by doing so, we bypass the glory of the
transfiguration.

Cyril of Alexandria puts it this way: "We must not think that he who descended into the limitation of manhood for our sake lost his inherent radiance
and that transcendence that comes from his nature. No, he had this divine ful-
ness even in the emptiness of our condition."[27] As John of Damascus affirmed,
Christ did not become *what he was not* before his transfiguration but appeared
to his disciples *as he was*, opening their eyes to his true nature.[28]

While the white garments testify that Jesus is the "sent one," they also represent the innocence of his soul, the purity of his life.[29] It is his very *being* that

24. John of Damascus, "Oration on the Transfiguration" (Daley, 219–20).

25. Leo the Emperor, "A Homily by Leo the Emperor" (Daley, 238, 251).

26. John Paul Heil, *The Transfiguration of Jesus: Narrative Meaning and Function of Mark 9:2–8,
Matt 17:1–8 and Luke 9:28–36*, AnBib 144 (Rome: Pontifical Biblical Institute, 2000), 78 (emphasis mine).

27. Cyril of Alexandria, *On the Unity of Christ*, ed. John Anthony McGuckin, Popular Patristics
13 (Crestwood, NY: St. Vladimir's Seminary Press, 2015), 123.

28. John of Damascus, *Exposition of the Orthodox Faith* (PG 96:564); Vladimir Lossky, *The
Vision of God* (Crestwood, NY: St. Vladimir's Seminary Press, 2013), 139.

29. Herman Melville reflects on the nature of the "white whale" in his book *Moby-Dick* (1851;
repr., New York: Book League of America, 1929), 208. Some argue that the whale is an image of
God. Interestingly, the "whiteness of the whale" maps onto God's incomprehensibility and fullness
of perfection. Melville writes, "Or is it, that as in essence whiteness is not so much a colour as the
visible absence of colour; and at the same time the concrete of all colours; is it for these reasons
that there is such a dumb blankness, full of meaning, in a wide landscape of snows—a colourless,
all-colour of atheism from which we shrink?" The whale embodies all these things by being the
white whale. It is terrifying, pure, excellent, frightening, mysterious, and incomprehensible. The
fullness of perfections are found in the whale just as the fullness of perfections are found in God.

pours forth whiteness into his garments. The splendor of his body makes the clothes whiter than white. They become luminous by proximity to his body. As Ephrem the Syrian says, "The brightness which Moses put on was wrapped on him from without, whereas . . . Christ was clothed in light from within."[30] That is why all the texts mention Jesus's shining face before they mention his bright clothes.

Jesus belongs elsewhere (in heaven) as much as he belongs here (on earth). He is a man who was *sent* from heaven (1 Cor. 15:48) and also made the heavens and eternally resides in the heavens.[31] The book of Revelation corroborates this line of thinking by describing the Son in terms previously used for the Ancient of Days in Daniel 7:9: the Son's hair is "white as wool," and his eyes are "like a fiery flame" (Rev. 1:14). But in the same scene John also uses language reminiscent of the transfiguration. John falls at Jesus's feet as a dead man, and the Son of Man says, "Don't be afraid" (Rev. 1:17), which mirrors Matthew 17:6–7. The dazzlingly white clothes assert not only that Jesus came from heaven but that he is the one who created the heavens.[32]

In the Hellenistic tradition, it was also common for gods to transfigure into a different form—though the transfiguration of a Greek deity differed essentially from the transfiguration of Jesus. In the Homeric Hymn to Demeter, the queen goddess disguises herself as an old woman to rescue her daughter Persephone from Hades, lord of the underworld. When she reveals her identity to a human, she is transformed: "When she had so said, the goddess changed her stature and her looks, thrusting old age away from her: beauty spread round about her and a lovely fragrance was wafted from her sweet-smelling robes, and from the divine body of the goddess a light shone afar, while golden tresses spread

---

30. St. Ephrem, *Church* 36.3–6, in Sebastian Brock, *The Luminous Eye: The Spiritual World Vision of Saint Ephrem the Syrian*, vol. 124 of *Cistercian Studies* (Kalamazoo, MI: Liturgical Press, 1992), 92.

31. Simon Gathercole's work on the "I have come" + purpose statements in the Gospels supports reading Jesus's preexistence in the Synoptic Gospels. Jesus is a preexistent heavenly being who has come to accomplish a mission on a cosmic scale. Jesus came to destroy the works of demons (Matt. 8:29; Mark 1:24), to preach to the world (Mark 1:38), to call the righteous (Mark 2:17), to fulfill the law (Matt. 5:17), to cast fire onto the earth (Luke 12:49), and to seek and save the lost (Luke 19:10).

32. Mike Bird (*Jesus among the Gods*, 254–74) asserts while there are correspondences between Jesus and angels (or heavenly figures), there are also differences. Jesus's name is venerated, he is declared to be God's Son, he is the mediator of creation, he has sovereignty over the cosmic powers, God brings salvation through him, and Jesus received cultic worship. Note that Matt. 25:31, a text connected to the transfiguration, distinguishes Jesus from angels, for "when the Son of Man comes in his glory, *and all the angels with him*, then he will sit on his glorious throne." In Revelation Jesus receives worship (Rev. 5:9–13) that angels refuse for themselves (19:10; 22:9). He sends angelic messengers rather than being sent as an angelic messenger (2:1, 8, 12, 18; 3:7, 14). Hebrews asserts that Jesus's name (Son) is superior to that of angels (Heb. 1:4–9). See also 1 Enoch 61:6–13, where the Elect One judges the works of the holy ones.

down over her shoulders, so that the strong house was filled with brightness as with lightning."[33]

Anyone familiar with such traditions would have understood what was happening when Jesus's figure shone and his clothes became white as light: Jesus had come down to earth in human form, and now he was revealing his true form. The difference, though, is that Jesus didn't just appear in human form. He became man and revealed his divinity *through* his humanity.

Messianic and Eternal Light

The transfiguration is a scene redolent with light. The light is not "merely decorative, but substantial and grounded in the being of God."[34] It both confirms Jesus's messianic status as the light that has come into the world (mission) and also reveals that Jesus is the eternal light (procession).

The brightness of the transfiguration therefore affirms both God's nature *ad intra* (in himself) and *ad extra* (in creation). The transfiguration combines both dogmatic realities (Jesus is God in himself) and biblical theological realities (he will accomplish redemption by being the light). The brightness of Jesus's face and his shining clothes are not merely ornamental; they unlock the very essence and meaning of transfiguration. However, even more can be said about Jesus's shining face.

The Face of God in the Scriptures

A unique emphasis on Jesus's face appears in the transfiguration episode. In Matthew's transfiguration account, he asserts that Jesus's face "shone" (17:2). Luke says that the appearance of Jesus's face "changed" (9:29). This is surprising, as very few texts speak of Jesus's face.[35] While most have attempted to interpret Jesus's luminous face through the biblical imagery of Moses, the theophanic theme of God's face remains untapped.[36]

The Old Testament recounts unique episodes where God interacts with his people "face to face" and fosters a longing for the day when humanity will do

33. Hesiod, *Hymn to Demeter* 275–80, trans. Hugh G. Evelyn-White, LCL (New York: Fletcher & Son, 1950), 308–9. See Adela Yarbro Collins, "Mark and His Readers: The Son of God among Greeks and Romans," *HTR* 93, no. 2 (2000): 91–92.

34. Dorothy A. Lee, "On the Holy Mountain: The Transfiguration in Scripture and Theology," *Colloquium* 36, no. 2 (2004): 154.

35. Matthew says that Jesus fell "facedown" in Gethsemane (26:39), and at Jesus's trial they spit on Jesus's face and blindfold him (26:67; Mark 14:65). In Luke, Jesus sets his face toward Jerusalem (9:51–53; 10:1).

36. Andrei Orlov, *The Glory of the Invisible God: Two Powers in Heaven Traditions and Early Christology* (London: T&T Clark, 2021), 124.

so once again.[37] The word for "face" is *panim* or *paneh* in Hebrew and *prosōpon* in Greek. The word can indicate someone's face, presence, or even person.[38] Often, it is simply translated as "presence" because someone's face may be the most intimate part of the human anatomy.[39] However, in the Old Testament, "face to face" is more than just a phrase to communicate relational closeness. It is an idiom for divine encounter.

Ian Wilson suggests the biblical theme of God's face has its origins in Genesis 3.[40] According to Sirach, Shem and Seth were glorified (*edoxasthēsan*) like Adam above every living thing in creation (Sir. 49:16).[41] When Adam and Eve sinned, the guilt and shame caused them to hide themselves from the "presence" or "face" (*panim*) of God (Gen. 3:8). The fall meant that God's face would be hidden and that humanity had lost an aspect of its glory. Salvation would mean seeing God's face again.

God does show his face in part to Israel. The first place the phrase "face to face" occurs is when Jacob wrestles God. After the wrestling match, the narrator says Jacob named the place "Peniel [from *panim*], 'For I have seen God face to face, . . . yet my life has been spared'" (Gen. 32:30). At Peniel, Jacob receives the name Israel. It is commonly understood that Israel means "one who strives with God," but the Philo and Origen both interpret "Israel" to mean "one who sees God."[42]

God also reveals his face to Moses on Mount Sinai. The Scriptures affirm that God spoke to Moses "face to face, just as a man speaks with his friend" (Exod. 33:11; see also Num. 12:8; 14:14; Deut. 5:4; 34:10). Because of the glorious face Moses sees on Sinai, the skin of his own face shines (Exod. 34:29). And yet the

37. The phrase "face to face" occurs in five places in the Hebrew Bible: Gen. 32:30 (Jacob); Exod. 33:11 (Moses); Deut. 34:10 (Moses); Judg. 6:22 (Gideon); Ezek. 20:35 (the people of Israel). Mark Wessner says that four elements occur in these episodes: divine initiation, profound intimacy, intentional solitude, and supernatural verification. Mark D. Wessner, "Toward a Literary Understanding of 'Face to Face' (פָּנִים אֶל־פָּנִים) in Genesis 32:23–32," *ResQ* 42, no. 3 (2000): 170. See also Apocalypse of Sedrach 2:4–3:2.

38. While Matthew Bates has argued that the "persons" language in trinitarian discourse may have stemmed from a certain reading strategy in the Old Testament where different *prosōpa* appear and speak in a text, it would also be worthwhile to reflect on the impact of the theme of seeing God "face to face" (person to person) for trinitarian discourse. Matthew W. Bates, *The Birth of the Trinity: Jesus, God, and Spirit in New Testament and Early Christian Interpretations of the Old Testament* (Oxford: Oxford University Press, 2016).

39. John and Paul tell their readers they wish to talk to them "face to face" (1 Thess. 3:10; 2 John 1:12; 3 John 1:14).

40. Ian Douglas Wilson, "'Face to Face' with God: Another Look," *ResQ* 51, no. 2 (2009): 107–14.

41. Genesis Rabbah 11 speaks of Adam's glorious face at creation, which he was deprived of when he was expelled from the garden. It quotes Job 14:20: "You change his appearance and send him away."

42. David H. Wenkel, *Shining Like the Sun: A Biblical Theology of Meeting God Face to Face* (Wooster, OH: Weaver, 2016), 23.

Lord said to Moses, "You cannot see my face, for humans cannot . . . see me and live" (33:20). It seems Moses saw the face of the Lord in some diminished way—in silhouettes and shadows (Num. 12:8; Deut. 5:4).

Priests also have a "face to face" relationship with the Lord. After the high priest had been in the presence of the Lord in the tabernacle, he was to give the priestly blessing: "May the LORD make his face shine on you and be gracious to you; may the LORD look with favor on you and give you peace" (Num. 6:25–26). English translations obscure that the word for face is employed in both parts of the blessing. Beneath the word "countenance" is the word *panim*, indicating that God will lift up his *face* upon them and give them peace.

The emphasis on a "face to face" relationship with God continues through the Hebrew Bible. The prophets speak of covenant curses in terms of God hiding his face and covenant blessings as God revealing his face to Israel.[43] The Old Testament ends with God's people waiting for the moment when God will shine his face on them again. When he does, their faces will "shine like the sun" (Matt. 13:43; see also Dan. 12:3). God's face signals his presence, glory, intimacy, and favor.

Arriving back at the transfiguration scene, we can now see the twofold significance of Jesus's shining face: his face shines because he has *received* glory as man, and his face shines because he *is* glory as God. The transfiguration unveils the Son.

The Face of Jesus in the Transfiguration

The most obvious Old Testament echo in Christ's transfigured visage is the shining face of Moses (Exod. 34:29–35). Both Jesus and Moses go up a mountain after six days, take three companions, meet with God, and are transfigured. Each scene includes a cloud, fear from the witnesses, and an audible heavenly voice. All the Synoptics include the command "listen to him," alluding to a Mosaic text (Deut. 18:15), and they both come down the mountain to find rebellion among the people.[44] Jesus's shining face also recalls Adam typology as several early Jewish texts link Moses's luminosity to the primordial glory of Adam.[45]

---

43. This begins with Moses's warnings in Deut. 31:17–19; 32:20. The prophets then pick up the theme of God revealing and hiding his face: Isa. 54:8; 59:2; 64:7; Jer. 18:17; 21:10; 33:5; 44:11; Ezek. 7:22; 39:23–24, 29.

44. See the parallels in Dale Allison, *The New Moses: A Matthean Typology* (Eugene, OR: Wipf & Stock, 2013), 243–48, and Patrick Schreiner, *Matthew, Disciple and Scribe: The First Gospel and Its Portrait of Jesus* (Grand Rapids: Baker Academic, 2019), 154–58.

45. See Linda Belleville, *Reflections of Glory: Paul's Polemical Use of the Moses-Doxa Tradition in 2 Corinthians 3.1–18* (London: Bloomsbury Academic, 2015), 50.

The shining face of Jesus thus signifies that he is the new Adam, the true humanity, and the righteous prophet like Moses, who has come. He is the "human one" chosen by God to enter the glory cloud. Jesus is the new mediator on the mountain who represents humanity to God. The shining face of Jesus implies that all of God's people will have gleaming faces; Jesus is simply the first fruit of humans beholding God's glory. In fact, the larger Jewish corpus affirms that the righteous will shine like the sun, indicating we will all be transformed into heavenly figures.[46] However, to note only how Jesus is akin to Moses and Adam is an exercise in missing the point. Jesus's shining face reveals that he is more than a blessed prophet of God, more than the new Adam.

The radiance of Jesus's face exceeds the sun: "Jesus's face is not compared to the sun, but the sun is compared to his face."[47] Jesus is the face of God revealed. There's a reason why art museums are filled with portraits: the face of a person reveals the person's identity. Similarly, in the transfiguration, the face of Jesus reveals that he is the Second Person of the Trinity. The shining face of Jesus discloses that he fulfills the longing to truly see God's face. As Jesus himself affirmed, "The one who has seen me has seen the Father" (John 14:9).

Jesus fulfills Adam and Eve's longing to see God again (Gen. 3:8), satisfies Jacob's affirmation that he has seen the face of God and not died (32:30), achieves Moses's request to see God's glory (Exod. 33:18), gratifies the priestly prayer that the Lord's face might shine on his people (Num. 6:25), fulfills David's desire to see something good (Ps. 73:28), reverses the prophets' pronouncement that God has hidden his face (Isa. 59:2), and achieves the new covenant promise that God will no longer hide his face (Ezek. 39:29).

The transfiguration is not merely about Jesus's correlation with Moses but about confirming that Jesus is what Moses *longed to see*. Moses said, let me see your glory (Exod. 33:18). God said, "No—not now. That will come later."[48] When Moses and Elijah appear with Jesus, they finally see the glory of the Father in the face of Jesus Christ. Jesus is the mediator of God's presence because he is the Son of God, the *prosōpon* of God. As Paul affirms, God "has shone in our hearts to give the light of the knowledge of God's glory *in the face of Jesus Christ*" (2 Cor. 4:6).

While Moses's bright face was a reflection, Jesus's brightness emanates from his being. Jesus's face is the sun; Moses's is the moon. As Gregory Palamas notes, "The Lord possessed that radiance in his own right. . . . The glory

---

46. See Dan. 10:6; 12:3; 4 Ezra 7:97; Apocalypse of Zephaniah 6:11; 2 Enoch 1:5; 19:1.
47. Thomas G. Weinandy, *Jesus Becoming Jesus: A Theological Interpretation of the Synoptic Gospels* (Washington, DC: Catholic University of America Press, 2018), 228.
48. Philagathos, "Homily 31, on the Saving Transfiguration" (Daley, 271).

processed naturally from his own divinity."[49] Or as John of Damascus says, "Glory did not come upon this body from outside itself, but from within."[50] Jesus's face radiates from its own brilliance, while Moses's face glitters with borrowed light.

Moses, Elijah, and Jesus are not a triumvirate of equals. The Son's luminosity is radically distinct from Moses's. Reflecting on the theme of God's face, John says, "For the law was given through Moses; grace and truth came through Jesus Christ. No one has ever seen God. The one and only Son, who is himself God and is at the Father's side—he has revealed him" (John 1:17–18). John affirms that the Son has revealed the Father. God has been revealed in the *prosōpon* of Jesus.[51] The old covenant was characterized by intermediaries (Moses, priests in the temple); now Jesus is the unmediated revelation of God.[52] God the Father is seeable in the Son, and the truth of the incarnation is revealed in the transfiguration.

The reason the Son can reveal the Father is because Jesus is God himself. Only God himself could truly reveal God. As Irenaeus affirms, the Son is "the visible nature of the Father" as the Father is "the invisible nature of the Son."[53]

The shining face of Jesus goes beyond our usual categories. Jesus is the greater prophet like Moses, who will accomplish a greater redemption. However, the shining face of Jesus also indicates that Jesus is God himself, thus asserting his double sonship. The Hebrew Bible is filled with people who longed to see God face to face—especially Moses. This thirst is finally satiated on the Mount of Transfiguration.

49. Gregory Palamas, *The Saving Work of Christ: Sermons by Saint Gregory Palamas*, ed. Christopher Veniamin (Waymart, PA: Mount Thabor, 2008), 44–45.
50. John of Damascus, "Oration on the Transfiguration" (Daley, 207).
51. This fits with Enoch's vision of the throne. Note how many correspondences there are between it and the transfiguration:
> And I observed and saw inside it a lofty throne—its appearance was like crystal and its wheels like the shining sun; and (I heard?) the voice of the cherubim; and from beneath the throne were issuing streams of flaming fire. It was difficult to look at it. And the Great Glory was sitting upon it—as for his gown, which was shining more brightly than the sun, it was whiter than any snow. None of the angels was able to come in and see the face of the Excellent and the Glorious One; and no one of the flesh can see him—the flaming fire was round about him, and a great fire stood before him. No one could come near unto him from among those that surrounded the tens of millions (that stood) before him. (1 Enoch 14:18–22, in *The Old Testament Pseudepigrapha*, 2 vols., ed. James H. Charlesworth [New Haven: Yale University Press, 1983, 1985], 1:21)
52. Jesus bringing about an unmediated vision of God does not contradict 1 Tim. 2:15, since Jesus is God. He mediates a vision of the Father.
53. Irenaeus, *Against Heresies* 4.6.6. "Yet all saw the Father in the Son: for that which is invisible of the Son is the Father, and that which is visible of the Father is the Son." Irenaeus, *Five Books of St. Irenaeus: Against Heresies*, trans. John Keble (Cambridge: James Parker and Co., 1872), 323.

The Bright Cloud

The Synoptics also report that a cloud appears on the mountain. Matthew calls it a "bright" (*phōteinē*) cloud (17:5). All the Evangelists mention that the cloud overshadows them (*episkiazō*, Matt. 17:5; Mark 9:7; Luke 9:34). Luke further explains that the disciples enter the cloud. And from this cloud, the Father speaks.

The cloud symbolizes divine presence—more specifically, the Holy Spirit. However, it does so in two ways. The Spirit continues to lead, direct, and glorify Jesus, but most importantly the cloud shows the union of the Father, Son, and Spirit. On the mountain, the Father speaks, the Son shines, *and* the Spirit presides as a theophanic cloud. In all the Scriptures, only here and at Jesus's baptism are all three persons of the Trinity distinctly manifested.

The transfiguration contains a triple three: the triune Father, Son, and Spirit; the triptych of Moses, Jesus, and Elijah; and the triad of Peter, James, and John. As Bede notes, on the mountain the whole mystery of the Holy Trinity is declared.[54]

The Holy Spirit's role in communing with and seeing God has been neglected in the transfiguration narrative and discussions of seeing God more generally. However, as our trinitarian grammar affirms, the light of God is revealed *through* the Son and *in* the Spirit. Maybe the cloud is just a mass of water drops or ice crystals suspended in the atmosphere, but maybe not. Four arguments support a connection between the cloud, theophanies, divine presence, and the Spirit.

The Cloud and the Spirit

First, clouds are often associated with God's presence in the Scriptures—and with the Spirit's presence specifically.[55] In Exodus, the Lord goes ahead of Israel in a "pillar of cloud" (Exod. 13:21–22; 14:19, 24). The Lord looks down from the pillar, and the glory of the Lord is in the cloud (14:24; 16:10). The text closely correlates the angel of the Lord with the pillar. In Exodus 14:19 the angel of God, who went in front of the Israelites, moves behind them along with the cloud.

This cloud also appears in the Sinai story. On Mount Sinai the Lord appears to Moses "in a dense cloud" (Exod. 19:9). Interestingly, the Greek has the word "pillar" (*stylos*) for the Hebrew word "dense" (*av*). The cloud also appears in the tabernacle and temple narrative. When Moses entered the tabernacle, "the

---

54. See John A. McGuckin, *The Transfiguration of Christ in Scripture and Tradition* (Lewiston, NY: Mellen, 1987), 113–14.

55. Walter A. Maier, "The Divine Presence within the Cloud," *CTQ* 79, nos. 1–2 (2015): 79–102. Augustine (*De Trinitate* 2.35) warns that we should not be dogmatic in deciding what person of the three appeared in created form. People forget that he also said this was the case unless the whole context of the narrative provides us with probable indications.

cloud would come down . . . , and the LORD would speak with Moses" in the tabernacle (33:9). Later, the cloud is connected to the glory and presence of the Lord (40:34–38; Num. 9:15–17, 21–23; 14:14; 16:42), and in this cloud God speaks to Moses (Exod. 33:9–11).

God instructs Aaron not to come into the tabernacle whenever he wants, for he will die *because* God's cloud is above the mercy seat (Lev. 16:2). Later, when Solomon dedicates the temple, the cloud fills the holy place, and the priests are unable to continue ministering because of the Lord's glory (1 Kings 8:10–12; 2 Chron. 5:13–14). Ezekiel likewise sees God wrapped in a huge fire cloud (Ezek. 1:4, 20, 28). In his vision, a man goes into the temple, a cloud fills the inner court, the glory of the Lord rises from above the cherubim, and the court is filled with brightness (10:3–4). In Daniel, the Son of Man comes with the clouds of heaven (Dan. 7:13).

The exodus story explicitly states that the pillar of cloud is a manifestation of God's presence. This doesn't necessarily mean that the cloud *is* the Spirit. However, later prophets and commentators tie the angel, the cloud, and the Spirit closely together. John Levison has argued that Isaiah correlates the Holy Spirit with the cloud.[56] This can be seen in Isaiah 63:10–14 (ESV):

> *But they* [Israel in the wilderness] *rebelled*
> > and grieved his Holy Spirit;
> therefore he turned to be their enemy,
> > and himself fought against them.
> Then he remembered the days of old,
> > of Moses and his people.
> Where is he who brought them up out of the sea
> > with the shepherds of his flock?
> *Where is he who put in the midst of them*
> > *his Holy Spirit,*
> who caused his glorious arm
> > to go at the right hand of Moses,
> who divided the waters before them
> > to make for himself an everlasting name,
> > who led them through the depths?
> Like a horse in the desert,
> > they did not stumble.
> Like livestock that go down into the valley,
> > *the Spirit of the* LORD *gave them rest.*
> So you led your people,
> > to make for yourself a glorious name.

56. John R. Levison, *The Holy Spirit before Christianity* (Waco: Baylor University Press, 2019), 30.

Three references to the Spirit occur in this passage. Most importantly, the prophet says that the Spirit was "in the midst of them." The prophet Haggai employs similar language. Drawing on the exodus tradition, Haggai speaks of God's presence with Israel both in the present and in the past: "Work, for I am with you, declares the LORD of hosts, according to the covenant that I made with you when you came out of Egypt. *My Spirit remains in your midst. Fear not*" (Hag. 2:4–5 ESV). When Haggai recalls Israel's past in Egypt, he says that the Spirit "remains" (lit. "stands") in their midst. The verb Haggai employs is important. Usually the Spirit rushes, rests, blows, or is poured out on people. Here, the Spirit *stands* in their midst.

Exodus 14:19 lies behind this terminology: "The pillar of cloud moved from in front of them and *stood* behind them." Using Spirit language, Haggai and Isaiah identify the cloud from Exodus. In their reading of Exodus, *the Spirit* was with Israel in the wilderness as a pillar of cloud by day and as a pillar of fire by night.

While this might seem far-fetched, the correlation between the cloud and Spirit continues in the New Testament. Paul follows this interpretive move when he states that Israel was baptized into Moses in the cloud and in the sea (1 Cor. 10:2). Being baptized in the cloud under the old covenant is correlated with being baptized in the Spirit under the new covenant. Also, in Acts the Spirit comes at Pentecost with a cloud (Acts 2:19).

In summary, the cloud in the Scriptures is an emblem of God's presence generally and the Spirit particularly. Isaiah 4:5 predicts that in the new age, the cloud will return on God's mountain (see 2 Macc. 2:8). Therefore, readers of the transfiguration story should at least ponder whether the cloud is more than a meteorological phenomenon.

Second, most early Christian interpreters unabashedly claim that the cloud was the Spirit. Origen says that the bright cloud signifies the glory of the Holy Ghost, which covers the saints as a tent.[57] Anastasius of Antioch walks through the Scriptures from the Sinai cloud to the cloud over the tent of meeting to the wilderness pillar to the temple cloud. He concludes, "We are to understand that these clouds mentioned in Scripture are related to each other—or rather, we must not hesitate to say that they are all one thing."[58]

Andrew of Crete affirms that the shining cloud is the same as the dove who came at the Jordan River. He explains that it is fitting for the Spirit to appear, for it is appropriate for the Father to be mirrored in the Son, and the Son in the Father, and for the Son to be revealed in the Spirit, since he

---

57. Origen, *Commentary on Matthew* 12.42 (*ANF* 9:473).
58. Anastasius of Antioch, "Homily on the Transfiguration" (Daley, 139).

shares with the Father and Son in the same substance, the same throne, and the same honor.[59]

Gregory Palamas upholds that the Father and the Holy Spirit were invisibly accompanying the Lord. The Father bore witness with his voice; the Holy Spirit joined his brilliance to Christ's in the cloud, and showed that the Son was of one nature with the Father and Himself united in their light.[60] John of Damascus says that the bright cloud was an image of the Spirit's flame or the cloud of the Spirit.[61] Philagathos argues deductively: If the Spirit is of the same substance with the Father and Son, *why would he not be on Mount Tabor?* He concludes that the cloud must be the Spirit, for many Scriptures refer to the Holy Spirit as a cloud.[62] Martin Luther affirms the same: "The entire Trinity appears here to strengthen all believers: Christ the Son in His glorious form, the Father in the voice declaring that the Son is Lord and Heir, the Holy Spirit in the bright cloud covering them or infusing faith."[63]

Third, the cloud should be associated with the Spirit because of the verb all the Evangelists employ: "overshadow" (*episkiazō*). This same verb is active in Exodus 40:35 (LXX) when the cloud "overshadows" the tabernacle and the Lord's glory fills it. Psalm 90:4 (LXX) says that the one who lives under the protection of the Most High dwells in the tent of God, and God will "overshadow" (*episkiasei*) them with his feathers. It is interesting to note that ornithological imagery, as in the Spirit's appearance as a dove in the baptism accounts, is side by side with the word "overshadow" in this psalm. The angel Gabriel uses this same verb when addressing Mary in Luke 1:35: "The Holy Spirit will come upon you, and the power of the Most High will *overshadow* you." Matthew also affirms that Mary became pregnant by the Holy Spirit (Matt. 1:18, 20). While Peter proposed to make three tents, God revealed a single, better, and very different tent—the cloud.[64] God, not Peter, decides how he will dwell with humanity.

Finally, the "cloud as Spirit" argument is bolstered by parallelism between the baptism and the transfiguration. In both, the Father speaks from heaven about his beloved Son—using nearly the exact same words (Matt 3:17; Mark 1:11; Luke 3:22). In the baptism, the Spirit descends upon Jesus as a dove (Matt. 3:16;

---

59. Andrew of Crete, "On the Transfiguration of Christ" (Daley, 197).

60. Gregory Palamas, *Homilies*, 268.

61. John of Damascus, "Oration on the Transfiguration" (Daley, 211, 228).

62. Philagathos, "Homily 31, on the Saving Transfiguration" (Daley, 273).

63. Martin Luther, *Annotations on Matthew 1–18*, ed. Christopher Boyd Brown, vol. 67 of *Luther's Works* (St. Louis: Concordia, 2015), 312.

64. Thomas Aquinas, *Summa Theologiae*, Pt. III, Q. 45; Origen, "Commentary on Matthew 12:36–43" (Daley, 63–64); Origen, *Commentary on Matthew* 12.42 (ANF 9.473). Origen calls the cloud both the Spirit and the power of God and the Savior. This is because the Father, Son, and Spirit always overshadow the genuine disciples of Jesus.

Mark 1:10; Luke 3:22), with Luke explicitly stating that the Spirit "descended in bodily form" (*sōmatikō eidei*). If the Spirit appeared at the baptism, it is appropriate for us to look for him at the transfiguration.

The Christian interpretive tradition demonstrates sound biblical arguments linking the Spirit with the cloud, and the close relationship between the baptism and transfiguration makes it reasonable to assume that all three persons of the Trinity are involved in the transfiguration. The Father speaks, the Son is transfigured, and the Spirit appears as a cloud.

The Bright Cloud and the Transfiguration

The cloud affirms both Jesus's vocational and divine identity. First, the cloud is an apocalyptic symbol of the new messianic era. As Israel was baptized in the water and cloud, so too Jesus is glorified by the Spirit. As the cloud led Israel, so too the Spirit leads Jesus. As the cloud remained with Israel, so too the Spirit rests on Jesus. As Moses entered the cloud of God's presence, so does the human Jesus. As the Son of Man was borne on the clouds of heaven, so will Jesus be in his ascension. The cloud will be vehicular for Jesus. The cloud signifies that Jesus is the messianic Son.

This messianic reading is confirmed by correlations to Jesus's baptism. Luke explicitly presents Jesus's baptism as the inauguration of his ministry (Luke 3:23). In the baptism, the Spirit equips Jesus as the God-man for his ministry (4:18–19). Jesus receives the Holy Spirit as a rite of purification for the priestly purpose of serving and saving others.

If baptism *prepared* Jesus for his ministry, culminating in the cross, then transfiguration *predicted* his future ministry, culminating in eternal enthronement. The transfiguration is a preview of Jesus's glory that he will receive when he ascends to the heavens. However, to only say this about the cloud is to bypass a lot of low-hanging fruit from the Hebrew Bible.

Second, the cloud ultimately displays that the transfiguration has a trinitarian texture. Peter calls the mountain "holy" because the sacred Trinity opened itself in that place. It also confirms our trinitarian grammar—everything is from the Father, through the Son, and in the Spirit. Around the luminous face of Jesus, the Father's voice echoes, and the Spirit's glory condenses.

Most fundamentally, the Spirit's presence as a cloud confirms that the transfiguration is a theophany, not simply an apotheosis. The cloud is the Old Testament *shekinah* cloud and symbolizes Jesus's union with both the heavenly realm and God himself. This claim is supported by several arguments.

To begin, our survey has indicated that the cloud is the habitation of God's presence. The cloud more than leads Jesus; the cloud is one with Jesus. No longer is God's presence hidden in the temple behind a heavy veil; it is found in the unveiled face of Jesus. The cloud overshadows Jesus, indicating that he is the new temple. In the Son, the Father's Spirit-filled priests will eternally serve.

Second, this not only a vehicular cloud but an oracular cloud: the Father speaks from the cloud.[65] This is how God communicated with Israel in the Old Testament during the wilderness wandering and at Sinai (Exod. 16:10–11; 19:9; 24:15–18). He spoke from the cloud at the tent of meeting (33:9; 40:35; Num. 9:18–23; 11:24–25; 17:7–10; Ps. 99:6–7) and even in Job and Ezekiel (Job 40:6; Ezek. 1:4, 28; 2:1). While Peter babbles about building tents, the glory cloud is God's way of saying, "I will make my own covering." Appropriately, the Father speaks *from* the cloud, just as we hear the voice of the Father *in* the Spirit.

Third, it is a "bright," "shining," or "radiant" (*phōteinos*) cloud. Divine light can only be seen with divine light (Ps. 36:9). As our trinitarian grammar indicates, not only are the Father and Son light but so is the Spirit. God shines forth his light in his triune nature, so it is proper that a bright cloud appears. When Moses went up Sinai, a "dense," "thick," or "heavy" cloud eclipsed it (Exod. 19:9, 16). The dark clouds denote God's hiddenness. Psalm 97:2 says, "Clouds and total darkness surround him."[66] However, the presence of the bright cloud on the Mount of Transfiguration signifies a scene of revelation and glory. What was concealed is now revealed. As Anastasius of Antioch says, the cloud makes the knowledge of the divine nature accessible to us by reaching down to us.[67]

However, it is a cloud of knowing and unknowing, of seeing but not seeing, a luminous darkness that both veils and discloses God.[68] It is a "landmark to limit curiosity, and to drive men off from approaching too near to pry into the divine secrets."[69] The light can be reckoned as darkness precisely because of

---

65. Heil (*Transfiguration of Jesus*, 143–48) also notes the vehicular function of the cloud, especially in relation to Moses and Elijah, tying the function of the cloud to Elijah, Enoch, Moses, and other figures (2 Kings 2:11; 1 Enoch 39:3; 1 Thess. 4:17; Acts 1:9–10; Rev. 11:12).

66. Some may wonder how God can be both light and surrounded by darkness. Douglas Koskela is right to note that darkness is not identified with God directly but *surrounds* him. He goes on to say that the imagery of darkness is noetic rather than ontological. Douglas M. Koskela, *The Radiance of God: Christian Doctrine through the Image of Divine Light* (Eugene, OR: Cascade Books, 2021), 11–14.

67. Anastasius of Antioch, "Homily on the Transfiguration" (Daley, 140).

68. Jamie Davies, "Apocalyptic Topography in Mark's Gospel: Theophany and Divine Invisibility at Sinai, Horeb, and the Mount of Transfiguration," *JTI* 14, no. 1 (2020): 140–48. Sonderegger argues that the "invisibility" of God preserves his immanence and omnipresence. Katherine Sonderegger, *The Doctrine of God*, vol. 1 of *Systematic Theology* (Minneapolis: Fortress, 2015), 50–70.

69. John Hackett, "The Sixth Sermon upon the Transfiguration," in *A Century of Sermons upon Several Remarkable Subjects by the Right Reverend Father in God John Hackett, Late Lord Bishop of Lichfield and Coventry*, ed. Thomas Plume (London: Robert Scott, 1675), 464. Calvin (*Commentary on a Harmony of the Evangelists, Matthew, Mark, and Luke*, trans. William Pringle, vol. 2 [Grand

the intensity of the light. The cloud expresses the inaccessible nature of God but at the same time points to the presence of God.

Fourth, the cloud reveals the triune God and divine glory in the face of Jesus. Though the Son is the only one visible, each person of the Trinity manifests perichoretically. All the divine persons occupy the same space. As Augustine puts it, "Each are in each, and all in each, and each in all, and all in all, and all are one."[70]

In this sense, the strongest argument for the cloud as the Holy Spirit is the appearance of the Son. We cannot see God without seeing all three persons at the same time. It is appropriate that *in the cloud* the disciples hear that Jesus is God's Son. By the Spirit (in the cloud), we see the glory of the Father in the face of Jesus Christ.

The cloud as the Spirit supports a traditional trinitarian perspective: in the Holy Spirit, we contemplate God. As Lossky says, "The whole vision of God [the beatific vision] will be trinitarian."[71] The object of the beatific vision will be the three lights that form the single light.[72] All three persons of the Trinity are fully in one another, and each possesses the divine essence.

While we usually turn either to the birth of Jesus or to Pentecost for our trinitarian texts, the transfiguration should play a more expansive role in our trinitarian theology. On the mountain, the three persons are present. The transfiguration shows they are united but also distinct. The Son is in the flesh, and the Father affirms the Son from the Spirit's cloud. The transfiguration reveals the glory of the triune God.

Moses and Elijah

The final glorious sign, in addition to the glorious appearance of Jesus and the cloud, is the mysterious presence of Moses and Elijah. It can be easy to treat them as peripheral figures. But as with the nativity, the transfiguration's significance lies in a coalition of symbols.

All three Evangelists recount Moses and Elijah's advent with only minor differences. Matthew and Luke list the figures in chronological order—Moses then Elijah—while Mark names Elijah before Moses. Luke is unique in saying they appeared in "glory" (*doxa*) and spoke of Jesus's "departure" (*exodos*).

Rapids: Eerdmans, 1949], 313) asserts that the cloud restrained their arrogance and acted as a bridle, that our curiosity might not indulge in undue wantonness.

70. Augustine, *On the Trinity* 6.12 (NPNF[1] 3:103).

71. Lossky, *Vision of God*, 81.

72. Gregory of Nazianzus, Oration 39.11 (NPNF[2] 7:355).

Significantly, only *after* Jesus is transfigured do they appear. Their arrival is predicated on the transfiguration in some way. In this section, we will inspect why Moses and Elijah appear and how their presence supports Jesus's double sonship.

Interpretations of Moses and Elijah's Presence

Why do Moses and Elijah, specifically, appear? Theoretically, it could have been anyone—Adam and Eve, Enoch, Abraham, David, Daniel, or Esther, for example.

Theories about why Moses and Elijah appear with Jesus on the Mount of Transfiguration abound. Some propose a more covenantal interpretation of Moses and Elijah, pertaining to their roles in salvation history. Others emphasize events in their lives as individuals. While these two emphases ultimately can't be separated, they are distinct and reveal slightly different interpretations.

EIGHT INTERPRETATIONS OF WHY MOSES AND ELIJAH APPEAR

Covenantal Figures	Individuals
Moses and Elijah represent the Law and Prophets.	Moses and Elijah have remarkable deaths.
Moses and Elijah are servants, Jesus is the master.	Moses and Elijah represent authority over life and death.
Moses and Elijah are witnesses or royal representatives.	Moses and Elijah were transfigured.
Moses and Elijah represent the arrival of the new era.	Moses and Elijah both asked to see God.

Covenantal Figures

Many assert that Moses and Elijah appear because they are *covenantal figures who represent the Law (Moses) and the Prophets (Elijah).*[73] Throughout the New Testament, the phrase "the Law and the Prophets" summarizes all of Israel's

---

73. Proclus of Constantinople, "Homily on the Transfiguration of the Savior" (Daley, 89); Cyril of Alexandria, "Homily 51 on Luke" (Daley, 101); Anastasius of Sinai, "Homily on the Transfiguration" (Daley, 165). Calvin (*Harmony of the Evangelists*, 2:311) says that this single reason ought to satisfy us.

Scriptures.[74] Moses is the paradigmatic figure for the Law, while Elijah is a major prophet. Moses and Elijah therefore represent the harmony of the Bible and suggest that the Scriptures are completed in Jesus.

This interpretation has numerous strengths. Throughout the Gospels, especially Matthew, Jesus affirms that he fulfills of the Law and the Prophets (e.g., Matt. 5:17). Many debates with Jesus concern whether Jesus rightly interprets or enacts the Hebrew Bible. Therefore, the transfiguration scene verifies that Jesus fulfills Israel's Scriptures: even Moses and Elijah authorize Jesus's message.[75] Jesus is the Jewish Messiah who satisfies all of Israel's hopes.

The words from the Father also support this view. The Father says they need to "listen to him." This echoes Deuteronomy 18:15, which asserts that another prophet is coming and appears in the context of covenantal promises and curses.

The conversation between Moses, Elijah, and Jesus also bolsters "the Law and the Prophets" interpretation, because they speak of Jesus's *exodos* in Jerusalem. The Law and the Prophets predicted a figure who would suffer on behalf of Israel. The heavenly figures appropriately discuss Jesus's future and how it intersects with the Jewish Scriptures.

But this view also has a few weaknesses. Moses and Elijah as the Law and the Prophets doesn't present immediate implications for Jesus's divinity. Some think the scene is mostly about Jesus's being one with the Father. If so, the presence of Moses and Elijah representing the Law and the Prophets could be seen as off topic. Additionally, while some argue that Moses wrote much of the Law, Elijah didn't write any of the prophetic literature. The question must be raised as to whether Elijah normally represents all the prophets.

A second view sees Moses and Elijah *as servants of Jesus the master.*[76] This is a subpoint of the previous view, clarifying why Moses and Elijah appear as representatives of Israel's Scriptures as whole. The danger with the first view is that it leaves their appearance somewhat unspecified. However, when the Father says, "Listen to him," he speaks not only to the disciples but to Moses and Elijah as well, making them all subservient to Jesus. He is the archetype; they are a copy.

Many in Jesus's day were asking, "Does Jesus agree with Moses and Elijah?" The transfiguration narrative suggests that they needed to flip the question

---

74. Matt. 5:17; 7:12; 11:13; 22:40; Luke 16:16; 24:44; John 1:45; Acts 13:15; 24:14; 28:23; Rom. 3:21.

75. Chrysostom, "Homily 56 on Matthew" (Daley, 71).

76. Chrysostom says that Jesus is the master, while Moses and Elijah are servants. Chrysostom, "Homily 56 on Matthew" (Daley, 71); see also Cyril of Alexandria, "Homily 51 on Luke" (Daley, 101); Timothy of Antioch, "Homily on the Cross and Transfiguration" (Daley, 151); Philagathos, "Homily 31, on the Saving Transfiguration" (Daley, 269).

around: "Do Moses and Elijah agree with Jesus?" The answer is yes, but one voice is superior (Heb. 1:1–2). The appearance of Moses and Elijah, therefore, parallels the argument of Hebrews 3: "Jesus is considered worthy of more glory than Moses, just as the builder has more honor than the house. . . . Moses was faithful as a servant in all God's household, as a testimony to what would be said in the future. But Christ was faithful as a Son over his household" (3:3, 5–6).

Others argue that Moses and Elijah appear *to satisfy the legal requirement of two witnesses.* Deuteronomy 19:15 codifies the requirement for legal testimony: "One witness cannot establish any iniquity or sin against a person, whatever that person has done. A fact must be established by the testimony of two or three witnesses." Moses and Elijah function as faithful witnesses under the Torah to Jesus's future glory.

Additionally, Moses and Elijah are seen by many as "heavenly" witnesses who underwrite Jesus's divine identity, complementing Peter, James, and John as "earthly" witnesses.[77] All these witnesses flank Jesus as people would in a royal *parousia.* Calvin says that they rose not on their own account but to wait on Christ.[78]

While this point may have some merit, it still does not explain why Moses and Elijah *specifically* appear. The two witnesses could have been any of the Old Testament luminaries.

Others argue that Moses and Elijah appear *to represent the inauguration of a new era.* Israel's Scriptures predicted that both a Moses figure and an Elijah figure would emerge before the day of the Lord. Deuteronomy says a new prophet like Moses will arise in the last days (Deut. 18:18–19), and Malachi affirms that a new Elijah will appear (Mal. 4:4–6). The Synoptic Gospels, then, could be presenting the transfiguration as a fulfillment of these twin apocalyptic prophecies. Moses and Elijah are harbingers of the new age.[79] This provides more specificity than simply saying Moses and Elijah are a sign of the Law and the Prophets. The presence of these two figures signifies that the end has drawn near (Matt. 17:10; Mark 9:11). The context also places Jesus's transfiguration under the umbrella of the coming kingdom.[80]

---

77. Simon Lee, *Jesus' Transfiguration and the Believers' Transformation*, WUNT 2/265 (Tübingen: Mohr Siebeck, 2009), 14.

78. Calvin, *Harmony of the Evangelists*, 2:310.

79. Tertullian (*Against Marcion* 4.22.12, 13 [CCSL 1:603]) even ties the appearance of Moses and Elijah to the two olive trees from Zech. 4:14, which are "anointed ones who stand by the Lord of the whole earth." Peter Anthony, *Patristic Perspectives on Luke's Transfiguration: Interpreting Vision* (London: Bloomsbury T&T Clark, 2022), 86.

80. Additionally, this eschatological point might be reinforced by the presence of two witnesses in Rev. 11:3–7, 11–12. These witnesses have a ministry of judgment, and they perform similar signs to those performed by Moses and Elijah. Fire comes forth from them, they close the heavens

However, this view also has several weaknesses. Is the transfiguration about the inauguration of the new age, or is it a preview of the consummation of the new age? Jesus's glory is a proleptic view of the future, but the texts about a new Moses and Elijah appearing seem to focus on the beginning, not the end, of the new age. However, this objection may be dividing things too neatly, as the last day should be viewed holistically. Therefore, the argument still has some merit.

In summary, a covenantal view of Moses and Elijah begins with them representing (1) the Law and the Prophets. A deeper dive into this reality suggests Moses and Elijah are (2) servants to the master, (3) witnesses or royal representatives, and (4) omens of a new era.

Individuals

Some interpreters choose to emphasize events that occurred in the lives of Moses and Elijah. The strength of these positions is that they specify why Moses and Elijah appear and not other covenantal heads, like Adam, Noah, Abraham, or David.

For example, some say they appear because *they signify Jesus's authority over life and death*. Martin Luther says they appear to show that the second death couldn't harm them.[81] The transfiguration, in this way, is about the victory of life. Elijah and Moses appear because they have been translated to heaven and foreshadow the glory that will come to Christ at his resurrection and ascension.

Spatially speaking, Moses comes up from the dead, and Elijah comes down from heaven. Moses died and was buried, but Elijah went up to heaven in a whirlwind. The witnesses to Christ's glorious transfiguration come from heaven (Elijah), the earth (Peter, James, and John), and under the earth (Moses). Jesus thus demonstrates that he has authority over every realm (Phil. 2:10).[82] As Leontius says, "He lured Elijah down from above, he fished Moses up from

---

and turn the water to blood, and after they die, they go up on a cloud of heaven. Chrysostom ("Homily 56 on Matthew" [Daley, 73]) mentions how Moses and Elijah foreshadow Jesus and the apostles. For as Moses and Elijah spoke boldly to tyrants, so too will Jesus and his apostles. As Moses and Elijah had very few possessions, so too Jesus and his apostles have nowhere to lay their heads. While Moses divided the sea, Jesus and Peter walked on the sea. While Moses raised a dead man, Jesus and the apostles raised thousands.

81. Luther, *Annotations on Matthew 1–18*, 308.

82. Chrysostom notes this point, as do others: Chrysostom, "Homily 56 on Matthew" (Daley, 72); Cyril of Alexandria, "Homily 51 on Luke" (Daley, 102); Pantoleon, "Sermon on the Transfiguration of the Lord" (Daley, 111); Timothy of Antioch, "Homily on the Cross and Transfiguration" (Daley, 150); John of Damascus, "Oration on the Transfiguration" (Daley, 223); Philagathos, "Homily 31, on the Saving Transfiguration" (Daley, 269).

below, he set Peter and James and John alongside him from those still on the earth: for the whole is known from the extremes."[83]

Further, the presence of Moses and Elijah confirms that Jesus gives life. God "is not the God of the dead, but of the living" (Matt. 22:32). No realm can resist Jesus's resurrection life from conquering. He has been given "the keys of death and Hades" (Rev. 1:18) and the keys to the heavens (Eph. 1:20–23). Therefore, the point of Moses and Elijah appearing is Jesus's authority in relation to the different cosmic realms.

While this view is attractive, it still doesn't quite answer why Moses and Elijah appear. It also raises the question of whether the main point of the transfiguration is the *authority* of Jesus or his *glory*. The preamble to the transfiguration scene does speak of it as a preview of the kingdom arriving (Luke 9:27), and the command is to listen to Jesus (Matt. 17:5). Nonetheless, most of the imagery speaks more to his glory. But ultimately, we can't separate Jesus's authority and glory, so this view has some value.

Others say Moses and Elijah appear because *they both have questionable deaths*. Elijah was taken up to heaven before death (2 Kings 2:11). And although Deuteronomy 34:5–6 reports that Moses died, some mystery surrounds Moses's death. The statement that no one knows the location of his grave caused some interpreters to surmise that Moses didn't truly die.

The Jewish historian Josephus recounts Moses's death on Mount Nebo. He says a cloud stood over Eleazar, Joshua, and Moses, and suddenly Moses disappeared. Josephus acknowledges that Moses wrote in the Scripture of his death but says he wrote this out of fear lest people should say that because of his extraordinary virtue, he went to be with God.[84]

Philo likewise claims Moses was "taken away" (*analambanō*) and completed his journey to heaven.[85] In one text, Pseudo-Philo says that Moses's appearance was changed into a state of glory and that he died in glory.[86] Philo interprets the statement that no one knows the location of Moses's tomb to mean "he was entombed not by mortal hands, but by immortal powers so that he was not placed in the tomb of his forefathers."[87]

The view that neither of them "died" is problematic, since a New Testament text confirms Moses's death. Jude 9 says, "Yet when Michael the archangel was

---

83. Leontius, "Homily on the Transfiguration" (Daley, 126).

84. Josephus, *Antiquities* 4:326, in *The Works of Flavius Josephus*, new updated ed., trans. William Whiston (Peabody, MA: Hendrickson, 1987).

85. Philo, *On the Life of Moses* 2:291, in *The Works of Philo*, new updated ed., trans. C. D. Yonge (Peabody, MA: Hendrickson, 1993).

86. Pseudo-Philo, *Biblical Antiquities* 19:16, in *The Biblical Antiquities of Philo*, trans. M. R. James (New York: Ktav, 1971).

87. Philo, *On the Life of Moses* 2:291–92.

disputing with the devil in an argument about Moses's body, he did not dare utter a slanderous condemnation against him but said, 'The Lord rebuke you!'" Though the text is a strange one, the Old Testament indicates that the Lord buried Moses (Deut. 34:6), and Jude adds that there was a dispute over Moses's body.

The point is that we have testimony to Moses's death in both the Old and the New Testaments, so the view that he was taken up is unlikely. The most positive spin on this perspective is to say that both departures from the world were remarkable. Moses was buried by the Lord, and Elijah was physical transported. This would indicate that Jesus's transfiguration is a sign of the coming kingdom. All will be raised.

Others argue that *both Moses and Elijah were themselves transfigured*.[88] Moses was transfigured as he beheld the glory of God on Mount Sinai. His face shone as he came down the mountain, and this seemed to be a permanent change. Philo even affirms a metamorphosis for Moses at death. He portrays Moses's departure from the earth as follows: "Afterwards the time came when he had to make his pilgrimage from earth to heaven, and leave this mortal life for immortality, summoned thither by the Father who resolved his twofold nature of soul and body into a single unity, transforming [*metharmozomenos*] his whole being into mind, pure as sunlight."[89]

While the Scriptures only hint at Elijah's transfiguration, Jewish interpreters took it for granted. The flaming chariot that picked him up can be seen as a change in nature that Elijah undergoes as he travels to the heavens (2 Kings 2:11). Most Jews believed one could not enter heaven unless one's body was transformed. The physical body is not able to enter the heavens in its physical state. Humans must receive heavenly bodies, and therefore both Moses and Elijah were transformed (1 Cor. 15:35–58).

Luke affirms that both Moses and Elijah appeared in princely glory on the mountain (Luke 9:31). This implies that Jesus's glory was shared with Moses and Elijah. Moses and Elijah stand as presages of what will happen to Jesus's followers even though suffering awaits them. Both Moses and Elijah went through tribulation but won the crown of life. Hilary of Poitiers states that Moses appeared so that we might be shown the glory of the resurrection body.[90] In Jewish traditions, the righteous are believed to hold angelic status as immortal beings and shine like the heavens and stars to signify that they belong to heaven (Dan. 12:1–5). It is therefore appropriate that Moses and Elijah appear, because they were both transfigured themselves. Their presence indicates that Jesus shares his glory with others.

---

88. Heil, *Transfiguration of Jesus*, 98–113.
89. Philo, *On the Life of Moses* 2:288–91.
90. Hilary of Poitiers, *Commentary on Matthew* 17:2 (PL 9:1014).

While this view may have some merit, it is difficult to identify this as the major point of the transfiguration narrative. The point is Jesus's transfiguration, not Moses and Elijah's. There are repercussions related to these two men, but the narrative focuses on Jesus's splendor.

Finally, many argue that Moses and Elijah appear because *they both requested theophanies on mountains*. The narrative correspondences between the two figures make this view hard to refute. Both Moses and Elijah fast for forty days, both are on the same mountain (Sinai/Horeb), both have visions of God that include visual and aural realities, and both long to see more.

In Exodus 33:18, Moses asks to see God's glory.[91] Though the Lord has spoken to Moses face to face (33:11), Moses asks to see the substance of God, a full revelation of his glory. Moses has seen things in shadows and obscurities. Now he requests to see the glory of God in its fullness. God responds in Exodus 33 by detailing what Moses can see and what he cannot.

Positively, the Lord says he will make all his "goodness" (*ṭûb*; Gk. *doxa*, "glory") pass before him. Two things should be noted about this. First, his goodness will only be revealed as a passing or transient vision. It will not endure or be permanent. Second, this goodness is related to the Lord's name (his nature as gracious and compassionate) and his glory (Exod. 33:19; 34:6). The Lord's goodness, name, and glory are all related concepts. What Moses hears is as important as what he sees.

Negatively, though, God tells Moses that while this theophany would be impressive and extraordinary, it will also be limited. God tells Moses he can't see his "face" (*paneh*), for humans can't see his face and live (Exod. 33:20). The vision will be a limited exposure. Moses's request concerns God's glory, and God answers with a statement about his face. God doesn't have a face in the anatomical sense, so he must mean that Moses can't see him in the full way as Moses requests. Moses won't see God's face as the angels see God in heaven (Matt. 18:10) or as the redeemed will see him on the last day (1 John 3:2) until he sees it on the Mount of Transfiguration.

God then gives Moses directives to protect him. When God's "glory" (*kavod*) passes by, Moses will be put in a crevice of the rock, and God will cover him with his hand until his glory has passed. The Lord's hand will block his vision, but he will remove his hand for a moment so that Moses may see his back, but not his face (Exod. 33:21–23). The amount of concealment in stunning. The cleft in the rock protects Moses, the Lord's hand hides him, and the Lord's back, rather than his face, is revealed.

---

91. The text ties seeing God's glory with Moses knowing his "ways" (*derek*, Exod. 33:13). This pushes against a fully mystical view of God's presence. God is known by inexpressible communion with him, but he is also known by what he has done (his ways).

Moses therefore appears in the transfiguration scene because he requested to see the glory of God. While his request was answered in an extraordinary way, it was also limited. God revealed himself in part. On the Mount of Transfiguration, the Moses's request is granted in full.

A very similar event occurs in the life of Elijah. In 1 Kings 19, Elijah hears how Jezebel killed the prophets of God. Jezebel threatens to end Elijah's life, so Elijah flees. He goes into the wilderness (like Moses) and prays that he might die. God provides food for him not by bringing him manna but by having ravens feed him. Elijah sleeps under a broom tree, an angel of the Lord appears to him, he walks for forty day and forty nights, and he comes to "Horeb, the mountain of God" (1 Kings 19:8).

Elijah enters "a cave" or "the cave" and spends the night there. Many modern commentators argue that this is the same cave where Moses saw the back of God. The word of the Lord comes to Elijah asking him what he is doing in this cave. Elijah, like Moses, is troubled and needs reassurance. He comes to the same place to get his own glimpse of God. God tells Elijah to stand, and he will see the Lord's presence. "The LORD passed by" him (1 Kings 19:11). The Hebrew word employed for "pass by" (*over*) is the exact word employed in Exodus 33:22 when the Lord tells Moses that his glory will pass him by.

However, the appearance of God is surprising. First, a mighty wind tears through the mountains. Second, an earthquake shakes the mountains. Finally, a fire bursts forth on the mountains. After these events, a low whisper is heard. In this soft voice, the Lord appears. When Elijah hears the whisper, he wraps his face in his mantle. He is not able to stand unveiled in the presence of the Lord. He can't bear the sight of the Lord. The Lord's voice comes to him and tells him to go back and finish his ministry.

The correspondence between the Exodus 33 and 1 Kings 19 is uncanny, suggesting that Moses and Elijah appear on the Mount of Transfiguration because they both longed to see the glory of God. Now their desire is satiated.

Moses and Elijah and the Transfiguration

We have surveyed several explanations for the appearance of Moses and Elijah. While we might be tempted to pick one, more than one of them could coalesce. Indeed, this is the benefit of signs and symbols: they allow for a multivalence of meaning. However, it is also useful to note primary and subsidiary points and categorize them for the sake of simplicity.

While many of the views have legitimacy, it is useful to categorize them as *covenantal* and *individual*, because the strongest views correspond to Jesus's role as the messianic and eternal Son. At the risk of being reductionistic, if one capitalizes on Moses and Elijah as covenantal figures—the more common view—then one's interpretation leans toward highlighting Jesus's future glory. However, if we emphasize the *individual* experiences, then we underscore the divine aspects. Moses and Elijah emerge both as old covenant representatives *and* as individuals who had critical events happen in their lives.

Moses and Elijah appear as representatives of the Law and the Prophets and therefore point to Jesus as the messianic Son. The advent of Moses and Elijah beside Jesus symbolizes the relationship between the old and new covenants. The transfiguration is not only about Jesus being divine but about his role in salvation history.

However, to merely say this—as many commentaries do—is not specific enough. Moses and Elijah not only signify the unity of the covenants but demonstrate how Jesus completes the story. Under the old covenant, Moses and Elijah were servants. Under the new, Jesus is the master. Jesus is *the* prophet, priest, and king Israel has been waiting for. He speaks like them, heals like them, rescues like them, and is glorified like them. Their ministry points to him.

Moses and Elijah also appear to affirm Jesus's message and ministry as dual witnesses. They confirm that Jesus is the final word of God. They testify to Jesus as the one all the Law and the Prophets pointed to. The new age has arrived. In the new age, Moses's hopes are satiated.

As one example of this fulfilled covenantal hope, we can consider that this is the first time Moses sets foot in Israel's promised land. Moses died on Mount Nebo looking out over the promised land (Deut. 34:1). Now he finally arrives. As Anastasius of Sinai says, "Mount Sinai did not open up the land of promise for Moses, but Thabor led Moses into the land of promise."[92] But not only does Moses see Immanuel's land (Isa. 8:8); he sees Immanuel himself.

These covenantal points converge, rather than being in opposition, at the mountain's peak. The presence of Moses and Elijah signals that Jesus is the long-awaited messianic Son whom the Law and the Prophets foretold.

However, this is not all that should be said. *Moses and Elijah also appear as individuals who both asked to see God.* As Fitzmyer notes, "Jesus is not just Moses redivivus or Elijah redivivus; he is God's Son and Chosen One."[93] When we view them as individuals, the eternal nature of the Son comes to the forefront. Moses and Elijah's very appearance signifies Jesus's communion with the celestial world.

While both might have had extraordinary departures, it is hard to know the significance of this detail for a reading of the transfiguration. Certainly both come from different realms, but the primary point of this narrative doesn't seem to be Jesus's authority over those realms. While both are themselves transfigured, their transfiguration is based on their participation in God. Thus, the

---

92. Anastasius of Sinai, "Homily on the Transfiguration" (Daley, 167).
93. J. A. Fitzmyer, *The Gospel according to Luke 1–9* (New York: Doubleday, 1981), 793.

main reason Moses and Elijah appear seems not to be their departures or their transfigurations but because they both longed to see God.[94]

The transfiguration is *the* theophany par excellence. Moses and Elijah longed to see God; now they see the *eternally begotten Son*. Before, Moses saw only the "back" of God; now he sees the very "face" and "image" of God. Jesus's transfiguration is longing sated—because he has the same essence as the Father.

The church fathers argue that the transfiguration must be understood as the New Testament climax of God's threefold Old Testament self-revelation to Moses:

- God reveals himself to Moses in a burning bush.
- God reveals himself to Moses on Mount Sinai.
- God reveals himself to Moses in the cleft of the rock.

Each Old Testament theophany is a progressive revelation—going "from glory to glory" (2 Cor. 3:18)—leading to the transfiguration. John can say that no one has seen God because no one has seen the face of God until the transfiguration (John 1:18). The bush is aflame on Mount Horeb but not burnt; so Jesus becomes aflame with the glory of God but is not consumed by it. On Mount Sinai, God appears to Moses in the likeness of fire and cloud; now Moses sees the brightness of Jesus's clothes. In the cleft of the rock, Moses sees God's back; now Moses finally sees God's face in Jesus Christ. He sees not only the afterglow but its exact imprint.

Illumination—Divine Sight

We have examined the three signs in the transfiguration scene. However, we must avoid the temptation of grasping what these signs mean intellectually without asking how this knowledge is transformative (tropology). Christ's celestial light transfigures us.

The church fathers linked the disciples' vision with our own progress in grace. Origen says that Jesus's face shines like the sun so that he might appear to the children of light. Chrysostom tells us to put aside our soiled clothing and put on the armor of light. Anastasius of Antioch affirms that when Jesus's garments become white, they signal to us that we have been purified through him. Anastasius of Sinai says that we ought to say with Peter, "It is good we are

---

94. As an aside, it is also important that Jesus converses with Moses and Elijah as if he knows them and where they are from. If Jesus is not a preexistent or at least heavenly figure, then this detail would be odd.

here, where everything is full of light." Peter left worldly things behind when he beheld rays of the divine sunshine.[95]

The church has spoken of the stage after purgation as one of *illumination*. We put off sin *so that* we can ascend and see. We move from the ways of a child (purgation) to those of an adolescent (illumination) (see 1 Cor. 13:11–12). Illumination is "characterized by a radical shift of the deep dynamics of our being, a profound transformation of our relationship with God."[96] A new connectedness abides in our relationship with God. As the disciples experienced the glory of Jesus Christ on the mountain, so in illumination we now experience God in a state of absolute trust. The mind becomes more enlightened to spiritual things and the practice of virtue.

Thomas Merton put it this way: "We awaken not only to a realization of the immensity and majesty of God 'out there' as King and Ruler of the universe (which He is) but also a more intimate and more wonderful perception of Him as directly and personally present in our own being. . . . He loves us better than we can loves ourselves . . . yet in opposing Him we oppose our own deepest selves."[97]

If in purgation we detached ourselves from fleshly passions, in illumination we begin to put on virtues. As Paul says in Ephesians 5:8–14,

> For you were once darkness, but now you are *light in the Lord*. Walk as *children of light*—for the fruit of the *light* consists of all goodness, righteousness, and truth—testing what is pleasing to the Lord. Don't participate in the fruitless works of darkness, but instead expose them. For it is shameful even to mention what is done by them in secret. Everything exposed by the *light* is made visible, for what makes everything visible is *light*. Therefore it is said:
>
> > Get up, sleeper, and rise up from the dead,
> > and Christ will *shine on you*.

We live "as children of light," in "all goodness, righteousness, and truth" (Eph. 5:8–9). We put on the armor of light (Rom. 13:12). We walk in love, joy, peace, patience, kindness, goodness, faithfulness, gentleness, and self-control (Gal. 5:22–23). We walk in the light so that the darkness does not overtake

95. Origen, "Commentary on Matthew" (Daley, 57); Chrysostom, "Homily 56 on Matthew" (Daley, 81); Anastasius of Antioch, "Homily on the Transfiguration" (Daley, 137); Anastasius of Sinai, "Homily on the Transfiguration" (Daley, 169).

96. M. Robert Mulholland Jr., *Invitation to a Journey: A Road Map for Spiritual Formation* (Downers Grove, IL: IVP Books, 1993), 109.

97. Thomas Merton, *Contemplation in a World of Action* (Garden City, NY: Doubleday, 1971), 160–61.

us (John 12:35). For "what fellowship does light have with darkness?" (2 Cor. 6:14). We are children of the light (1 Thess. 5:5) and have been called out of darkness into God's marvelous light (1 Pet. 2:9). Good works are the hallmark of the illuminative way. When we behold the light, we don't walk in darkness but in brightness (1 John 1:5–7).

We know that we have been illumined if we keep Jesus's commands, for if we obey him, the love of God is made complete in us (1 John 1:5–7). The illuminative stage is often described as an increase in works of love. We become preoccupied with progress in the spiritual life, and the fruits of the Spirit begin to abound in us.

This growth is directly tied to our vision of God. We shine because God "has shone in our hearts to give the light of the knowledge of God's glory in the face of Jesus Christ" (2 Cor. 4:6). In the Spirit, we are illumined and taken up into glory. God causes light to dawn in us, and he lights the spiritual path to greater holiness. Prayer becomes the ebb and flow of our lives: "Miserable men are those that think to be transfigured without continual prayer."[98] As Paul says, we pray to the Father of *glory* for the Spirit of *revelation*, that we would be *enlightened* to know the *glorious* inheritance in the saints (Eph. 1:17–19). Drawing on Luke's account, Gregory Palamas explains that we procure this blessed vision in the present through prayer.[99] The four ascend the mountain to pray (Luke 9:28), and "*as* he was praying, the appearance of his face changed" (9:29).

When was the last time you simply sat and contemplated the goodness of God? Can we expect spiritual transformation without a willingness to seek his face continually in prayer? God desires a quietness of spirit in us, where we rest in the presence of his light. When we see the light, we too might tremble and fall on our faces before him.

CONCLUSION

The transfiguration is a scene full of splendor. Jesus's face shines, his clothes turn bright white, a bright cloud appears, and Moses and Elijah appear in glory. All these symbols suggest a dual meaning: Jesus is both the messianic and the eternal Son. He has a mission on the earth, and he eternally proceeds from the Father.

A trinitarian grammar allows us to speak about the light of the transfiguration with more precision. Jesus's white clothes and shining face suggest Jesus is both the Messiah in the mold of Moses and also of the same essence as the Father. He not only receives light but is light from light (God *ad intra*).

98. Hackett, *Century of Sermons*, 417.
99. Gregory Palamas, *Saving Work of Christ*, 44.

The overshadowing cloud represents the glory cloud and Holy Spirit. This cloud will transport the Messiah to the realm of heaven as the Danielic Son of Man. However, in the cloud, we also behold God the Father (from the thunderous voice), God the Son (by the unbearable light), and God the Holy Spirit (in the luminous cloud).

Finally, Moses and Elijah appear in glory. Jesus converses with both the earthly and the heavenly worlds. Their presence points to Jesus as the messianic Son who unites the old and new. Yet their unique experiences on Mount Horeb signify that Jesus is the face of God and the fulfillment of their requests to see God's glory.

The signs in the transfiguration are glorious. Now we must turn the glorious saying, which further decodes and gives support to these visual elements.

The Glorious Signs	Meaning
Shining face and white clothes	*Messianic sonship*: Jesus is the light of the world sent from the Father (as indicated by his bright clothes). His face shines as the new Mosaic mediator between man and God.
	Eternal sonship: Jesus is light from light, his face reveals the Father, and his bright clothes signify that he belongs in heaven as much as on the earth.
Bright cloud	*Messianic sonship*: The bright cloud evokes Jesus's exaltation as the Danielic Son of Man. It is a vehicular cloud.
	Eternal sonship: The bright cloud is also the Spirit from which the Father speaks—an oracular cloud. The scene is a theophany revealing the triune God.
Moses and Elijah	*Messianic sonship*: Moses and Elijah are representatives of the old covenant who prepare the way for the Messiah.
	Eternal sonship: Yet Moses and Elijah also longed to see God. This longing was only satisfied at the transfiguration.

4

The Glorious Saying

You are my Son, today I have begotten you.

—Psalm 2:7 ESV

My life at this stage consists of a lot of kids' movies. I'm not ashamed to admit that among my favorites is the Kung Fu Panda trilogy. Set in China, the animated films feature Po (Jack Black), a tubby, food-loving, clumsy panda who desires to be a kung fu warrior. The movies recount his flawed but endearing adventures. In the third movie, a warrior yak named Kai, empowered by the stolen chi (life force) of many kung fu masters, seeks to destroy Po. An ancient prophecy has foretold that Po is destined to stop him. In their great battle, Po sacrifices himself and brings Kai back to the spirit world. When they are in the spirit world, Po masters the art of chi and becomes full of light.

Kai looks at Po and asks incredulously, "Who are you?" Po replies, "I've been asking the same question. Am I the son of a panda? The son of a goose? A student? A teacher? It turns out, I'm all of them. I am the Dragon Warrior!" Full of light, Po goes on to defeat Kai because he has finally realized his identity.

As Jesus shines with light on the mountain, Kai's question also hangs on the lips of disciples: "Who are you?" The transfiguration contains not only signs but sayings. A declaration of Jesus's identity is pronounced when the Father proclaims, "This is my beloved Son. Listen to him!" (see Matt. 17:5; Mark 9:7;

93

Luke 9:35). The transfiguration is often remembered for its visual components. People forget about the proclamation.[1]

In fact, when Peter retells this scene in his second epistle, he says nothing about the Son's appearance; he cites the Father's declaration only (2 Pet. 1:16–18). Jesus receives honor and glory when the Father *speaks*.[2] We have considered the transfiguration's signs, but we also must exegete the words. Divine resplendence and the divine declaration conjoin on the mountain.[3]

In this chapter we will cover three sayings of the transfiguration: (1) the inglorious saying from Peter, (2) the glorious declaration of Jesus's sonship, and (3) the command to listen to Jesus. The sayings support the argument of this book: the transfiguration reveals Jesus as both the heavenly glorious Son and the earthly suffering messianic Son. While the signs benefited from a trinitarian grammar, the sayings will be explored using the parameters of a christological grammar. The hypostatic union will be our guiding light for exegesis.

A Christological Grammar

The purpose of this theological grammar is to give us categories for speaking more faithfully about the transfiguration and to provide scriptural guardrails for our reading. This is important because the transfiguration is a key text that tests one's dogmatic commitments.

Some might argue we should simply get on with the exegesis, but it is precisely this impulse that has kept modern interpreters from retrieving the riches of earlier theologians. Without salvaging these doctrines, our interpretation of the transfiguration may become lopsided, focusing on one aspect at the expense of another.

Possibly the most important doctrine to reintegrate into the transfiguration is Christology. As Aquinas notes, "All the knowledge imparted by faith revolves around these two points, the divinity of the Trinity and the humanity of Christ."[4] This section will provide four christological rules drawn from Scripture and

1. When Moses requests to see God's glory in the Old Testament, the Lord responds referencing both something visual and something auditory. Moses can't see the Lord's face, but the Lord will let all his goodness pass before him. That is the visual element. However, the Lord says he will also proclaim his name to him (Exod. 33:19).

2. Peter likely focuses on the words because his argument in the larger context is about the prophetic word. Therefore, the conclusion should not be that the visual element is unimportant.

3. I don't find it convincing to argue, as some do, that the aural element (or the visual element) of the scene is more important. The visual and aural elements intertwine, and the disciples' response is to both. Protestants tend to prioritize the voice and not the symbols.

4. Thomas Aquinas, *Compendium of Theology*, trans. Richard J. Regan (Oxford: Oxford University Press, 2009), 18.

articulated in the Chalcedonian Definition that will chaperone our interpretation of the transfigural sayings.[5]

Four Christological Rules

First, *the Son is truly God and truly man without confusion of those two natures.* The Son's nature as God and as man are "without confusion, without change, without division, and without separation." We can't separate the natures (Nestorianism) nor conflate them (Eutychianism). He is fully God and fully man, but his natures are not mixed. The property of each nature is preserved. For example, as man, the Son suffered; as God, he never suffered. As man, he grew in wisdom and experienced gaps in his knowledge; as God, he knew all things. As man, he hungered and thirsted; as God, he never needed anything.

The transfiguration can thus have implications for him as a man and as God. Only interpretations of the mountaintop scene that take into account "his true and proper deity; his true and proper humanity; the union of deity and humanity in one person; and the proper distinction of deity and humanity in one person" will satisfy.[6] This doctrinal rule allows us to affirm something about Jesus's humanity and his divinity in the transfiguration without confusing the two.

Second, *the Son is truly God and truly man, but in one subject.* While we must not confuse the two natures of Christ, Chalcedon also reminds us not to separate them. They meet in one person. Jesus is a single divine subject. Arguing against Nestorianism, Cyril of Alexandria asserts, "He is the one and only Son, not one son alongside another son, considered in this way to be one person

---

5. The Council of Chalcedon (451) met to confront christological errors and offered a concise clarification regarding the church's teaching about Jesus's two natures:

> We, then, following the holy Fathers, all with one consent, teach men to confess one and the same Son, our Lord Jesus Christ, the same perfect in Godhead and also perfect in manhood; truly God and truly man, of a reasonable [rational] soul and body; consubstantial [coessential] with the Father according to the Godhead, and consubstantial with us according to the Manhood; in all things like unto us, without sin; begotten before all ages of the Father according to the Godhead, and in these latter days, for us and for our salvation, born of the Virgin Mary, the Mother of God, according to the Manhood; one and the same Christ, Son, Lord, Only-begotten, to be acknowledged in two natures, inconfusedly, unchangeably, indivisibly, inseparably; the distinction of natures being by no means taken away by the union, but rather the property of each nature being preserved, and concurring in one Person and one Subsistence, not parted or divided into two persons, but one and the same Son, and only begotten, God the Word, the Lord Jesus Christ, as the prophets from the beginning [have declared] concerning him, and the Lord Jesus Christ himself has taught us, and the Creed of the holy Fathers has handed down to us. (Philip Schaff, *Creeds of Christendom*, vol. 2 [Grand Rapids: Baker, 1984], 62–63)

6. Louis Berkhof, *The History of Christian Doctrines* (London: Banner of Truth, 1969), 102.

[*prosōpon*]."[7] To speak of the transfiguration only as a proleptic vision of the glory of the Son of Man would be to divorce his two natures and commit the Nestorian error. There are not two Sons but one Son. Divine and human attributes exist in the one person.

Chalcedon speaks of Jesus having two natures but "concurring in one Person and one Subsistence," and it speaks of "one and the same Son, our Lord Jesus Christ." That is why the declaration of Jesus's sonship can be a statement both about his divine nature and about his human mission: because there are two natures, human and divine, in one person.[8]

Third, *the Son is doubly begotten*. Chalcedon speaks of two begettings. Jesus was "begotten before all ages of the Father according to the Godhead." This refers to his eternal begotten nature—his procession from the Father. To speak of the "Son" and the "Father" is to speak both of what is common between these persons of the Godhead (divine essence) and of what distinguishes them (paternity vs. generation). Relational and kinship categories should be primary when we hear Jesus spoken of as the Son on the Mount of Transfiguration.

However, Chalcedon immediately continues, "*and* [begotten] in these later days, for us and for our salvation." Though the Greek, like the English, doesn't carry over the verb "begotten," it is implied. The creed continues by describing Jesus's earthly birth: "born of the virgin Mary, the mother of God." Ignatius of Antioch affirms, "Jesus Christ . . . before the ages was with the Father and appeared at the end of time."[9] Jesus is doubly begotten—eternally and then in Mary's womb.[10] This second begetting concerns the Son's mission on the earth.

---

7. Cyril of Alexandria, *On the Unity of Christ*, ed. John Anthony McGuckin, Popular Patristics 13 (Crestwood, NY: St. Vladimir's Seminary Press, 2015), 83.

8. Palamas speaks of the transfiguration in this way: "The glory that proceeds naturally from his divinity was shown on Tabor to be shared with his body as well because of the unity of his person. Thus, his face shone like the sun on account of this light." Gregory Palamas, *The Saving Work of Christ: Sermons by Saint Gregory Palamas*, ed. Christopher Veniamin (Waymart, PA: Mount Thabor, 2008), 45.

9. Ignatius, *Epistle to the Magnesians* 6.1, in *The Apostolic Fathers: Greek Texts and English Translations*, 3rd ed., trans. Michael W. Holmes (Grand Rapids: Baker Academic, 2007), 206–7. John of Damascus says, "We venerate his double generation—one from the Father before the ages . . . and one in these latter days for us and like us and beyond us." *On the Orthodox Faith*, trans. Norman Russell (Yonkers: St. Vladimir's Seminary Press, 2022), 178–79.

10. Jesus wasn't "born" from the Father in the way we think of birth. Hilary of Poitiers puts it this way: "For God [Christ] is not born from God [the Father] by the ordinary process of a human childbirth." Jesus's begetting is "the birth of living nature from living nature. It is God going forth from God. . . . For the proceeding forth of God from God is a thing entirely different from the coming into existence of a new substance" (Hilary of Poitiers, *On the Trinity* 6.35 [*NPNF*[2] 9:111]). John Chrysostom also reminds us that even though there is a temporal word in

The two begettings must remain distinct yet intertwined in our interpretation. Adonis Vidu argues that the Son's mission manifests the procession.[11] In other words, Jesus's mission to the earth is an extension of his begotteness from the Father. It was fitting for the Son to be born as a human because he is begotten of the Father. Sonship implies unity and equality but also distinction and order. A christological grammar allows us to excavate this *sonship* of Jesus.

Fourth, *the "net profit" of the incarnation is not a decrease of the Son's divinity but an exaltation of his humanity.* When Chalcedon says Jesus is "the same perfect in Godhead and also perfect in manhood," it implies that Jesus added human flesh; he did not subtract deity.[12]

The fathers were careful to delineate the ways in which Christ's divine and human properties communicate (*communicatio idiomatum*). Immortality, light, and glory are communicated to his flesh because human nature can receive these properties. Other attributes, however, such as eternity, immensity, and ubiquity, could not be communicated to him without destroying his human nature.

Consider the analogy of an iron in the fire. Iron takes on the form of fire when it is heated—it brightens and glows. Yet the iron does not blacken the fire. The iron becomes enflamed without changing the property of the fire. Likewise, Jesus's human nature is enflamed, but the weakness of humanity is not transferred to his divinity. When Jesus is transfigured, his body brightens, revealing his divine nature through his humanity.

It is not wrong for Jesus to *receive* glory, to *become* Lord, to *be exalted* by the Father because of the hypostatic union. To be a recipient of all things from God is to be fully human. Cyril explains that Jesus indeed participated in the fullness of flesh so that mankind might participate in his received sacred and divine honors.[13] As John of Damascus taught, "The Son eternally begotten of the Father possesses the natural and eternal ray of divinity; yet the glory of the divinity has become also the glory of the body."[14] Jesus's divine nature brings resplendence to his human nature.

---

the phrase "eternal generation," we must not think of it in terms of time. "Let us not change the ancient boundaries which our fathers set, but let us yield everywhere to the laws of the Spirit. . . . If He begot in human fashion, it would be necessary that there be some interval between the one begetting and the begotten, but, since He begets ineffably and as befits God, leave out the words 'before' and 'after,' for these are terms belonging to time, and the Son is the Maker of all ages." John Chrysostom, "Homily 7 on St. John's Gospel" (*NPNF*[2] 14:28).

11. Adonis Vidu states, "The divine operations *ad extra* follow from, are grounded in, the immanent processions." Adonis Vidu, *The Same God Who Works All Things: Inseparable Operations in Trinitarian Theology* (Grand Rapids: Eerdmans, 2021), 95.

12. This is against kenoticism, which affirms the opposite—that Christ's divinity was lessened when he assumed a human nature.

13. Cyril of Alexandria, *On the Unity of Christ*, 101.

14. John of Damascus, *Homily in Transfiguration* 12 (PG 96:564b).

Avoiding a Slip in Our Christological Grammar

Christology is always a balancing act, and Chalcedon aids our equilibrium on the rope. A christological grammar of the transfiguration will therefore reject three mistaken views of Christ.

First, it will rebuff the interpretation that Jesus was a divine being wrapped in a human body (Apollinarianism). The Son has a fully human nature and even glorifies human nature.

Second, it will reject the view that the human person and divine person operate independently (Nestorianism). While we can speak of Jesus in his human and divine nature, the two natures are brought together in true union. The glory the disciples see is therefore both united and distinguishable. As Cyril of Alexandria says, there is both one Christ and one Son, though each retains his respective characteristics.[15]

Third, a christological grammar of the transfiguration will also reject that Jesus has two natures combined into a single nature (Eutychianism). This is the opposite of the error of Nestorianism. We can't speak of the single nature of Jesus in the transfiguration. Jesus has two natures; it is therefore appropriate to speak about two glories uniting in one person.

Peter's Inglorious Saying

Before we hear what is *true* in the transfiguration scene, we turn first to what is *wrong*—namely, Peter's reaction. In response to the *proper* divine signs, Peter responds with an *improper* human proposal.

The three heavenly witnesses (the Father, Moses, and Elijah) are contrasted with the three earthly onlookers (Peter, James, and John). Heaven speaks truth, but earth misstates. All the Synoptics record Peter's reaction, with remarkable similarities.[16]

Matthew 17:4: "Lord, it's good for us to be here. If you want, I will set up three shelters here: one for you, one for Moses, and one for Elijah."

Mark 9:5–6: "'Rabbi, it's good for us to be here. Let's set up three shelters: one for you, one for Moses, and one for Elijah'—because he did not know what to say, since they were terrified."

---

15. Cyril of Alexandria, *On the Unity of Christ*, 77, 83, 91.

16. It is tempting to read into the address that Peter employs. For example, in Mark the title "Rabbi" could be viewed in a negative light, as it is clear from this scene that Jesus is more than their Rabbi, and Mark tends to portray the disciples negatively. However, Peter addresses Jesus as "Lord" in Matthew and as "Master" in Luke. Possibly, all the titles are insufficient. Only the name "Son" is sufficient.

Luke 9:33: "'Master, it's good for us to be here. Let's set up three shelters: one for you, one for Moses, and one for Elijah'—not knowing what he was saying."

Before we examine Peter's blunder, we must give him partial credit. Peter speaks better than he knows when he blurts out, "It is *good* we are here." Indeed, the three earthbound disciples are in the presence of Goodness itself. His words are laden with the longing of all of humanity for a return to the good of the garden where they walked with God (Gen. 1:31). Peter's words reflect the heart of Psalm 84:1–2:

> How lovely is your dwelling place,
> LORD of Armies.
> I long and yearn
> for the courts of the LORD;
> my heart and flesh cry out for the living God.

The fact remains, however, that Peter had zeal, but it was not according to knowledge (Rom. 10:2). Mark and Luke specify that Peter did not know what he was saying, and Mark adds that it was because "they were terrified" (Mark 9:6). Yet even in his incoherence, Peter provides a lesson. His hasty words model how we too might *mis*understand the Son. Peter's poorly chosen words reveal the Son's glory by contrasting it against falsehood.

Interpretations of Peter's Words

There are several common ways of interpreting Peter's statement.[17] To begin, it is important to recognize that "*while* [Peter] was still speaking," the voice from heaven thus interrupted and corrected him (Matt. 17:5; see also Luke 9:34). The most persuasive view will integrate Peter's words with the Father's response.

First, some think Peter's request to set up three shelters recalls *the Jewish Feast of Tabernacles*. Peter's inclination to build three tabernacles to house Jesus, Moses, and Elijah is an allusion to Israel's tent-dwelling days in the wilderness. *Sukkoth* commemorates what God did for Israel by sustaining them for forty years following the exodus. This reading ties in all our previously discussed connections: the presence of the Lord dwelling with his people, the glory cloud, the exodus theme, and the Moses imagery. Additionally, by Peter's day, the Feast of Tabernacles had acquired eschatological significance.[18]

17. This list of differing views on Peter's response follows Dorothy Lee's list. Dorothy Lee, *Transfiguration* (New York: Continuum, 2004), 19–21.

18. Amos asserts that the Lord will restore the fallen tent of David (Amos 9:10–14). Zechariah says that a day will come when the nations will celebrate the Festival of Shelters (Zech. 14:16–19). John predicts that the one on the throne will shelter his people (Rev. 7:15–17).

Two problems arise with this interpretation. The first is that it might be pressing Peter's thoughtless statement too far to see a new Feast of Tabernacles expressed by his few words. The second is a matter of arithmetic: If Peter was thinking of the Feast of Tabernacles, why did he only offer to build three tents and not six? Maybe they will bunk together, but the language in all the Synoptics makes clear that one is for each individual: "one for you, one for Moses, and one for Elijah" (Matt. 17:4; Mark 9:5; Luke 9:33). Furthermore, Peter specifically says that the tents would be for the heavenly figures. Clearly, the tents would be more suitable for the three disciples than the heavenly figures if a renewal of the Feast of Tabernacles was in view.

Others propose Peter's request alludes to *the tent of meeting in the wilderness*. The tabernacle was a particular tent where God dwelt among his people (Exod. 33:7–11; Deut. 31:14–15). In saying he will build tents, Peter recognizes Jesus's unique status. His request, then, could be read as a well-intentioned attempt at the restoration of God's dwelling with his people.

The problem with this interpretation is again arithmetic. Peter offers to make three tents, not one. The tent of meeting was meant for God and God alone. Even in his most bewildered state, we should credit Peter with knowing that it would be blasphemy to place Moses and Elijah on the same level as Yahweh. And if Peter didn't understand Jesus to be Yahweh in this moment, then his offer to construct tents for three "co-servants of the Lord" would have no connection to a new tent of meeting.

The third option speculates that Peter was thinking of *the eternal tents in which the righteous will dwell with angels at the end time* (Luke 16:22; John 14:2). The Testament of Abraham speaks of paradise as a place where the righteous dwell in tents and God dwells with his people (Testament of Abraham A 20:14). First Enoch also foretells that the dwelling place of the saints is with the angels at the end (1 Enoch 39:3–8; 71:16). Perhaps this was Peter's line of reasoning?

The problems with this interpretation are similar to those above. Did Peter believe he could make tents suitable for *heavenly figures*? And if he was envisioning *eternal* dwellings for the righteous, why didn't he offer to build six tents?

Peter's Blunder: The Singularity and Suffering of the Son

We will commit our own blunder by tethering Peter's offer too strictly to the Feast of Tabernacles, the Tent of Meeting, or even an eschatological dwelling. Peter's mistake is more elementary. His error is found both in the *number* (three) and in the *nature* (tents) of what he proposes. Peter's request reveals that he misunderstands both the *singularity* and the *suffering* of Jesus.[19]

Peter's blunder begins with the number of tents he offers to make.[20] When Moses and Elijah are removed, the voice points out that Jesus is the one and only: "*This* is my beloved Son." Jesus is not in a triumvirate of equals with Moses and Elijah. He is exclusive. Even Peter's recognition of Jesus as the Messiah doesn't go far enough. Thus, Peter doesn't understand the relationship between Moses, Elijah, and Jesus. He attempts to put Jesus on the same level as men. God won't allow it. The voice from heaven makes it plain: Jesus is not equal to Moses and Elijah; he is far superior to them. He is the *singular* Son.

Sonship primarily has to do with Jesus's eternal relationship to the Father, not his role in redemptive history. Affinity to the Father makes the Son singular. God reenforces this reality by withdrawing Moses and Elijah (Matt. 17:8; Mark 9:8; Luke 9:36). Jesus stands alone as God's Son. While Jesus, Moses, and Elijah are all servants of Yahweh, all are anointed prophets, and all speak the word of the Lord, Jesus is the only beloved Son.[21]

Timothy of Antioch captures this idea in an imaginative retelling of the scene: "But the Lord said to him, 'What are you saying, Peter? Have you decided to construct three tabernacles? Do you treat me in the same way as them? Do you make the master equal to slaves? You offer an opportunity for blasphemy to Arius and Eunomius, in wanting to make my dwelling place with creatures! Shall I dwell here, even though it is outside my Father's bosom?'"[22]

Peter's mistake is related not only to Jesus's singularity but to his *suffering.* His error lies in his basic proposal to make *tents.* Peter's misstep pertains to his attempt to prolong the glory of the scene *ad finitum.*[23] Peter envisions this mount

19. Calvin asserts that (1) Peter did not comprehend the design of the vision; he thought it would endure forever; (2) he put servants on the level of their Lord; and (3) he sought to build fading tabernacles for men who had already been glorified (Calvin, *Commentary on a Harmony of the Evangelists, Matthew, Mark, and Luke,* trans. William Pringle, vol. 2 [Grand Rapids: Eerdmans, 1949], 312–13). Randall E. Otto claims that the tents were for protection and that Peter did not want the vision to continue. Otto, "The Fear Motivation in Peter's Offer to Build *Treis Skēnas,*" *WTJ* 59, no. 1 (1997): 101–12.

20. Augustine capitalizes on it being a single cloud in contrast to the three tabernacles Peter proposed to build. Augustine, Sermon 78.3 (PL 38:401).

21. Proclus of Constantinople, "Homily on the Transfiguration of the Savior," in *Light on the Mountain: Greek Patristic and Byzantine Homilies on the Transfiguration of the Lord,* trans. Brian Daley, Popular Patristics 48 (New York: St. Vladimir's Seminary Press, 2013), 91; Gregory Palamas, *Saving Work of Christ,* 51.

22. Timothy of Antioch, "Homily on the Cross and Transfiguration" (Daley, 151).

23. John Chrysostom notes that Peter wanted Jesus to remain there always; that is why he mentions the tents. John Chrysostom, "Homily 56 on Matthew" (Daley, 75); see also Cyril of Alexandria, "Homily 51 on Luke" (Daley, 103); John of Damascus, "Oration on the Transfiguration" (Daley, 226).

as the new Bethel, the dwelling place of God, which should last into eternity. But Christ's light cannot be domesticated. His flashing glory will inhabit the whole cosmos. Peter lobbies for Jesus to stay *here* so that he might not depart for *there*.[24] He attempts to hold on to the moment too tightly. As Palamas says, "The time for all things to be restored had not yet come, but even when it does, we shall not need tents made by hand."[25] Peter believes he is witnessing the full realization of God's kingdom—a kingdom come without the cross. He mistakes a preview for a final act. He cannot comprehend that Jesus's suffering will lead to his glory.[26]

This interpretation is also supported by the response from the Father. Peter wants Jesus to establish the kingdom's glory now and skip the cross. Upon the mountain, the Father's voice speaks of the "beloved" Son. This is a direct allusion to the mountaintop sacrifice of Abraham's "beloved" son Isaac (Gen. 22). By adopting the verbiage from Mount Moriah, the heavenly voice affirms Jesus's messianic mission to Golgotha. Glory is seen at the transfiguration, but final glory, humanly speaking, will only come by suffering.

In summary, Peter's error lies in his confusion about Jesus's *singularity* and his *suffering*. The voice from heaven confronts Peter's ill-formed conception of Jesus's unique divine status and his messianic mission. The voice from heaven brings fatherly correction: "Moses and Elijah are mere servants. *This* is my only Son" (see Heb. 3:5–6). Peter can't domesticate God's light.

"This Is My Beloved Son"

A heavenly voice interrupts Peter with the declaration of Jesus's nature and vocation. In his second letter, Peter acknowledges that the voice he heard from heaven that day belonged to the Father (2 Pet. 1:17). As Peter stammered about the three tents, the Father declared the unique identity and role of the Son.

The signs of the transfiguration seem obscure to us. Light, a shining face, a cloud, and the presence of Moses and Elijah need to be correlated with the words surrounding them. The transfiguration, in the most important respect, is about the sonship of Jesus.

24. Pantoleon, "Sermon on the Transfiguration of the Lord" (Daley, 111); Anastasius of Antioch, "Homily on the Transfiguration" (Daley, 138).

25. Gregory Palamas, *Saving Work of Christ*, 51.

26. The fact that Peter still wants to bypass the cross makes his comment about the goodness (*kalon*) of them being there ironic (Mark 9:5). The use of *kalon* may be interpreted innocently, but shortly after this, Jesus will explicate what is "good" (*kalon*) about discipleship. It includes self-denial. Jesus says that if their hands cause them to fall away, they should cut them off because it is "better" (*kalon*) for them to enter life maimed than to have two hands and go to hell, the unquenchable fire (9:43; 9:45, 47). "Good" discipleship is painful discipleship.

Interestingly, the words of the Father are *not* new words. They are drawn from the Hebrew Scriptures. However, they differ slightly in each account:

Mark 9:7: "This is my beloved Son."

Luke 9:35: "This is my Son, the Chosen One."

Matthew 17:5: "This is my beloved Son, with whom I am well-pleased."

2 Peter 1:17: "This is my beloved Son, with whom I'm well-pleased."

Joel Green celebrates these varied pronouncements as a "virtual choir of intertextual voices whose presence is so forceful that they threaten to drown out the narrator's own voice."[27] The slight variations form a majestic harmony of the Law (Deut. 18:15), the Prophets (Isa. 42:1), and the Psalms (Ps. 2:7). This section will examine these intertextual echoes in relation to the transfiguration.

In all these intertexts, Jesus is presented as the messianic Son. However, even in the Old Testament there are also adumbrations that he is more than the messianic Son. While these are not always explicit, they are suggestive.

Most argue the transfiguration is primarily about Jesus's vocation, not his ontology. However, the two can't be divorced. As implied in our christological grammar, our task is not only to ask how Jesus in his human nature has been glorified (a vertical question) but also to ask the question of *relations* (a horizontal question). The title "Son" connotes both the mission and the procession of the one person Jesus.

Genesis 22:2 and the Suffering Son

When the Father says, "This is my beloved Son," in Mark's and Matthew's accounts, he alludes to several Old Testament texts. One that is sometimes overlooked is Abraham's sacrifice of his son Isaac in Genesis 22:2: "'Take your son,' he said, 'your *only* son [*yakhid*; Gk. *agapētos*] Isaac, whom you *love* ['*ahav*; Gk. *agapaō*], go to the land of Moriah, and offer him there as a burnt offering on one of the mountains I will tell you about.'"[28]

The Lord commands Abraham to take his *only* and *beloved* son and sacrifice him on the mountain. The links to the transfiguration are hard to miss: (1) sacrificial imagery, on (2) a mountaintop, accompanied by (3) beloved-son language, and (4) future glorification.

In the Jewish tradition, Isaac is seen as a sacrificial figure. The story is called the Akedah, from the Hebrew term for the binding of Isaac. In Jewish thought,

27. Joel B. Green, *The Gospel of Luke*, NICNT (Grand Rapids: Eerdmans, 1997), 377.

28. For an analysis of the Isaac echoes, see Leroy Huizenga, *The New Isaac: Tradition and Intertextuality in the Gospel of Matthew* (Leiden: Brill, 2012), 209–35.

the Akedah became the supreme example of self-sacrifice in obedience to God's will and a symbol of martyrdom.[29] The context of the transfiguration also indicates that Jesus voluntarily goes to the cross and obeys the will of his Father.

Further, both scenes take place on a mountain. On Mount Moriah, God provides a substitutionary lamb, prompting Abraham to name the place "The Lord Will Provide" (Gen. 22:8, 14). The only other place Mount Moriah appears in Scripture is 2 Chronicles 3:1, where it forms the foundation of Solomon's temple. This connection to Solomon's temple encourages us to scan the transfiguration for any sacerdotal hues. Each Evangelist notes the brightness of Jesus's face and clothes (like a priest), the appearance of a cloud (the glory cloud), and Peter's reference to tents (like the tabernacle). In some ways, the transfiguration is the new Mount Moriah: the new locale full of glory. Jesus is the new anointed priest who communicates God's presence to God's people and who will build God's spiritual house (see 1 Pet. 2:5). The Lord has again provided.

While the sacrificial imagery and mountain setting are suggestive, the theme of *sonship* is loud and clear. Eleven times, Genesis calls Isaac Abraham's "son."[30] Isaac is Abraham's beloved and only son; Jesus is the Father's beloved and only Son.[31] Both stories concern kinship, descendants, and inheritance. The power resides in the *relationship* between father and son. The Isaac story foreshadows what is to come: God intercedes before the sacrifice of Isaac as if to show Abraham's offspring a path that the Father alone will one day tread. To sanctify a new people, the Father will sacrifice his only Son.

Finally, both stories employ suffering-glorification patterns. Isaac was to be sacrificed, but instead he became the foundation of a large nation. Jesus is sacrificed, and through his sacrifice he becomes a cornerstone of the new temple. Suffering and glory thus come together both in the Isaac narrative and in the transfiguration narrative. Therefore, the voice from heaven affirms that Jesus is a new sacrificial Isaac who will bless his people and make their offspring "as numerous as the stars of sky" (Gen. 22:17).[32]

The allusion to Genesis 22 therefore has the effect of amending Peter's theology of glory with a theology of the cross. The two must come together.

29. See Josephus, *Antiquities* 1:232, in *The Works of Flavius Josephus*, new updated ed., trans. William Whiston (Peabody, MA: Hendrickson, 1987).

30. Gen. 22:2, 3, 6, 7, 8, 9, 10, 12, 13, 16, 20.

31. Readers may wonder how this can be the case, since Abraham also fathered Ishmael. However, Isaac is still Abraham's "only begotten Son" because he is his father's only legitimate heir. Charles Lee Irons, "A Lexical Defense of the Johannine 'Only Begotten,'" in *Retrieving Eternal Generation*, ed. Fred Sanders and Scott R. Swain (Grand Rapids: Zondervan Academic, 2017), 108.

32. In the Eastern tradition, the promise of Abraham's descendants being "as the stars" (Gen. 15:5; 22:17; 26:4) is not only a comment on the *number* of descendants but a comment on their future *nature*. This is then connected to Dan. 12:3 and Matt. 13:43.

The transfiguration is not only about Jesus's essential glory but about his mission to redeem a new people and bless the world. Without the cross, there will be no people as numerous as the sand of the seashore; without suffering there will be no splendor like that of the stars.

While Genesis 22 doesn't contain explicit indications of Jesus's preexistent glory, and we need to be careful of overarguing the point, the language from the Isaac story may have paved the way for a deeper understanding of sonship. Easter eggs can be found.

In many Greek translations and interpretations of Genesis 22:2, the word *agapētos* (beloved) is substituted for *monogenēs* (only begotten). Aquila's translation of Genesis 22:2 has *monogenēs*, as does Symmachus in Genesis 22:12. Hebrews 11:17 employs *monogenēs* to interpret this scene, and so does Josephus in *Antiquities* 1:222. This is because the word in Hebrew—"only" (*yakhid*)—can be translated in the LXX both as *agapētos* (beloved) and as *monogenēs* (only begotten). Three times in the Old Testament *yakhid* is translated with *agapētos* (Jer. 6:26; Amos 8:10; Zech. 12:10), and once it is translated as *monogenēs* (Judg. 11:34). Early interpreters and translators thus viewed "beloved" and "only begotten" as somewhat mutually interpreting. To say that Isaac is the beloved son is connected to him being the only begotten son.

THE TRANSLATION AND INTERPRETATION OF *YAKHID* (ONLY ONE) IN GENESIS 22:2

Hebrew (BHS)	Greek (LXX)	Greek (NA[28])	Greek (Aquila)	Greek (Symmachus)	Greek (Josephus)
yakhid = only	agapētos = beloved (Gen. 22:2; see also Jer. 6:26; Amos 8:10; Zech. 12:10) monogenēs = only begotten (Judg. 11:34)	agapētos = beloved (Matt. 3:17; Mark 1:11; Luke 3:22) monogenēs = only begotten (Heb. 11:17)	monogenēs = only begotten	monogenēs = only begotten	monogenēs = only begotten

Note: The references in the LXX don't pertain to Genesis 22 but are simply Greek translations of *yakhid*.

This detailed look at the specific words might seem unimportant, but when we turn to the Gospels, these words begin working extra hard (as Humpty

Dumpty tells Alice when she encounters him in Wonderland, "When I make a word do a lot of work like that . . . I always pay it extra").[33]

The Synoptic tradition tends to employ the adjective form, *agapētos*, to describe Jesus in the baptism and transfiguration scenes. However, John substitutes the word *monogenēs* to signify what sort of sonship Jesus has (John 1:14, 18; 3:16, 18).[34] That John avoids the adjective form *agapētos* is somewhat surprising, because John was on the mountain with Jesus and heard the Father's voice declare that Jesus is the *agapētos*! Why wouldn't he employ the same words from the Father? The answer is perhaps that John transports the word into a different frame, nodding toward a deeper meaning.[35] The beloved Son is the eternally begotten Son. Jesus has a double sonship, as the creeds affirm, because he is doubly begotten.

Genesis 22:2 primarily points forward to Jesus's messianic sonship. He is the suffering Son like Isaac. However, the language in Genesis 22 may have been generative for New Testament authors to reflect on the deeper sense of Jesus's sonship.

Isaiah 42:1 and the Suffering Son

Genesis 22:2 is not the only text the transfiguration accounts allude to. The heavenly voice calls Jesus the "chosen" Son (Luke 9:35) in whom God delights (Matt. 17:5, my trans.). This echoes a similar pronouncement in Isaiah 42:1, which speaks about another suffering servant: "This is my servant; I strengthen him, this is my *chosen one* [*bekhiri*; Gk. *eklektos*]; I delight in him. I have put my Spirit on him; he will bring justice to the nations."

In its historical context, this prophecy speaks to an exiled Israel. Yet Yahweh promises to redeem not only Israel but the nations. Key to this mission is his servant. God will send a "chosen" servant in whom he delights. This spirit-filled

33. Lewis Carroll, *Through the Looking-Glass* (Mineola, NY: Dover, 1999), 58.

34. John does speak of the Father's love for the Son in the verbal form (John 3:35; 10:17; 15:9; 17:24), but he avoids the adjective *agapētos*. Interestingly, the Synoptic Gospels largely avoid the adjective *monogenēs*, except in Luke to speak of the "only son" of the widow of Nain (Luke 7:12), the "only daughter" of Jairus (8:42), and the father who pleads for his "only child," who is demon-oppressed (9:38).

35. Twentieth-century scholarship has claimed that *monogenēs* means not "only begotten" but "only one of his kind" or "unique." Dale Moody, "God's Only Son: The Translation of John 3:16 in the Revised Standard Version," *JBL* 72, no. 4 (1953): 213–19; Richard N. Longenecker, "The One and Only Son," in *The NIV: The Making of a Contemporary Translation*, ed. Kenneth L. Barker (Grand Rapids: Zondervan, 1986), 119–26; Gerard Pendrick, "MONOGENĒS," *NTS* 41, no. 4 (1995): 587–600. It has been argued that the Greek adjective is derived not from *monos* ("only") + *gennaō* ("beget") but from *monos* ("only") + *genos* ("kind"). However, Irons ("Lexical Defense," 98–116) has shown that this is mistaken. The Greek term's "'fundamental meaning' is 'only begotten' or 'only child' in the sense of having no siblings." Additionally, the term *genēs* strongly encodes notions of derivation, offspring, and begetting. Irons affirms that *monogenēs* should be understood in John as supporting the Nicene confession that Jesus is eternally begotten from the Father. While we should be careful of proof texting and only relying on one word (as it is not the only argument for this doctrine), it's an important one.

chosen servant will be a light to the nations; he will open blind eyes and bring prisoners out from the dungeon (Isa. 42:7).

Isaiah later identifies how this servant, in whom God delights, will bring light to the world *by suffering* (Isa. 52:13–53:12). Paradoxically, the servant will be greatly exalted amid his suffering (52:13). Servants are typically of low estate, but this servant will be glorified—glorified *because* he becomes low, despised, and rejected.

When the Father speaks from the cloud in Luke and Matthew, he affirms Jesus as the Chosen One, and the one in whom God delights, from Isaiah (Luke 9:35; see also Matt. 17:5; 12:18–21). Though Jesus will suffer at the hands of the chief priests and scribes, though he will be crucified on a Roman cross, God will highly exalt him. He is God's *eklektos*, his chosen and glorified messianic Servant.

The disciples on the mountain get a preview of this exaltation to give them hope in the face the coming suffering. As Isaiah affirms, "After his anguish he will see light and be satisfied. . . . He will receive the mighty as the spoil because he willingly submitted to death" (53:11–12). The words from Isaiah 42:1, spoken from the cloud on the mountain, affirm that Jesus is the suffering messianic Servant, Son, and Chosen One.

While Isaiah gives little indication that the servant is a preexistent being, two realities are interesting to note. First, when the servant acts, God acts. God's agency is manifested in the servant's agency. After the servant has redeemed God's people, Israel praises God for his salvation. After the servant has redeemed Israel, they "sing a new song to the LORD" (Isa. 42:10). They "give glory to the LORD" because it is *he* who "advances like a warrior" (42:12–13). However, on the Mount of Transfiguration, a deeper understanding of Isaiah's prophetic servant is brought to light.

Second, this Isaianic servant has a unique relationship to the Spirit. The Spirit *rests* on him (Isa. 11:2), is *put* on him (42:1), and is *on* him (61:1). The servant is defined not only by his relationship to the Father but by his relation to the Spirit. While the Spirit empowers this servant as a man, the Spirit is also uniquely *united* to him.

As Old Testament readers hear about this servant, they will ask, "Who is this that was predicted to be wholly faithful to God's covenant? Who will act on God's behalf? Who will redeem us as God redeemed us before? Who will have the Spirit rest on him?" The transfiguration scene reveals that Jesus is none other than Isaiah's Chosen One.

Daniel 7:13–14 and the Exalted Son

Genesis 22 and Isaiah 42 concern a suffering Son and Servant. Lurking in the background is another text that interpreters often overlook, Daniel 7:13–14, which also speaks of a "son"—an exalted human son.

References to "the Son of Man" bookend the Synoptic transfiguration narratives (Matt. 16:28; 17:9; Mark 8:38; 9:9; Luke 9:26, 44). Additionally, both Daniel 7 and the Synoptics contain the imagery of a cloud and the exaltation of a human figure. When the voice booms with the declaration "This is my beloved Son," it evokes the exaltation of the Son of Man from Daniel 7.

Old Testament theophanies also support a connection to the Son of Man. When figures in the Old Testament see the throne room in heaven, they see a bright human figure sitting on the throne. Ezekiel saw "on the throne, high above, someone who looked like a human" (Ezek. 1:26). John asserts that Isaiah saw the glory of Jesus when he peered into heaven (John 12:36–41; see also Isa. 6:1–8). Moses saw the "form" of the Lord on Sinai (Num. 12:8), while the others heard the voice (Deut. 4:12). Daniel 7 fits into the pattern of these visions.

While exiled in Babylon, Daniel dreams of four animals, representing worldly kingdoms (Dan. 1:17; 7:1, 13). As Daniel watches, the Ancient of Days takes his seat to judge these nations. His hair is white with wisdom and his throne aflame with power. The court is convened, the books are opened, and the nations are judged for breaking God's law. At this moment, Daniel sees one "like a son of man" (7:13)—a human figure—approach the Ancient of Days. The human one contrasts with the beasts. He is pure and simple. He has kept the covenant. He has not corrupted God's good creation. This Son of Man is given dominion, glory, and an eternal kingdom.

Daniel's scene is called a vision (Dan. 7:13), and Matthew 17:9 also calls the transfiguration a "vision" (*horama*).[36] The words "this is my beloved Son" reverberate with the significance of Daniel's vision. It is the sound of the Ancient of Days confirming Jesus as the Son of Man, who, through perfect obedience to the law, will receive all the kingdoms of the earth.

This intertextual connection thus stresses Jesus's humanity, his messianic vocation, and his future splendor. Though the kings of the earth vie for glory and power, only Jesus will be honored. He is the human king predicted long ago who will be exalted. The transfiguration previews the exaltation of the Son of Man.

While Daniel 7:13–14 doesn't detail where this Son of Man comes from, two clues suggest he is more than simply a "human one." While some take a minimalist approach to the identity of Daniel's Son of Man, I take a maximalist approach.[37]

---

36. The burning-bush moment with Moses is also labeled a vision (Exod. 3:3; Acts 7:31). See also the Abraham narrative (Gen. 15:1) and the Jacob narrative (46:2). However, also note that God shows himself to Moses in more than a vision, for Moses beholds the form of the Lord (Num. 12:6–8).

37. The identity of Daniel's Son of Man has been highly contested. Some argue the phrase simply refers to a "human being" in general without reference to any particular individual. Others argue that the Son of Man is not a human figure but rather an angelic or heavenly figure. Others view the Son of Man as a representative of a group of people.

To begin with, the Danielic Son of Man is closely, almost too closely, associated with Yahweh himself. He shares in his throne, power, and authority. In fact, we have later Jewish literature that reflects on these verses and even asserts that this Son of Man is a preexistent figure. The earliest known manuscript of the Old Greek translation of Daniel (MS 967) says that the Son of Man was like the Ancient of Days and thus divine. In the Similitudes of Enoch (1 Enoch 37–71), a text clearly reflecting on Daniel 7, the Son of Man has a highly exalted position. He is preexistent (48:2–3, 6–7),[38] is ascribed glory (49:2; 51:3), and is seated on God's own throne of glory (45:3; 51:3; 55:4; 61:8; 62:2–3, 5). He acts as the last-day judge of sinners and angels (55:4), and he receives worship (46:5; 48:5; 62:6, 9).

Crispin Fletcher-Louis has drawn attention to these texts as particularly eyebrow-raising—a figure receiving devotion alongside God in *pre-Christian Judaism*.[39] In other words, some precedence exists for Jews having a theological category for a figure who would stand in the place of Yahweh, share his identity and authority, and receive his worship.

If we pull this canonical thread, Revelation draws together the identities of Daniel's Ancient of Days *and* Son of Man in the one person Jesus Christ. His hair is white as wool, his eyes are like flames, and he calls himself "the First and the Last" (Rev. 1:14, 17; see also Dan. 7:9). This Son of Man has a face that shines like the sun, and John falls as though dead before him (Rev. 1:16–17). Later this same Son of Man is seen seated on the cloud with a golden crown on his head (14:14).

How could this human figure be so closely aligned with God? The church fathers pointed to the hypostatic union. This Son must exist as two natures united in one person. Therefore, it is fair to read the language of Daniel 7 as intentionally vague, leaving the door open for a future Son who is both human and more than human. This mystery is revealed in the incarnation and put on glorious display in the transfigured Son of Man.

---

38. "At that hour, that Son of Man was given a name, in the presence of the Lord of the Spirits, the Before Time; even before the creation of the sun and the moon, before the creation of the stars, he was given a name in the presence of the Lord of the Spirits" (1 Enoch 48:2–3). It continues:

> For this purpose he became the Chosen One; he was concealed in the presence of (the Lord of the Spirits) prior to the creation of the world, and for eternity. And he has revealed the wisdom of the Lord of the Spirits to the righteous and the holy ones, for he has preserved the portion of the righteous because they have hated and despised this world of oppression (together with) all its ways of life and its habits in the name of the Lord of the Spirits; and because they will be saved in his name and it is his good pleasure that they have life. (48:6–7, in *The Apocrypha and Pseudepigrapha of the Old Testament*, trans. R. H. Charles [Oxford: Clarendon, 1913])

39. Crispin Fletcher-Louis, *Jesus Monotheism*, vol. 1, *Christological Origins: The Emerging Consensus and Beyond* (Eugene, OR: Cascade Books, 2015), 171–205. While there is debate about the date of the Similitudes, according to Fletcher-Louis the new consensus is that they are pre-Christian.

Psalm 2:7 and the Exalted Son

When the Father says, "This is my beloved Son," he alludes to several Old Testament texts, some of which refer to Jesus's suffering and others of which point to his exaltation. The most important "Son" intertext may be Psalm 2:7.

> I will declare the LORD's decree.
> He said to me, "You are my Son;
> today I have become your Father."

The transfiguration's meaning, and more precisely the meaning of sonship, is largely dependent on how we interpret Psalm 2. The second psalm and its declaration of sonship has a depth of meaning that can be deceiving. Its expansive meaning can be viewed through the temporal reference "today." When is today?[40] Today is far more than a twenty-four-hour time period. Rather, it refers to time past, present, and eternal.[41]

Time past. At the historical level, the reference to "today" in Psalm 2:7 points to the installation of Israel's king on earth *in the past.* In this sense, "today" refers to a time contemporary with the speaking. This psalm was appropriately recited on Israel's royal coronation days.

Multiple unmarked speakers appear in Psalm 2. Verse four introduces Yahweh's retort. He laughs at the kings of the earth, speaking to them in his anger, saying, "I have installed my king on Zion, my holy mountain" (2:6).

In response to the rage and rebellion of the nations, the Lord sets his king—the king of Israel—on his "holy mountain" (Ps. 2:6; see also 2 Pet. 1:18). God establishes his ruler who will possess all the nations. Psalm 2:7 is part of the Lord's response to the uprising of the nations.

Psalm 2:7 also begins with a first-person singular referent, "I," leading readers to assume Yahweh is again speaking. However, the "I" here says, "I will declare *the LORD's* decree." The speaker in verse 7 recounts what the Lord said to him on coronation day: "You are my Son; today I have become your Father." Kings were known as "sons of God." The gods established kings over nations and called them their sons. In the same way, Israel's king was a "son of God"—the chosen human ruler of Yahweh.[42]

---

40. Admittedly, the voice from heaven omits the phrase, "Today, I have begotten you." Some say this is to avoid any adoptionism. However, the allusion more likely refers to the whole verse, and sonship naturally implies begetting.

41. For a good chapter on the use of "today" in Hebrews, see Madison Pierce, "Hebrews 1 and the Son Begotten 'Today,'" in *Retrieving Eternal Generation*, ed. Fred Sanders and Scott R. Swain (Grand Rapids: Zondervan Academic, 2017), 117–31.

42. Second Sam. 7:10–14; 1 Chron. 17:13; Pss. 89:4, 26; 132:11–12, 17–18; Psalms of Solomon 17:4; 4Q174 3, 7–13; 4 Ezra 7:28; 13:32, 37, 52.

The literal sense of "today" concerns Yahweh's words to Israel's king in the past. Israel's king is God's son, and God is his father. The Davidic figure hears the declaration of sonship and understands that God has enthroned him.

Time present. However, the "today" in Psalm 2:7 is more expansive. "Today" should also be understood metaphorically to denote *an ever-present day.* This spiritual interpretation is confirmed when New Testament authors apply these words to Jesus.

Paul cites Psalm 2:7 at Antioch Pisidia, preaching that God kept his covenant promise to his people Israel "by raising up Jesus as it is written in the second Psalm: 'You are my Son; today I have become your Father'" (Acts 13:33). Paul claims Jesus's resurrection day is the fulfillment of Psalm 2:7. Likewise, Hebrews cites Psalm 2:7 as God's declaration of Jesus's eternal priesthood (Heb. 5:5). Along with Paul, Hebrews affirms that the "today" of Psalm 2:7 is a transcendent present. This installation psalm points beyond Israel's past to Israel's ultimate king and priest in the present—Jesus the Son.

The "today" therefore has a present meaning. It refers not only to a Davidic king in the past but to a Davidic priest-king in the present. Jesus's reign is even more extensive than the past king's. He reigns not only on earth but in heaven. He is not only Israel's king but the world's king. He sits not only on Mount Zion but on the highest throne in heaven. He is not only Israel's priest but the world's mediator. He enters not only the earthly temple but the heavenly temple. The Father's declaration confirms that the human Jesus has fulfilled Psalm 2 in his resurrection and ascension.

The implication for the *present* meaning of "today" is that when the Father declares that Jesus is his Son in the transfiguration, he designates him as Israel's true human king foretold in Psalm 2. Jesus is the new David, the messianic Son that Israel has longed for. He will establish the kingdom. This Son will be vindicated and glorified. All nations will be called to his side. Jesus will defeat death and ascend to the heavens. The Father's words affirm that *Jesus is the long-awaited human king* who will be glorified. The transfiguration is a foretaste of this glory, a picture of his coronation day.

Time eternal. The meaning of these words goes even deeper. "Today" also speaks about an *eternal* day.[43] This reading of Psalm 2 helps us grasp how the transfiguration platforms the divine eternality of the begotten Son.

---

43. Admittedly, the claim that this Psalm refers not only forward in time but backward is debated. Arguments for an eternal time include J. V. Fesko, *The Trinity and the Covenant of Redemption* (Fearn, UK: Mentor, 2016), 95–106; Kevin Giles, *The Eternal Generation of the Son: Maintaining Orthodoxy in Trinitarian Theology* (Downers Grove, IL: InterVarsity, 2012), 56, 79. Giles says, "Psalm 2:7 read critically and historically does not speak of the eternal begetting of the Son of God." He points to its use in Acts 13:33, Heb. 1:5, and Heb. 5:5 as being fulfilled in Jesus's exaltation

Richard Bauckham points out the dearth of Old Testament texts citing Israel's king, or even the messiah, as God's Son. Alone, these texts fail to explain why the Gospels give such prominence to the title "Son of God." However, if "Son of God" refers not merely to an office but to "a profound relationship that binds Father and Son together,"[44] then sonship is not primarily *kingship* language but *kinship* language.[45] Several arguments support this interpretation of Psalm 2.

First, Hebrews 1:1–5 employs Psalm 2 to link Jesus's messianic sonship with his eternal sonship.[46]

In these last days, he has spoken to us by his **Son** [introducing the Son].

> God has appointed him heir of all things [messianic sonship]
> *and made the universe through him* [divine sonship].
> *The Son is the radiance of God's glory* [divine sonship]
> *and the exact expression of his nature* [divine sonship],
> *sustaining all things by his powerful word* [divine sonship].

> After making purification for sins [messianic sonship],
> he sat down at the right hand of the Majesty on high [messianic sonship].
> So he became superior to the angels [messianic sonship],
> just as the name he inherited is more excellent than theirs [messianic sonship].
> For to which of the angels did he ever say [messianic sonship],

You are my **Son***; today I have become your Father* [messianic and divine sonship]. (Heb. 1:2–5)

Hebrews 1:2 begins by introducing us to the title the author will expound: Son. After saying that in the past God spoke by the prophets at various times and in various ways, but now he has spoken through his Son, the author then pauses to explicate who this Son is. Some of the statements about the Son label

---

(resurrection and ascension). However, he also defends patristic exegesis, saying that the church fathers build on apostolic and christological exegesis by extending generation into eternity and affirming that the historical meaning of a biblical text does not exhaust the meaning of a text. For a contrary view see Paul R. Williamson, "The *Pactum Salutis*: A Scriptural Concept or Scholastic Mythology?," *Tyndale Bulletin* 69, no. 2 (2018): 259–81.

44. Richard Bauckham, *Who Is God? Key Moments of Biblical Revelation* (Grand Rapids: Baker Academic, 2020), 77.

45. "Eternal generation" is also kinship language. "Son" as kinship language picks out from among possible contenders who is the Father's true Son.

46. R. B. Jamieson, *The Paradox of Sonship: Christology in the Epistle to the Hebrews* (Downers Grove, IL: IVP Academic, 2021), 51–75.

him a *passive recipient*: he has been appointed (1:2), he has inherited a name, and he became superior (1:4). In others, he is an *active agent*: the Son sustains the universe by the word of his power, he made purification for sins, and he sat down at the right hand of Majesty (1:3). Maybe most important are the statements about his *ontology*: he "is the radiance of God's glory and the exact representation of his nature" (1:3).

The author of Hebrews links the Son's messianic vocation with his eternal sonship and employs Psalm 2:7 as support. The Son has *been* appointed (vocation) but also *is* the radiance of God's glory (ontology). He became superior to angels (vocation) but also is the exact imprint of God's nature (ontology). He has made purification for sins (vocation) but also sustains all things (something only Yahweh does).[47]

Readers should note that Hebrews 1 contains a variety of transfiguration echoes. The chapter speaks about Jesus as the radiance of God's glory (the eternal Son) and also as one who has been appointed at the right hand of the "Majesty on high" (the messianic Son; see also 2 Pet. 1:17). The only two explicit references to "Son" (*huios*) in Hebrews 1:1–5 are found in 1:2 and 1:5, thus framing the argument. Hebrews is not afraid to link the identities. This is the paradox of sonship.[48] In summary, Hebrews provides an early and canonical interpretation of Psalm 2 that includes both a messianic and a divine reading of sonship in Psalm 2.

Second, the author of Hebrews sets a hermeneutical precedent, as Madison Pierce has argued, for reading "today" as an eternal present.[49] In Hebrews 3–4, the author quotes Psalm 95:7–11 to warn God's people not to be like the Israelites who fell in the wilderness:

> *Today*, if you hear his voice:
> Do not harden your hearts as at Meribah,
> as on that day at Massah in the wilderness
> where your ancestors tested me;
> they tried me, though they had seen what I did.
> For forty years I was disgusted with that generation;
> I said, "They are a people whose hearts go astray;
> they do not know my ways."
> So I swore in my anger,
> "They will not enter my rest." (Ps. 95:7–11)

47. As D. A. Carson states, "Thus the sonship language applied to Christ in the prologue cannot be restricted to a strictly Davidic-messianic horizon. . . . Sonship language in the prologue to Hebrews assigns transparently divine status to the Son and speaks of his pre-existence." D. A. Carson, *Jesus the Son of God* (Wheaton: Crossway, 2012), 62.
48. Jamieson, *Paradox of Sonship*.
49. Pierce, "Hebrews 1," 129.

Hebrews 3 capitalizes on the word "today" and makes it ever present. "Encourage each other daily, while it is still called today, so that none of you is hardened by sin's deception" (Heb. 3:13). For Hebrews, "today" is forever. Today is always present. Therefore, when the Father says, "Today, I have become your father," it implies a past, present, and maybe even eternal meaning.

Third, many of the church fathers read the declaration of sonship in Psalm 2 as an eternal statement. This "eternal" interpretation of Psalm 2:7 is part of the text's reception.[50] Indeed, many of the church fathers asserted that Psalm 2 is about eternal generation. Augustine is a representative example: "The word *today* denotes the actual present, and as in eternity nothing is past as if it had ceased to be, nor future as if it had not yet come to pass, but all is simply present, since whatever is eternal is ever in being, the words, 'Today I have begotten you,' are to be understood of the divine generation. In this phrase, the orthodox catholic [i.e., universal] belief proclaims the eternal generation of the Power and Wisdom of God who is the only-begotten Son."[51]

This interpretation carries over into reflection on the transfiguration narrative. John of Damascus asserts that sonship means the Son is before the ages and has come forth eternally and timelessly from God the true begetter. Jesus always existed from the Father and in him and with him.[52] Timothy of Antioch affirms the following about Jesus, based on the Father's words at the transfiguration:

> He is unique. . . . This who is of one substance with me, his Father, in every way—he is not like those whom some heretics have reduced to a slave! This one pre-existed along with me, before the ages. This one put the world together by his Spirit. This one shaped Adam, when he and I together planned to make human beings. This one took mud from the earth and formed the human person. This one transported Enoch in a marvelous way from human company. This one is seen and understood. This one exists with me, and stands on the mountain. This one has walked in your company, and is not separated from the one who begot

50. The Reformer Juan de Valdes says that Jesus's sonship means his generation is divine and he is of the same substance as the Father. Jason K. Lee and William M. Marsh, eds., *Matthew*, Reformation Commentary on Scripture: New Testament 1 (Downers Grove, IL: IVP Academic, 2021), 222–23.

51. Augustine, quoted in Pierce, "Hebrews 1," 129.

52. John of Damascus, "Oration on the Transfiguration" (Daley, 228); see also Philagathos, "Homily 31, on the Saving Transfiguration" (Daley, 278): "This is my beloved Son, who is before the ages; who has come forth eternally and timelessly, only-begotten, alone from the alone, from me his begetter; who always exists from me and in me and with me, not a moment later in his existence. He is from me as from his Father and cause, begotten of my substance and hypostasis, and therefore 'of the same substance.' He is begotten in me, inseparably and without coming forth from me; he exists with me as a complete hypostasis."

him. This one is without time, without beginning, without successor, eternal, unchangeable, incomprehensible, ineffable beyond thought. This one is; he did not come to be, he was not created. He is by nature, not by grace. He is, without having his being in time. He is, for he also was and existed before. For I did not become Father in time, but I always exist as Father. And if I am always Father, then this one is always Son, and the Holy Spirit also always is—who is adored along with me and with the Son, and glorified along with us, always and to the unending ages of ages. Amen.[53]

Gregory the Sinaite also says that the Father's words mean that Jesus is divine:

This is my Son, the Beloved, the only One, transfigured today on Mount Thabor in his humanity; this is the stamp of my individual being, the radiance of my glory, the unchanging image of my super-substantial being. This is my strong right arm, my all-powerful right hand. This is my personified wisdom and power; through whom I created the ages and brought all things into being from nothing, in whom I am well pleased and through whom I have saved you, through whom I appeared and in whom I shed light on the world and create it anew, in whom I have come to be known and through whom I was glorified, in whom I continue to receive glory and through whom I glorify you and will glorify you again. He is the one who reveals my name among men and women, and I revealed him and bore witness to him and showed him forth at the Jordan; he gave me glory, and I gave him glory today, and will glorify him in the inaccessible light. He lives in me without confusion, and I in him without change, flashing forth in a way that befits a triune God; he is in me singly and I in him in a threefold sense—the first because of the assumption of humanity, the second because of the existence of the divinity. He is the begotten light, I the unbegotten; he the only Son, I the unbegotten Father, source of all things; he is the Word in the beginning, and is God in the beginning, before all ages, I the beginning of the beginning and Father of the Word, the Mind that is above all mind and all substance. He is the light, I am the spring of light; he is the life, I am the cause of life; he is the sun of justice who shines forth in me, I am known in him as the light of three suns, beyond all substance, and in him I shine with all the fullness of the Godhead, in a bodily way. In him I am well pleased, and in him I have willingly chosen you; I remain in him without change, without confusion, without separation, without alteration. I shine out in him, I reveal and foreknow and cleanse and enlighten you, I make you holy in him. In the light of his glory you will see me, the inaccessible light.[54]

53. Timothy of Antioch, "Homily on the Cross and Transfiguration" (Daley, 152–53).
54. Gregory the Sinaite, "Discourse on the Transfiguration" (Daley, 337–39).

Fourth, the multiple unmarked speakers in Psalm 2:7 led many church fathers to argue that the whole Psalm is an intratrinitarian conversation before time began and that continues in Jesus's appointment. The Father speaks, the Son speaks, and the Spirit conveys the scene. As Bates affirms, this text finds its "theodramatic setting before the dawn of time."[55] Clement of Rome declares that the Master spoke to the Son, meaning that the Father spoke to the preexistent Jesus. Justin reports the words of Psalm 2:7 are spoken by David in the *prosōpon* (person) of the preexistent Christ as the Son reports the words of God the Father. Irenaeus affirms that David did not speak from himself. The Spirit of God, conforming himself to the person of the Son, spoke.[56] Early Christian authors thus concluded that David spoke in the person of the Son and reported the speech of the Father, who had previously addressed these words to the Son. Psalm 2:7 was seen as a conversation in eternity past between the Father and Son and reported by the Spirit.

In summary, the words of Psalm 2:7 operate in three temporal locations: a historical statement *in the past* about a Davidic king, a statement in the *present* fulfilled in Jesus's resurrection and ascension, and a statement of *eternal time* about Jesus's eternal relation to the Father. Genesis 22, Isaiah 42, Daniel 7, and Psalm 2 are all suggestive of Jesus's eternal sonship.

THE POLYVALENCE OF PSALM 2:7

"You are my Son; today I have become your Father."

Past	Historical meaning	"Son" refers to Israel's king coronated on Mount Zion.
Present	Messianic meaning	"Son" refers to Jesus as king coronated over heaven and earth.
Eternal	Eternal meaning	"Son" refers to Jesus as the only begotten Son from the Father.

Thus, the declaration of sonship in the transfiguration is about both Jesus's messianic sonship and his eternal sonship with the Father. As our christological grammar indicated, the divine personal names "Father" and "Son" don't communicate that one has divine nature and the other lacks it. These titles signal the

55. Matthew W. Bates, *The Birth of the Trinity: Jesus, God, and Spirit in New Testament and Early Christian Interpretations of the Old Testament* (Oxford: Oxford University Press, 2016), 67.

56. First Clement 36:4 (in Holmes, *Apostolic Fathers*, 92–93); Justin, *Dialogue with Trypho* 88.8, trans. Thomas Halls, ed. Michael Slusser (Washington, DC: Catholic University of America Press, 2003), 138; Irenaeus, *On the Apostolic Teaching*, trans. John Behr, Popular Patristics 17 (Yonkers: St. Vladimir's Seminary Press, 2003), 49. Bates (*Birth of the Trinity*, 71) also points to Origen and Tertullian for this interpretation.

relationship between two persons sharing divine essence. The Son radiates God's glory because he is eternally generated; yet because he is eternally generated, he is of the same *ousia* as the Father.

The names "Father" and "Son" signal both what they hold in *common* and what *distinguishes* them. As Basil asserts, "The divinity is common, but the paternity and the filiation are properties. . . . Thus, when we want to speak of an *unbegotten light*, we think of the Father, and when we want to speak of a *begotten light*, we conceive the notion of the Son. As light and light, there is no opposition between them, but as begotten and unbegotten, one considers them under the aspect of their opposition."[57]

Notably, Luke asserts it is while Jesus is praying that he is transfigured. While the brilliance comes forth from Jesus, it is not apart from his prayerful communion with his Father. "The Father, being the Father, fathers his glory within his Son and in the fathering of the Son."[58]

When the Father declares Jesus as his Son, he affirms both Jesus's vocation and his ontology. Chalcedon reminds us that when we speak of the Son, we must affirm that his two unmixed natures reside in a single subject. The Son has equality and unity *with* the Father but also an order and distinction *from* the Father.

"Listen to Him"

The declaration of Jesus's sonship is not the only pronouncement heard on the Mount of Transfiguration. Because Jesus is the Son, the Father also issues a command: "Listen to him" (*akouete autou*, Matt. 17:5; Mark 9:7; Luke 9:35). Though many elements of the transfiguration are visual, the command from heaven directs the onlookers to Jesus's *voice*. The irony is that Jesus never speaks in this scene. In fact, in all the Gospels, the transfiguration is one of the only episodes after the commencement of his ministry in which Jesus doesn't speak.

Heil argues that the whole orientation and final focus of this scene centers on this specific mandate.[59] While this point is likely overstated, this is a climactic command that we must pay proper attention to. We obey by listening

---

57. Basil, *Against Eunomius* 2.28, quoted in Gilles Emery, *The Trinitarian Theology of St Thomas Aquinas* (Oxford: Oxford University Press, 2010), 45.

58. Thomas G. Weinandy, *Jesus Becoming Jesus: A Theological Interpretation of the Synoptic Gospels* (Washington, DC: Catholic University of America Press, 2018), 229.

59. John Paul Heil, *The Transfiguration of Jesus: Narrative Meaning and Function of Mark 9:2–8, Matt 17:1–8 and Luke 9:28–36*, AnBib 144 (Rome: Pontifical Biblical Institute, 2000), 51. Heil compares the transfiguration to a number of Old Testament epiphanies that include commands: Balaam's (Num. 22:31–35), Joshua's (Josh. 5:13–15), and Heliodorus's (2 Macc. 3:22–34).

until we see him face to face. We will examine three aspects of this command. The first two relate to Jesus's messianic sonship, and the last points to his eternal sonship.

The Imminent Cross

In the surrounding context of the transfiguration narrative, the command "Listen to him" concerns Jesus's predictions of the looming cross. Listening to Jesus means discerning the importance of the suffering Son. Four arguments support this.

First, the command is an interruption. Peter wants to build tents, to camp out on the glorious mountaintop forever, thus bypassing the cross. This is in keeping with Peter's mindset just before the group's ascent up the mountain. When Jesus predicts he will suffer, Peter takes Jesus aside and says, "Oh no, Lord! This will never happen to you" (Matt. 16:22; see also Mark 8:32). Jesus calls Peter Satan and tells him to get out of his way.

This reference to Satan evokes the garden of Eden, where the serpent also offered a shortcut to Adam and Eve, saying that there was another way to be "like God" (Gen. 3:5). The serpent's proposition, to be like God, was not misguided; the problem was the means by which he offered it. In the same way, Peter offers a substitute path to glory for Jesus. At Caesarea Philippi, Jesus calls Peter Satan because he suggests the same shortcut as Satan. The command from heaven, "Listen to him!," is a heavenly "Amen!" to what Christ has already told Peter: suffering must precede glory.

Second, the command to listen directly refers to Jesus's suffering because the declaration of sonship alludes to Genesis 22:2 and Isaiah 42:1. Genesis 22 is about the sacrifice of Isaac, and Isaiah 42:1 is about the servant who will suffer on behalf of Israel. The command to listen is grounded in Jesus's vocation.

Third, the command to listen has to do with the cross because when Moses and Elijah appear, they speak to Jesus about his *exodos* (Luke 9:31). The two saints could have conversed with Jesus about anything: the nature of the Trinity, the essence of the new creation, or the timing of the last day. However, they speak about the epitome of all saving knowledge—the death of Christ.

Fourth, the context of the transfiguration narrative supports that these words concern Jesus's suffering. In all the Gospels the story of Jesus's passion prediction and the command for the disciples to take up their cross come just before the transfiguration (Matt. 16:21–28; Mark 8:31–9:1; Luke 9:22–27).

In Matthew, two references to the Son of Man frame the transfiguration narrative. Immediately preceding the transfiguration, Jesus speaks about the coming glory of the Son of Man (Matt. 16:28). Then just after the transfiguration, Jesus tells the disciples that the Son of Man is going to suffer at the hands of his opponents (17:12). The command to listen to Jesus is thus directly related to Jesus's teaching about his cross.

These four arguments imply that the words "listen to him" concern the relationship between Jesus's suffering and glory. The disciples must listen to Jesus's words about the imminent cross. Jesus reveals his future glory as the messianic Son, but he will not be exalted if he does not suffer. The transfiguration is about Jesus's supremacy through suffering.

Jesus's Teaching as the New Prophet and Mediator

The command to "listen" to Jesus certainly encompasses more than his passion predictions. It is an unqualified heavenly commendation of all Jesus's instruction. Jesus is the new prophet who proclaims the Torah. This reality comes into focus through several avenues.

First, Jesus is identified as the new prophet in this command because of the obvious allusion to Deuteronomy 18:15–19:

> The LORD your God will raise up for you *a prophet* like me from among your own brothers. *You must listen to him.* This is what you requested from the LORD your God at Horeb on the day of the assembly when you said, "Let us not continue to hear the voice of the LORD our God or see this great fire any longer, so that we will not die!" Then the LORD said to me, "They have spoken well. I will raise up for them *a prophet* like you from among their brothers. I will put my words in his mouth, and he will tell them everything I command him. I will hold accountable whoever *does not listen to my words that he speaks in my name.*"

Moses foretells a time when a new prophet will arise. God's people must listen to this new figure because he speaks on God's behalf. In fact, Moses ties this future voice to a mountain scene. Israel asked not to hear the voice of God on Sinai, for they were terrified. God's response is that he will raise up a prophet who will speak for him. Like the prototype, a new figure must descend from heaven to proclaim God's Word.

Now, on another mountain, the promise is fulfilled. A new prophet like Moses has arisen. Elijah and Moses *bear witness* to him. Jesus mediates the new covenant and faithfully delivers the Torah. Under the old covenant, the people couldn't stand to hear the Father's voice or see his great fire, but under the new covenant they behold God in the face of Jesus Christ and hear the Father's affirmation of the Son. On Sinai, the word of God was written on tablets of stone; on Tabor they see the glorious word on the tablet of flesh. The new covenant is "enfleshed rather than inscribed."[60]

Additionally, the command is a pointed response to Peter's inclination to build *three* tents. The voice doesn't say, "Listen to *them*" but "Listen to *him*." The singular object is important. This is somewhat shocking considering the mountain is populated with a "who's who" of apostles and prophets (see Eph. 2:20). Moses was the mediator of the Torah. Elijah was one of the greatest prophets. Peter, the rock, is also on the mountain—not to mention James and John. Ignoring the rest, the Father declares, "Listen to *him*."

As Bruner says, "Peter, Rock that he is, is never to be the church's final voice of authority."[61] Jesus is the *sole teacher* of the church. Or as Cyril comments, Jesus himself is the end of the law as well as the prophets.[62] While Christ "came to maintain the authority of the Law and the Prophets, yet he holds the highest rank."[63] By keeping the referent singular, the Father subordinates Moses, Elijah, and Peter.

However, listening to Jesus means listening to whomever he says to listen to. This helps us avoid the heretical Marcionite pitfall of dispensing with the Law and Prophets. While Jesus is the ultimate and final revelation of God, Jesus also affirms the ministry of the apostles and prophets. As if to head off misunderstanding, he explains in the Gospels that he comes to fulfill the teaching of Moses and Elijah, not to abolish it (Matt. 5:17–20). When we listen to Jesus, he tells us to listen to Moses and Elijah.

It is similar with Peter. While Jesus is the final teacher of the church, he is not its only teacher. Jesus himself gives secondary authority to his church. Jesus says that the keys of the kingdom of heaven have been given to Peter and to the gathering of believers (Matt. 16:19; 18:18–20). The church, under the direction of Jesus's words, has delegated authority. Therefore, the command in the transfiguration mints Jesus as the new and superior prophet.

Second, the same command is given to Israel concerning the angel of the Lord. Andrei Orlov notes that while the Mosaic connections have been acknowledged, the angel of the Lord traditions have consistently escaped attention. Israel is commanded to listen to an authority above Moses—God's angelic messenger who is the divine voice.[64] In Exodus 23:20–22 God says, "I am going

60. Richard Hays, *Echoes of Scripture in the Letters of Paul* (New Haven: Yale University Press, 1989), 129–30.

61. Frederick Dale Bruner, *Matthew: A Commentary*, vol. 2, *The Churchbook: Matthew 13–28*, rev. ed. (Grand Rapids: Eerdmans, 2004), 176.

62. Cyril of Alexandria, "Homily 51 on Luke" (Daley, 104).

63. Calvin, *Harmony of the Evangelists*, 2:315.

64. Andrei Orlov, *The Glory of the Invisible God: Two Powers in Heaven Traditions and Early Christology* (London: Bloomsbury T&T Clark, 2021), 140–42.

to send an angel before you to protect you on the way and bring you to the place I have prepared. Be attentive to him and *listen to him*. Do not defy him, because he will not forgive your acts of rebellion, *for my name is in him*. But if you will carefully obey him and do everything I say, then I will be an enemy to your enemies and a foe to your foes."

Like Moses, the angel is a mediator. Yet the identity of the angel is curious. He is both distinguished from Yahweh and brought into union with him. He speaks in the first-person as God, receives worship and sacrifices, and makes the ground holy. The angel is both a visual representation and a visible presence of Yahweh. He is the "form" of God to Israel and serves as God's voice. God is the speaker, but the voice is the angel's. The angel serves as a sort of loudspeaker and visual image of God.

The Hebrew Bible often conflates the actions and speech of Yahweh and the angel.[65] For example, in the burning bush episode, it is an angel of the Lord who appears to Moses (Exod. 3:2), but then the Lord himself speaks to Moses out of the bush (3:4–14). In Judges 6:20–22, the angel of God speaks to Gideon, and Gideon cries out, "Oh no, Lord GOD! I have seen the angel of the LORD face to face!" When the angel of the Lord stretches his hand out over Jerusalem to destroy it, the Lord relents from destroying the people (2 Sam. 24:16). Beginning with the earliest church fathers, the consensus was that the angel of the Lord was the second person of the Trinity.[66] When God says about the angel in Exodus 23, "My name is in him," it is hard not to make correlations with "This is my Beloved Son." The angel embodies Yahweh; so does the Son.

While we might balk at this, we must remember that when we think of angels, we think in terms of ontological categories. But the view in antiquity was more functional. This is evidenced by the reality that *angelos* means "messenger." In our minds, angels are superhuman spirits, but in antiquity they were "sent ones." In John's Gospel, Jesus speaks of being sent no less than twenty-six times.[67] In the literature, angels do recognize their subordinate positions in relation to God (Col. 2:18; Rev. 22:8–9; Apocalypse of Zephaniah 6:15; Ascension of Isaiah 7:21; 9:31). Therefore, the ontological category of "angel" was not completely absent in ancient thinking. Nevertheless, even if we can't be certain about the identity of the angel of the Lord, the correlations are intriguing.[68] At the most

---

65. Along a different line of thought, Charles A. Gieschen argues that early Christians used Jewish angel motifs to describe the significance of Jesus. Gieschen, *Angelomorphic Christology: Antecedents and Early Evidence* (Waco: Baylor University Press, 2017).

66. Günther Juncker, "Christ as Angel: The Reclamation of a Primitive Title," *TrinJ* 15, no. 2 (1994): 221–50.

67. The predicted child in Isa. 9:6 is called *angelos* (messenger) in the LXX: "angel/messenger of great counsel."

68. See the appendix for a discussion of Old Testament Christophanies.

basic level, the angel is another mediator of Yahweh to whom Israel is called to listen. And the angel of the Lord and his connection to this text again raise the question, "Who is this Son?"[69]

The New Shema

We have examined the narrow context (prediction of suffering) and wide context (new prophet and mediator) for the command from the Father. Both are based on Jesus's messianic mission, while the "angel of the Lord" tradition suggests even more. However, the command is ultimately grounded in Jesus's divine identity. The Son is greater than Moses, the servant; therefore, the disciples must listen.

Some might wonder whether Jesus's divine identity is assumed in the heavenly command. But as one widens one's perspective and considers another Old Testament echo, the command becomes at least evocative. If the declaration of sonship has a double meaning, then the related command likely does as well.[70]

The Old Testament contains an iconic text that also calls Israel to listen: the Shema, found in Deuteronomy 6:4–5. The title "Shema" is based on the first Hebrew word of the text, which means "listen," "hear," or "obey": "Listen [shemaʿ], Israel: The LORD our God, the LORD is one [ekhad]. Love the LORD your God with all your heart, with all your soul, and with all your strength." The Shema is akin to the transfiguration in a variety of ways. Like the transfiguration, the Shema asserts something about the ontology of God and then calls for an appropriate response.

Consider the ontological statement "The LORD is one." The small caps indicate the name "Yahweh," which was revealed to Moses at the burning bush. This confession of God's oneness should be understood with respect to two different dimensions.

First, it refers to God's *uniqueness*. God is one in that there is no other god like him. There are other spiritual beings who are called gods (*elohim*) in the Hebrew Scriptures. However, the writers of the Old Testament insist that their God, Yahweh, is the supreme being, the uncreated creator and sustainer of all

---

69. This question should also arise because whenever the New Testament compares Jesus to Moses, it makes clear that Moses is subordinate to Jesus. Hebrews claims, "Jesus is considered worthy of more glory than Moses, just as the builder has more honor than the house. . . . Moses was faithful as a servant in all God's household. . . . But Christ was faithful as a Son" (Heb. 3:3, 5–6). This all amounts to Jesus being more than a servant like Moses. He is a Son, and Hebrews says its audience must listen to this Son.

70. Admittedly, Israel is also called to listen to Moses, and this does not mean he is divine. However, they are called to listen to him because he is divinely appointed. Jesus is also divinely appointed, as the last section argued. However, he is also the divine Son.

things. That is why Isaiah can also say there is no God but one (Isa. 43:10; 44:6; 45:5). God is one in that he is supreme.

Second, God's oneness also refers metaphysically to God's *nature*. He is one substance, one essence, not composed of parts. Paul seems to take it this way in 1 Corinthians. He is comfortable speaking both of Yahweh's uniqueness in comparison to other gods and of the oneness of God in the relationship between the Father and the Son. After he has asserted that God is the creator and sustainer of all and that we exist for him, Paul includes Jesus in this oneness: "There is one Lord, Jesus Christ. All things are through him, and we exist through him" (1 Cor. 8:6). Paul has included Jesus in both the *supremacy* and the *unity* of God in the oneness of God. The Father is one, but so is the Son.

Paul thinks that the supremacy and simplicity of God relate. God is one because he is one. Or to put this more clearly, God is unique and supreme because he is metaphysically simple. Because of these realities (God's uniqueness and his nature), the Old Testament and the New Testament both call on God's people to listen to God. God's nature, his being, demands unreserved devotion.

All of this informs the transfiguration scene. The command "Listen to him" given on the mountain is the new covenant Shema. Because of the oneness of the Father and Son, because of the identity of the Son, the disciples are called, like Israel of old, to heed his voice. They listened to Yahweh in the Old Testament. Now they listen to Yahweh in the New Testament through the Son.

The first chapter of Hebrews maintains this view of sonship. Long ago, God spoke to his people by the prophets, but now he has spoken to us by his Son (Heb. 1:1–2). The Son is affirmed to be on both the "God side" of the divide and the "creature side." Because his identity is the Son, God's people are to "listen."[71]

> Hebrews 2:1: "For this reason, we must *pay attention* all the more to what we have *heard*, so that we will not drift away."
>
> Hebrews 3:7 (see also 3:15; 4:7): "Therefore, as the Holy Spirit says: 'Today, if you *hear His voice,* do not harden your hearts as in the rebellion.'"
>
> Hebrews 12:25–26: "See to it that you do not reject *the one who speaks*. . . . His *voice* shook the earth at that time, but now he has promised, 'Yet once more I will shake not only the earth but also the heavens.'"

Hebrews links the nature and mission of God with hearing, listening, and heeding. All these texts are instructive for how we are to understand the

---

71. For more on the theme of divine speech in Hebrews, see Madison N. Pierce, *Divine Discourse in the Epistle to the Hebrews: The Recontextualization of Spoken Quotations of Scripture*, SNTSMS 178 (Cambridge: Cambridge University Press, 2020).

command from the cloud. The disciples are to listen to Jesus not simply because of his messianic mission; more fundamentally, they are to listen to him because he is the one true God of Israel.

Jesus is God's Son sent to the earth. Yet he is also God's Son eternally. The Father and Son exist in fully mutual relationship. The disciples are to listen to the one true God, who has revealed himself in the Son's shining face.

Union—Partaking in the Divine Nature

The goal of the transfiguration is union. Right before the transfiguration, Jesus speaks about how in the last day "the righteous will shine like the sun in their Father's kingdom" (Matt. 13:43; see also Dan. 12:3). The transfiguration is not only about Jesus's transformation but about ours. Our future is revealed in the face of Jesus.

We have examined two different stages of formation. The journey begins with *purgation*—our spiritual ascent. We are called to go up on the mountain with the disciples and seek the things that are above by ridding ourselves of fleshly passions. The next stage is tied to what Peter, James, and John saw on the mountain—*illumination*. As we progressively see the face of Jesus, we grow in virtue and charity and walk in the light as he is in the light. If purgation is pulling apart the darkness, and illumination is letting light shine in, then *union* is being overwhelmed, enveloped, and encompassed by the light.

Union is where our minds are drawn away from all temporal things and we enjoy peace in the presence of God. We experience oneness with God and find ourselves caught up in something beyond understanding. In John Jesus says, "Remain in me, and I in you" (John 15:4) and, "Remain in my love" (15:9). Jesus prays, "I am in them and you are in me, so that they may be made completely one, that the world may know you have sent me and have loved them as you have loved me" (17:23). This is a gift; it is not procured by works. We sense that it is no longer we who live, but Christ who lives in us. We are completely pliable in the hands of God.

Athanasius writes, "Christ was made a man in order that we might be made God"—or as Peter said, we partake in the divine nature (2 Pet. 1:4).[72] Other

---

72. Athanasius, *On the Incarnation* 54.3 (NPNF[2] 4:65). There can be many misunderstandings and miscalculations about metamorphosis, but metamorphosis does not abolish the gulf between the divine and the human natures. It is important to remember the surprising nature of the incarnation here. While collapsing the distinction between Creator and creature is one error, the other error is to not respect the union that has occurred in the incarnation. Before the incarnation, a strict separation between the divine and the human existed. However, after the incarnation, the paradigm was radically altered. In the incarnation, the two realities meet. They are united in

church fathers tie Jesus's transfiguration to our own metamorphosis. John Chrysostom says that we ourselves shall see Christ, not in the same way the disciples did on the mountain but much more gloriously.[73] Proclus affirms that Jesus was transfigured not simply to be so "but that he might show us the transfiguration of our nature that is to come."[74] Anastasius of Sinai urges us also to "flash like lightning before spiritual eyes . . . [to be] transformed along with him in order to be like him, always being deified, always changing for the better."[75]

Humanity was created to be in the form of its archetype: Christ.[76] Human beings were created in the image of *the* Image. The divine image in humanity is marred in the fall, but the goal is to be remade in the divine image. Many of the church fathers spoke of how we are "deified by participation in the divine radiance, not transferred into the divine essence."[77] The truth of humanity lies in the person it represents. Since humankind is the image of God, our real being is defined in the Son.

The transfiguration is therefore a preview not only of Christ's future glory but of ours. Jesus shows what will happen to humanity on the mountain: "that ineffable mystery, how man can be taken into God, how God can dwell in man, and fill him with the glory of his Father."[78] So how does one begin "partaking of the divine nature"?

First, while we typically push transfiguration toward the future, the transfiguration narratives remind us that there is an already and a not yet. Transfiguration begins even now. Paul tells us that we are metamorphosized from glory to glory as we behold Christ (2 Cor. 3:18) and that light is given through the gospel (2 Tim. 1:10). John asserts that the true light is already shining (1 John 2:8). Our transfiguration begins in our union with Christ, which, Paul tells us, *happens by the Spirit.* Though only Israel stood at the foot of the mountain, only Moses went into the glory cloud, and only Peter, James, and John witnessed the transfiguration, now all Christians enter the glory cloud and see the face of Jesus by the Spirit. The people of Israel had a veil shrouding their hearts, but the veil is now taken away in Christ (2 Cor. 3:15–16). Paul says that not only Moses and

---

Christ. The immaterial one is made flesh so that we might put on immateriality. The immortal one dies so that the mortal ones might not die.

73. John Chrysostom, "Homily 56 on Matthew" (Daley, 79).

74. Proclus, "Homily on the Transfiguration" (Daley, 93).

75. Anastasius of Sinai, "Homily on the Transfiguration" (Daley, 169).

76. Panayiotis Nellas, *Deification in Christ: Orthodox Perspectives on the Nature of the Human Person,* Contemporary Greek Theologians 5 (New York: St. Vladimir's Seminary Press, 1987), 33.

77. John of Damascus, *On the Orthodox Faith,* 130.

78. Bouverie Pusey, "Sermon 87," quoted in John Gatta, *The Transfiguration of Christ and Creation* (Eugene, OR: Wipf & Stock, 2011), 18.

Paul can behold the glory of the Lord but "we all" can by the Spirit. Paul relays, "This [namely, our transfiguration] is from the Lord who is the Spirit" (3:18).

The only way we can be transformed is by the Spirit who metamorphosizes us. When the Spirit enters our being, a divine person has entered a creature. God then permeates the believer to such an extent that his presence transfigures us. Basil ties together the light of God with our metamorphosis:

> Just as when a sunbeam falls on bright and transparent bodies, they themselves become brilliant too, and shed forth a fresh brightness from themselves, so souls wherein the Spirit dwells, illuminated by the Spirit, themselves become spiritual, and send forth their grace to others. Hence comes foreknowledge of the future, understanding of mysteries, apprehension of what is hidden, distribution of good gifts, the heavenly citizenship, a place in the chorus of angels, joy without end, abiding in God, the being made like to God, and, highest of all, the being made God.[79]

Second, this union continues through the ordinances. We display this newness in baptism, where we *participate* in Christ's death and resurrection. Through regeneration and baptism, we are given new spiritual senses that conform to Christ's body. That is what it means to be born again: it is to be born into the image of Christ. And that is why it is proper and fitting that only those who have repented and believed in the gospel be the subjects of baptism.

Baptism doesn't mean that our bodies are destroyed but rather that they begin to be transfigured. That is why our *bodies* are baptized. Metamorphosis is the restoration and heightening of our true humanity, not its diminishment or abandonment. In being baptized into Christ, we begin to become like Christ. In Christ's body, we begin to function as part of Christ.

Third, the bread and wine keep us in Christ as a means of grace. In communion, we receive Christ himself. The Eucharist is the center of our Christian life, where the whole person is joined to the body of Christ. The one who eats of Jesus's flesh and drinks of his blood remains in Jesus and Jesus in him (John 6:56).

The bread and wine assimilate us to Jesus. As Paul says, "It is no longer I who live, but Christ who lives in me" (Gal. 2:20). We now have the mind of Christ (1 Cor. 2:16). Christ speaks in us (2 Cor. 13:13). We have the affection of Christ (Phil. 1:8). We are in Christ (Rom. 8:1). We become Christified.

While our union begins now, there will always be a longing for consummation. This is why Paul says that we look "as in a mirror" (1 Cor. 13:12; see 2 Cor. 3:8). The point is not that our viewpoint is distorted but that it is incomplete.

---

79. Basil, *On the Holy Spirit* 23 (NPNF[2] 8:15–16).

A mirror in this context likely implies indirect knowledge. Indirect knowledge is not necessarily inaccurate, but it is mediated. We can't see Jesus's face physically in the present, but the gospel message communicates it to us. The gospel is therefore the "mediator." On the last day, we will see him "face to face" and become as he is (1 John 3:2). We see a reflection now, and thus it is provisional. Direct vision awaits at the end of the age.

But even in eternity, there will continue to be growth. Gregory of Nyssa employs the term *epektasis*, which refers to our perpetual spiritual ascent. *Epekteinomai* means to reach forward, to stretch and strain toward a goal (see Phil. 3:13–14). It is the soul's perpetual act of striving toward our inexhaustible God. For Gregory, perfection is not static but continual movement toward God. To quote C. S. Lewis, it is about going "further up and further in."[80]

Since God is infinite, our sight of God will always be progressive, even in the eternal state.[81] We will be changed and continuously changed as we behold God. Our future will be infinite progress toward the perfection that exists in God. Gregory writes, "For this is truly perfection: never to stop growing towards what is better and never placing any limit on perfection."[82] While it may sound like a state of never being fulfilled, the idea is rather that once we have reached one degree of fulfillment, we then long for more. We arrive at joy and then realize deeper joy awaits us still.

Union is both a present reality and a future hope. We are truly "in" Christ and seated with him in the heavenly places (Eph. 2:6). Yet we still long for more. We long for the day when we are "caught up together" with the saints in the clouds and "meet the Lord in the air" (1 Thess. 4:17); then we will "shine like the sun in [the] Father's kingdom" (Matt. 13:43).

CONCLUSION

Jesus's glory and his double sonship are communicated both by his appearance *and* by the Father's testimony about him. This chapter has focused on Peter's response, the Father's declaration of sonship, and the command to listen.

I have argued that all three support the early confessions that Jesus is both the messianic and the divine Son. Peter misunderstands both the *mission* and the *metaphysics* of the Son. The Father corrects Peter: Jesus is his beloved and chosen Son. These words go back to several Old Testament texts. Some of them

---

80. C. S. Lewis, *The Last Battle* (London: Bodley Head, 1956).

81. It is important to acknowledge that the church has not unanimously held this view through the ages. For example, following Aristotle, Aquinas denies progression on the grounds that any natural desire must have some corresponding terminal fulfillment.

82. Gregory of Nyssa, *On Perfection* 214.4–6 (FC 58:122).

speak to the Messiah's suffering. Others express the Messiah's future glory. The texts also suggest that this Messiah will be linked to Yahweh himself. They are hyper-fulfilled in Jesus.

Finally, the command "listen" affirms Jesus's double sonship. Since Jesus is the Messiah, the disciples must listen to his words about his suffering and his teachings on the Torah. However, Jesus is greater than Moses, for the command is the new covenant Shema.

These exegetical conclusions fit remarkably well with our christological grammar. To say that Jesus is the Son of the Father is to affirm both a *closeness* between the Father and Jesus and some *distance*. The closeness relates to what they share in common: sons and fathers share in being. The distance relates to their distinctness: sons are begotten by their fathers. Jesus is the filial and eternal Son of the Father, who shares in his very essence.

Yet the eternal Son took on flesh and was therefore doubly begotten. The Son has a unity and equality with the Father but also a distinction and order. Jesus is both truly God and truly man, but he exists in one subject. Two things can be true about him at once because he has a double ontology. His human nature is exalted by this union and therefore he shines. We see God in the human face of Jesus Christ.

The Glorious Saying	Meaning
The inglorious saying	*Messianic sonship*: Peter doesn't recognize the necessity of the suffering preceding Jesus's glory in his messianic mission (three *tents*).
	Eternal sonship: Peter doesn't recognize the supremacy of Jesus; he is the Son while Moses and Elijah are the servants (*three* tents).
"This is my beloved Son"	*Messianic sonship*: Jesus is the earthly, suffering Davidic Son who will be glorified.
	Eternal sonship: Jesus is also the eternally begotten Son, who always possessed glory.
"Listen to him"	*Messianic sonship*: Jesus is the new prophet in the mold of Moses and the new mediator (angel of the Lord) to whom God's people must listen.
	Eternal sonship: Jesus is also *the* Word of God, to whom a new Shema commands obedience.

5

The Transfiguration
and Theology

He wraps himself in light as if it were a robe.

—Psalm 104:2

I mentioned at the beginning of this book that the transfiguration is one of those events we can never seem to plumb the depths of. I have focused on the setting, the signs, and the sayings and how each of them displays the double sonship of Jesus. However, the transfiguration also has implications that go far beyond these arguments.

The transfiguration has repercussions for our nature (anthropology), for our identity (ecclesiology), for how we are saved (soteriology), and for what will happen in the future (eschatology). In the transfiguration, all the diverse fields meet. G. B. Caird was right when he said, "A satisfactory explanation of the Transfiguration must do justice to its connection with the Baptism, Caesarea Philippi, Gethsemane, the Crucifixion, the Resurrection, the Ascension, and the Parousia; and with the persecution of the disciples and their share, present and future, in the glory of the risen and ascended Christ."[1] Not enough

---

1. George B. Caird, "Expository Problems: The Transfiguration," *ET* 67, no. 10 (1956): 292.

interpretive work has been done on this important event, and so many books beg to be written.[2]

In this chapter I will slightly veer from the main argument about Jesus's double sonship by relating the transfiguration to creation, the incarnation, Jesus's baptism, Gethsemane, the cross, the resurrection, Jesus's ascension and return, and finally the new creation. As it is set alongside these events, the significance of the transfiguration becomes even clearer.

Creation

While I have spoken to some extent about the relationship of the transfiguration to creation, one other thread is worth pursuing. When God created human beings, he made them in his image and likeness (Gen. 1:26). Both terms point to the idea of "reflection." Humanity is the icon of God. We are meant to represent God to creation.

This is one reason the second commandment forbids forging an "idol" or "graven image" (Exod. 20:4). God has already created an image of himself in humanity. Humans are to embody God's glory to all of creation, to be a mirror of who he is and to release his light on all creation.

In the Apocalypse of Adam, Adam recounts his former Edenic glory. Adam says he and Eve were like the great eternal angels (1:2–3). However, when they fell, the glory of their hearts deserted them; glory fled from them (1:5–6). But God made a promise to Noah that his seed would again stand in glory, and then they would be like "the cloud of great light" (3:9–10). Early interpreters followed this tradition, viewing Adam and Eve as being clothed in a primordial "robe of light" or "glory." They lost aspects of this glory and needed to be reclothed.[3]

This view was an extensively held interpretation of the garden scene. When Adam and Eve fell, their glory departed from them. They didn't stop being the image of God, but the image was distorted. If we adopt this view, then the shining face of Moses was a "restoration" of God's image and likeness. When Moses came down the mountain, he was reinstated with the glory possessed

2. PhD students could consider doing work on angelomorphic imagery in the transfiguration, press more deeply into the Moses traditions (especially in Philo) and how they relate to the transfiguration, research the abundance of light imagery in the fathers when they describe the Trinity, investigate early interpretations of Adam and Eve as full of light, consider the relationship between Jesus's resurrection/ascension body and the transfiguration, or compare Roman and Greek literature in which gods take another form and then reveal themselves.

3. See Allison, who notes all the texts that speak of Adam, Abraham, and Joshua's radiance (Dale Allison, *The New Moses: A Matthean Typology* [Eugene, OR: Wipf & Stock, 2013], 246–47). See also the Syrian tradition in Sebastian Brock, *The Luminous Eye: The Spiritual World Vision of Saint Ephrem the Syrian*, Cistercian Studies 124 (Kalamazoo, MI: Liturgical Press, 1992), 85–90.

in the garden. However, humanity was not ready to perceive that glory. Moses had to veil his face, just as the tabernacle filled with the glory cloud was veiled (Exod. 34:29–35).

The transfiguration thus recalls the garden. Jesus is the true image of the invisible God, the new Adam cloaked in light (Col. 1:15). Jesus reestablishes the glory lost at the fall as his face and clothes shine. Pseudo-Chrysostom interprets Jesus's transfigured form as a revival of human nature:

> And why did he appear to them this way? To show them that the Lord of all things had put on the whole Adam and had wiped him clean of sin, and had whitened what had become scarlet in Adam's descendants. And having cleansed him from all stain, he showed him to his own disciples, being transfigured then on the mountain to be as Adam was when he had just been formed. For this is how Adam was before his disobedience, just as Christ appeared in his transfiguration; and this was the reason Christ appeared in this way.[4]

Adam was clothed with glory, but then he had to put on animal skins. Now the Son dons himself in robes of light—the same robes he will put on us in the age to come.[5] As John Chrysostom says, our first parents were "clad . . . in ineffable glory, which adorned them better than any clothing."[6] Ephrem the Syrian connects Christology to the fall of Adam and Eve in this way:

> All these changes did the Merciful One make,
> Stripping off glory and putting on a body;
> For He had devised a way to reclothe Adam
> in that glory which Adam had stripped off.
> Christ was wrapped in swaddling clothes,
> Corresponding to Adam's leaves,
> Christ put on clothes, instead of Adam's skins;
> He was baptized for Adam's sin,
> His body was embalmed for Adam's death,
> He rose and raised up Adam in his glory
> Blessed is He who descended, put Adam on and ascended![7]

4. Pseudo-Chrysostom, "Discourse for the Transfiguration," in *Light on the Mountain: Greek Patristic and Byzantine Homilies on the Transfiguration of the Lord*, trans. Brian Daley, Popular Patristics 48 (New York: St. Vladimir's Seminary Press, 2013), 320.

5. Gregory Palamas, *The Saving Work of Christ: Sermons by Saint Gregory Palamas*, ed. Christopher Veniamin (Waymart, PA: Mount Thabor, 2008), 50.

6. John Chrysostom, *On Genesis* 16.3, in *Homilies on Genesis, 1–17*, The Fathers of the Church 74, trans. Robert C. Hill (Washington, DC: Catholic University of America Press, 1986), 208.

7. St. Ephrem, *Nativity* 23.13, quoted in and translated by Sebastian Brock, *The Luminous Eye: The Spiritual World Vision of Saint Ephrem the Syrian*, Cistercian Studies 124 (Kalamazoo, MI: Liturgical Press, 1992), 85.

The transfiguration foretells the future by employing symbols from the garden. Humanity was robed in glory at creation, but this was stripped from them. What was lost by the first Adam is reinstated by the Second Adam.

The Incarnation

The transfiguration and the incarnation have a distinctive relationship. This is because Jesus's *sōma* (body) is transfigured. "Divine glory blazed through the sackcloth covering his humanity."[8] Jesus took the "form" (*morphē*) of a slave to "transform" (*metamorphē*) it. Through the transfiguration, we see the incarnation in new light.

First, *the transfiguration displays divinity as revealed through humanity*. Jesus's body is not discarded, peeled back, or put aside to show his divinity. Divinity does not even overwhelm humanity, thereby erasing it. No, Jesus's deity is displayed *in* his humanity. "The uncreated is received by the creature in a created mode."[9] As Matthew Levering says, "In Christ, God has made himself definitely perceivable; there is no beatific vision unmediated by the humanity of Christ. The humanity of the Son is the instrument by which the vision of God transpires. God's perceivable form in Christ fulfills the entirety of God's revelation in history."[10]

God reaches down to us in the incarnation in a way we can understand. The face of Jesus is how we see God.[11] Gregory of Nyssa affirms that divine power is made accessible through the covering of the flesh, not in spite of it.[12] Through covering himself in flesh, the Son made divine glory accessible. The light of God's glory is seen in the face of Jesus the Messiah (2 Cor. 4:6). While most assume that this refers more generally to the incarnation, it more properly and precisely refers to the transfiguration. The *light of God's glory* is seen in Jesus's luminous body.

However, did Jesus's flesh also hide his divine nature? Palamas says that Jesus "possessed the splendor of the divine nature hidden under his flesh" until it was

---

8. S. Lewis Johnson, "Transfiguration of Christ," *BibSac* 124 (1967): 133.

9. Cory Hayes, "*Deus in se et Deus pro nobis*: The Transfiguration in the Theology of Gregory Palamas and Its Importance for Catholic Theology" (PhD Diss., Duquesne University, 2015), 190, https://dsc.duq.edu/etd/640/.

10. Matthew Levering, *The Achievement of Hans Urs von Balthasar: An Introduction to His Trilogy* (Washington, DC: Catholic University of America Press, 2019), 65.

11. Anastasius of Antioch ("Homily on the Transfiguration" [Daley, 136]) says the following: "Now [in the transfiguration] he restores the form of a servant to its natural appearance—not putting aside the substance of the servant, but making it radiant with divine characteristics."

12. Gregory of Nyssa, *The Great Catechism* 23 (NPNF[2] 5:486–87).

revealed at the transfiguration.[13] This is also true. Jesus hid his divinity under the veil of flesh, yet at the transfiguration, this veil is not subtracted. Rather, his divinity is exposed *in* his flesh. Leo the Emperor alludes to Moses and Elijah narratives when he says: "They saw what is impassible mingled with matter, and matter aflame with divine fire without being consumed—the presence of God formed as if from a light breeze, gently and noiselessly communicating through the flesh."[14]

Second, *the transfiguration displays the purpose of the incarnation: the future perfection of the flesh.* The transfiguration reveals that flesh, the *sarx*, shares in the hope of redemption, the hope of metamorphosis. This is the ultimate purpose of the incarnation.

As the obedient human, Jesus bears the light and becomes what humanity was always meant to be. Jesus bridges the expanse between heaven and earth, between divine and human. Humanity is made more itself in Christ, not less. Our flesh will not be annihilated but fulfilled, not destroyed but renewed.

We are tempted to think that Jesus's divinity overcomes his humanity, that his veil of flesh is vanquished for a moment. The transfiguration corrects us. God perfects flesh; he doesn't destroy it. The transfiguration shows us it is wrong to think that the incarnation represents a limitation to the Son. His physicality is an "icon of his celestiality."[15]

The Son takes on flesh without any alteration of his divinity, but in so doing he perfects and sanctifies it. The transfiguration does not move us past Jesus's humanity; it reveals to us how the flesh will be glorified.[16] Our bodies likewise will be not destroyed but transformed. By becoming radiant, Jesus indicates that flesh is not canceled, rejected, or demeaned when it is glorified. It is transfigured.

Jesus's Baptism

The most similar scene to the transfiguration is not Jesus's resurrection, ascension, or return. It is his baptism. The baptism and the transfiguration are correlated in a variety of ways. Most noticeably, in both scenes a divine voice from

---

13. Gregory Palamas, *Saving Work of Christ*, 45. Aquinas (*Summa Theologiae*, Pt. III, Q. 14, a. 1, ad. 2) notes that while the natural consequence of the beatific vision (which he affirms the Son possessed) is full glorification, Christ, by an act of divine will, contained the effects of the beatitude in the depths of his soul so that he might be capable of suffering.

14. Leo the Emperor, "A Homily by Leo the Emperor" (Daley, 239).

15. Dorothy A. Lee, "On the Holy Mountain: The Transfiguration in Scripture and Theology," *Colloquium* 36, no. 2 (2004): 157.

16. Proclus affirms that Christ was transfigured to show the transfiguration of our nature that is to come. Proclus of Constantinople, "Homily on the Transfiguration of the Savior" (Daley, 93).

heaven declares, "This is my beloved Son" (Matt. 3:17; Mark 1:11; Luke 3:22). One begins the first stage of Jesus's ministry; the other begins the second stage.

However, other parallels exist. Prior to Jesus's baptism, John the Baptist bears witness to Jesus; prior to his transfiguration, Peter bears witness to Jesus. Both scenes foreshadow the new exodus, one by showing Jesus passing through water and the other by speaking about the exodus. These are the only two moments in the Synoptic Gospels when the Father speaks from heaven. Both have Elijah figures (John the Baptist and Elijah himself). Both see the Spirit descend, one as a dove and one as a cloud. Both are trinitarian theophanies. Both are followed by a showdown with demonic forces; Jesus is tempted after his baptism and casts out a demon after descending Mount Tabor. In Jesus's temptation, Jesus is brought to a high mountain and offered glory by Satan (Matt. 4:8–9). Now, on another high mountain, Jesus is given glory and vindicated by God.

PARALLELS BETWEEN THE BAPTISM AND THE TRANSFIGURATION

The Baptism	The Transfiguration
Before: John the Baptist witnesses to Jesus.	*Before*: Peter witnesses to Jesus.
Foreshadows the new exodus (passing through water).	Foreshadows the new exodus (speaks of Jesus's exodus).
The Father speaks from heaven declaring Jesus his Son.	The Father speaks from heaven declaring Jesus his Son.
The three persons of the Trinity are present.	The three persons of the Trinity are present.
After: Jesus is brought to a high mountain and offered glory.	Jesus is brought to a high mountain and glorified.
After: Showdown with demonic forces (the temptation).	*After*: Showdown with demonic forces (casts out a demon).

All the parallels imply that these two scenes are "hot spots" where the identity of Jesus is publicized. However, we also must distinguish them. The transfiguration is not simply a repetition of the baptism. An advancement occurs. If the baptism initiates Jesus into priesthood, then the transfiguration declares his great high priesthood over God's house. If the baptism initiates Jesus into his prophetic vocation, then the transfiguration declares that all must listen to this prophet. If the baptism initiates Jesus into kingship, then the transfiguration reveals that Jesus is the true Son.

While the baptism *begins* Jesus's earthly ministry and the ascension *ends* it, the transfiguration is the *gateway* to the saving events of Golgotha. While the baptism kickstarts Jesus's ministry, the transfiguration prepares the disciples for Jesus's death. One initiates Jesus's ministry; the other inaugurates the climactic phase—Jesus's journey to Jerusalem. The baptism resides in the phase of testing, but the transfiguration's refrain is vindication.

This can be partially confirmed by the audience of each event. In the baptism, the Father's voice speaks *to Jesus* and identifies him as the messianic Son. In the transfiguration, the identity of Jesus is revealed to the three disciples. Tabor is not the moment where Jesus receives the Spirit; the Spirit now transforms Jesus. Jesus is designated as the Son before witnesses, and he displays the result of his submission: glory. Jesus is not only the servant but also the glorified Son.

All these parallels should cause readers to ask what we can learn from the ties between these two scenes. The biggest difference is that in the transfiguration, Jesus is transfigured! The transfiguration is full of light, the baptism full of water. The water symbolizes death; the light symbolizes glory. As Israel went through the water to get to Sinai to see God, so Jesus went through water to reveal God. The baptism, in this way, foreshadows the death and resurrection; the transfiguration foreshadows the ascension and return.

Baptism = death and resurrection

Transfiguration = ascension and return

The baptism is appropriately placed at the beginning of Jesus's ministry while the transfiguration is placed at the beginning of the end of Jesus's ministry. Correlating the baptism and the transfiguration brings clarity to the purpose of both.

Gethsemane

Jesus's journey to Jerusalem appropriately begins with the transfiguration. His final moment before his arrest, in the garden of Gethsemane, also has many parallels with the transfiguration (Matt. 26:30–46; Mark 14:26–42; Luke 22:39–46; John 18:1–12).[17]

---

17. Anthony Kenny, "The Transfiguration and the Agony in the Garden," *CBQ* 19, no. 4 (1957): 444–52. Kenny notes that the transfiguration narrative provided the fathers with arguments against the Arians and Nestorians, while Gethsemane was an arsenal against Docetists and Monophysites.

In both accounts, Jesus takes with him the three disciples—Peter, James, and John—who become sleepy. Both occur on a mountain and at night.[18] Both mention Jesus's face. In both, Jesus speaks with heavenly beings, and his physical appearance changes. Peter plays a special part in both. The disciples don't quite understand what is happening, and people fall before Jesus. Both reference the Son of Man. And while the voice in the transfiguration designates Jesus as the Son, Jesus addresses his prayer to his "Father" in Gethsemane. Jesus is left alone in the garden; in the transfiguration, Jesus is left alone when Moses and Elijah disappear.

Adamic and priestly themes also exist in both. John's Gospel calls the Mount of Olives a "garden," tying it to Eden (John 18:1). In Luke Jesus tells the disciples to pray that they might not fall into temptation (Luke 22:46). Gethsemane is a new testing place for the Son of Man. The transfiguration also has priestly and temple themes. It occurs on a high mountain, Jesus's garments turn bright like a priest's robes, his face shines like Moses, and the glory cloud appears.

PARALLELS BETWEEN GETHSEMANE AND THE TRANSFIGURATION NARRATIVES

On a mountain at night.

Three disciples accompany Jesus.

Peter plays a prominent role.

The disciples don't understand.

People fall before Jesus.

Jesus is left alone.

Jesus's face is focused on.

Jesus addresses his Father; the Father addresses his Son.

The physical appearance of Jesus is changed.

However, differences also exist in the narratives. While both seem to take place at night, light fills the transfiguration scene. Alternatively, Jesus calls the garden a dominion of darkness (Luke 22:53). Jesus is full of glory in the transfiguration; he is full of grief and sorrow in Gethsemane. The Father speaks to the Son in the transfiguration; the Son speaks to the Father in the garden.

18. It is debated whether the scene occurs at night (Luke 9:32). Chrysostom rejects that it was at night, for the disciples' eyes were dimmed by the overpowering brightness. "Homily 56 on Matthew" (Daley, 76).

All these correspondences should encourage readers to compare the narratives. The Evangelists linked these scenes to confirm that the glory and humiliation of Jesus are allies, not enemies. Before the resurrection, the climax of the revelation of Jesus's glory is the transfiguration; before the cross, the climax of Jesus's humiliation is Gethsemane. On the Mount of Transfiguration we see the form of God; on the Mount of Olives, we see the form of a slave. In Gethsemane, Jesus is the man of sorrows; on the Mount of Transfiguration, he is the man of glory.[19]

The two narratives illustrate the complementary truths of the incarnation: Jesus is in both the form of God and the form of a slave (Phil. 2:6–11). He has two natures united in one person. Jesus's glory will only come through suffering. Light is the result of darkness. Connecting Gethsemane with the transfiguration displays that Jesus is the slave and the sovereign. Sacrifice leads to splendor.

The Cross

One key to understanding the transfiguration is to place it next to another parallel: the cross. As Ware notes, "Between the two hills Tabor and Calvary there is no great distance."[20] If we divorce these hills, we distort the meaning of both.

The transfiguration is the light to the darkness of the cross. One is revealed to three disciples; the other in public spectacle. One is a scene full of glorification; the other is filled with humiliation. In both, there are two figures flanking Jesus: in one, two Old Testament luminaries; in the other, two common thieves.[21]

Both events occur on a high place, one in Jerusalem and one outside of Jerusalem. One mountain has a bright cloud, the other has darkness over the land. One references the sixth day, the other the sixth hour. In one Jesus takes others with him; in the other Jesus is taken by others. In one Peter is thrilled to be there, saying it is good they are there (Matt. 17:5). In the other Peter hides and denies Jesus. In both there are onlookers, and in both Jesus is confessed as the Son of God. In both Elijah is referenced, and in both people are afraid. Jesus is declared the Father's Son in the transfiguration, but on the cross he cries out to his God, who has forsaken him.

---

19. Thanks to Quinn Mosier for pointing out this language in a private conversation.

20. Kallistos Ware, "Safeguarding the Creation for Future Generations," Orthodox Fellowship of the Transfiguration, June 8 2002, https://www.orth-transfiguration.org/safeguarding-the-creation-for-future-generations/. In fact, the Feast of the Transfiguration on August 6 is likely on that date because the celebration of the cross is forty days later (September 14).

21. As Anastasius of Sinai says, "Just as on Golgotha, he stood between two living creatures, conformed to a cross, so here he stands between Moses and Elijah in a way conformed to God." Anastasius of Sinai, "Homily on the Transfiguration" (Daley, 165).

THE TRANSFIGURATION AND THE CROSS

The Transfiguration	The Cross
Audience: the three disciples.	Audience: a public spectacle.
Locale: a mountain outside of Jerusalem.	Locale: a high place in Jerusalem.
Entourage: Moses and Elijah flank Jesus.	Entourage: two criminals flank Jesus.
Cosmic sign: a bright cloud appears.	Cosmic sign: darkness covers the land.
Peter: thrilled to be there.	Peter: hides and denies Jesus.
Elijah: appears next to Jesus.	Elijah: people think Jesus is calling out for Elijah.
Declaration: the Father asserts that Jesus is his Son.	Declaration: the centurion asserts that Jesus is the Son of God.
Declaration: the Father asserts that Jesus is his Son.	Declaration: Jesus says that the Father has forsaken him.

In some ways, the cross is the reverse of the transfiguration. One shows us Jesus's ultimate disgrace, and the other his ultimate honor. While the face of Christ bore shame at his passion as he was spit on, beaten, and pierced with thorns, his face brightened with honor at the transfiguration. While his garments were scornfully stripped from him on Calvary, they shone with unspeakable purity on Tabor.

In linking the scenes, the Gospels bring Jesus's glory and suffering together into a paradoxical union. Metamorphosis demands an encounter with affliction. The chief purpose of the transfiguration for the disciples was to remove their stumbling concerning the cross.

Mysteriously, the cross was part of Jesus's glorification. The parallels demonstrate that darkness cannot engulf the light. When Jesus is nailed to the cross, the meaning of the transfiguration shines.[22] Moreover, the cross itself is transfigured. It is no longer a mere instrument of torture, defeat, and death but an emblem of beauty, triumph, and life.

Philagathos juxtaposes the cross and the transfiguration in this way:

He [Jesus] strengthened them by this miraculous apparition, so that—when they could see him betrayed and in agony and praying that the cup of death might pass and dragged into the courtyard of the high priest—they might think back on their

22. Daley, introduction to *Light on the Mountain*, 20–21.

climb up Mount Thabor, and realize that he who had been surrounded in the glory of divinity, and attested as beloved Son of God, had not been betrayed to death against his will. If they should see his face slapped and spit upon, let them no longer be scandalized, since they had stored in their memories his brilliance that outshone the sun. If they were to see him clothed in purple as mockery, let them affirm him to be the one who, on the mountain, was "wrapped in light as in a robe." If they should see him fixed on a scaffold between two criminals, let them recognize him here as Lord, standing in majesty between Moses and Elijah. If they should know him as a corpse, hidden away in the earth, let them remember him overshadowed by a brilliant cloud. These are the reasons, then, for which the Transfiguration took place.[23]

The cross and the transfiguration are not two competing visions but two complementary pictures of the Messiah. If the rulers of this age had understood who Jesus was, they would not have crucified the *Lord of glory* (1 Cor. 2:8).

The Resurrection

We have associated the transfiguration with creation, the incarnation, baptism, Gethsemane, and the cross. However, critical scholars have proposed that the transfiguration is a misplaced resurrection narrative. I have hardly engaged with this view, as it is an unfruitful interpretation deserving little attention.[24]

Yet the two events should be associated. Jesus tells the three disciples not to tell anyone about the vision until he is raised from the dead (Matt. 17:9; Mark 9:9). Many therefore say that the glory seen on the mountain is a preview of Jesus's resurrection body.

To begin with, the context of the transfiguration includes Jesus's predictions of his death *and* resurrection. In this sense, the transfiguration is a sign that he will rise from the dead, that he possesses abundant life.

Second, the resurrection scene is introduced by angels appearing in clothing very similar to the way Jesus is described in the transfiguration. This implies that heaven has come down to earth. Paul tells of heavenly bodies with reference to the resurrection of the dead (1 Cor. 15:42). Peter speaks of Jesus's life in two frames: his suffering and subsequent glories, which seem to include the resurrection (1 Pet. 1:11, 21).

23. Philagathos, "Homily 31, on the Saving Transfiguration" (Daley, 263–64).
24. Stein gives the reasons why the transfiguration is not a replaced resurrection account. Robert H. Stein, "Is the Transfiguration (Mark 9:2–8) a Misplaced Resurrection-Account?," *JBL* 95, no. 1 (1976): 79–96.

Third, after his resurrection, Jesus's appearance seems to have changed in some ways. The two disciples don't recognize Jesus on the Emmaus road, Mary doesn't recognize him in the garden, and the eleven disciples don't recognize him as he stands on the shore. When Jesus does appear and people recognize him, they are startled, afraid, think they are seeing a ghost, and fall down before him.

Fourth, the declarations of divine sonship in other parts of the Scriptures are associated with the resurrection. Paul claims that Jesus was appointed to be the Son of God at the resurrection of the dead (Acts 13:33; Rom. 1:4).

Finally, we may also surmise that even in Jesus's resurrected body, since heaven had not come to earth in full, he still veiled his full glory so that others could look at him. This could help partially explain why the disciples couldn't recognize Jesus on Emmaus road. Throughout the Christian tradition, it has been common to argue that people can't behold Jesus's glory until they receive their glorified bodies. The transfiguration and resurrection would thus be only a partial preview of the resurrected body.

If that is the case, the transfiguration may embody the metaphysics of resurrection bodies that Paul speaks of in 1 Corinthians 15. Paul asserts that there are heavenly bodies and earthly bodies, but the "splendor [*doxa*] of heavenly bodies is different from that of the earthly ones" (1 Cor. 15:40). "One glory is of the sun, another of the moon, another of the stars. For one star differs in glory from another star. So also in the resurrection of the dead. Sown in decay, raised imperishable. Sown in dishonor, raised in glory. Sown in weakness, raised in power" (15:41–43, my translation).

Paul says that this will happen on the last day, at the last trumpet (1 Cor. 15:52). The dead will be raised incorruptible, and our bodies will be changed. If Christ is the first fruits of this change, then Jesus received his glorified body at his resurrection. The glory Jesus reveals in the transfiguration is thus a preview of Jesus's resurrection body. He shows the witnesses his *doxa* body. His face shines and his clothes are turned white as a screening of Jesus's heavenly physique.

While the resurrection is a major part of Jesus's victory and glorification, the transfiguration more readily connects with Jesus's ascension and return. After all, *Jesus is not described as having a* doxa *body in the resurrection appearances*, though his body is uniquely changed.[25]

When people see Jesus after he has been raised, they don't see him as a bright light and full of glory. When Jesus meets the women, they take hold of his feet and worship him, but the text doesn't describe the way Jesus looks (Matt. 28:9–10). Jesus then appears to his disciples on the mountain of Galilee, but

---

25. While 1 Cor. 15:42 ties the heavenly body to the resurrection, it also links this body to the final trumpet and the last day (15:52). The process may have been unique for Jesus, since he was raised but not yet glorified, but our resurrection and glorification will coincide.

nothing is said about his appearance. Some worship, others doubt (28:17). Only the angel of the Lord is described as being like lightning and wearing clothing as white as snow (28:3).

On the Emmaus road the disciples are "prevented from recognizing him" (Luke 24:16). Later, their eyes are opened. They recognize him, but Luke doesn't describe his appearance as bright glory (24:31). Jesus then appears to all the disciples. They are startled and terrified because they think they are seeing a ghost (24:37).

In John's Gospel, Mary comes to the tomb and doesn't find Jesus there. When she turns around, she thinks she sees the gardener, but it is Jesus. She doesn't recognize Jesus until he speaks her name (John 20:11–17). Jesus then appears to the gathered disciples and shows them his hands and side. The scene doesn't describe how Jesus looks, but the Scriptures usually note if someone looks like a heavenly being (20:12).

In John 21, Jesus reveals himself by the Sea of Tiberias. Jesus comes to the disciples while they are fishing. He is on the shore, and they don't recognize him. He gives them instructions, they haul in many fish, and then Peter recognizes that it is the Lord. They then eat with Jesus on the shore.

Strikingly, all the narratives refrain from describing Jesus as full of light. This is even more arresting since the angels are described in heavenly clothing in these scenes (Matt. 28:2–3; Luke 24:4; John 20:12). While their appearance could be seen in continuity with Jesus, maybe giving some support for Jesus's bright body at the resurrection, no text explicitly says that anyone is blinded by the light of Jesus's body. All this might be explained by the simple reality that Jesus still concealed his glory after his resurrection. The Emmaus road experience, where the disciples eyes are opened, may support this (Luke 24:31).

Alternatively, the resurrection might not be the consummation of the unveiling process. Maybe a future day is coming when his glory will be manifested more fully (Luke 24:26; Phil. 3:21; Col. 3:4). Certainly, Jesus demonstrates supernatural features, as he can appear or vanish suddenly (Luke 24:31, 36) and even appear through closed doors (John 20:19), but arguably he doesn't reveal his *doxa* body.

Origen held to a three-stage understanding of Christ's visibility. First, everyone can see Christ's physical body donned in the incarnation. Second, there is a glorified but only semi-spiritualized body shown at the transfiguration and between the resurrection and ascension, and only the spiritually mature can perceive it. Third, there is the body of Jesus that has ascended into the heavens, which is fully spiritual and can only be seen by those who have assumed "spiritual" bodies.[26]

---

26. Peter Anthony, *Patristic Perspectives on Luke's Transfiguration: Interpreting Vision* (London: Bloomsbury T&T Clark, 2022), 93.

Thus, although there are some parallels between the resurrection and the transfiguration, the difference in Jesus's visible glory prevents us from too tightly correlating the events. The next section explains why I think the transfiguration more aptly previews the ascension and Jesus's return.

Jesus's Ascension and Return

While most have focused on Jesus's transfiguration as a preview of his resurrection glory, a good argument can be made that the transfiguration more precisely points to Jesus's *ascension and return*.[27] Several arguments support this view.

First, the context of the transfiguration is closely related to Jesus's ascension and return. Right before the transfiguration, Matthew says the disciples won't "taste death until they see the Son of Man coming in his kingdom" (Matt. 16:28). All the Synoptics reference the "coming" (*erchomai*) of the Son of Man with his holy angels in this context (Matt. 16:27; Mark 8:38; Luke 9:26). Meanwhile, angels are continually referenced in the context of Jesus's return (Matt. 13:39, 41, 49; 16:27; 24:31; 25:31; Mark 13:27, 32). The Synoptic Gospels speak of the return of the shining Son of Man with the clouds of heaven and with great power and glory (Matt. 24:27, 30; Mark 13:26).[28] Luke is the most detailed. He says: "Then there will be signs in the sun, moon, and stars; and there will be anguish on the earth among nations bewildered by the roaring of the sea and the waves. People will faint from fear and expectation of the things that are coming on the world, because the powers of the heavens will be shaken. Then they will see the Son of Man coming in a cloud with power and *great glory*" (Luke 21:25–27).

Second, the transfiguration's imagery (mountain, cloud, glory, brightness) more naturally points to Jesus's ascension. In Luke 24:51, while Jesus is blessing the disciples, he is carried up to heaven. Acts 1:9–10 describes the ascension by saying "a cloud took him out of their sight," and "two men in white clothes" appear. The cloud is allied to God's glory throughout the Bible. It also points forward to his return (1:11).[29] First Timothy 3:16 explicitly affirms that Jesus was "taken up in glory." Philippians says that God highly exalted Jesus and gave

27. Ultimately, it may be hard to divorce the resurrection, ascension, and return, as they are all part of Jesus's exaltation.

28. Matthew 24:30 speaks of the sign of the Son of Man "shining" (*phainō*), which can also mean "appearing."

29. Many have in fact seen the discussion of Jesus's "exodus" in Luke as a reference to the ascension. This might be supported by the proximity of the reference to Jesus being "taken up" in Luke 9:51. Additionally, both the transfiguration narrative and the ascension narrative include the phrase "behold, two men" (Luke 9:30; Acts 1:10 ESV). John G. Davies, "Prefiguration of the Ascension in the Third Gospel," *JTS* 6, no. 2 (1955): 229–33.

him the name above every name (Phil. 2:9). Hebrews asserts that Jesus was "exalted above the heavens" (Heb. 7:26), and in Acts, Peter claims that Jesus has been exalted to the right hand of God (2:33; 5:31).

Interpreters should also note that when Jesus appears again after his ascension, he appears as light. When Stephen sees the ascended Lord, he sees the glory of God and Jesus standing beside God (Acts 7:55). When Paul sees the ascended Lord, he sees light (9:3). When John sees the ascended Lord in Revelation, he sees the Son of Man "dressed in a robe and with a golden sash around his chest. The hair of his head was white as wool—white as snow—and his eyes like a fiery flame. . . . He had seven stars in his right hand; . . . and his face was shining like the sun at full strength" (Rev. 1:13–14, 16).

Third, the imagery also closely parallels Jesus's return. As *lightning* comes from the east and west, so will be the coming of the Son of Man (Matt. 24:27). He will come "with the *clouds* of heaven" (Mark 14:62) and with power and great glory (Matt. 24:30; 16:27; 26:64). Revelation affirms that Jesus is returning "with the *clouds*," and "every eye will see him" (Rev. 1:7). He will come riding on a white horse, and his eyes will be *blazing* with fire (19:11–16). The epistle to Titus says we await our blessed hope and his "*glorious* appearing" (Titus 2:13 KJV). In 2 Thessalonians, Paul asserts Jesus will return "in *flaming fire*." Those who deny him will be away from "his *glorious* strength" when he comes "to be *glorified* by his saints" (2 Thess. 1:8–10). Those who are left will be caught up "in the *clouds*" (1 Thess. 4:17). Paul says in Romans that on the last day, God will render to each according to their works. Those who do well will receive *glory, honor, immortality,* and *eternal life* (Rom. 2:6–7).

Fourth, our earliest interpretations of the transfiguration tie it to the return of Christ.[30] The apostle Peter references the transfiguration in the context of

---

30. Nearly all our earliest interpretations of the transfiguration associate it with Jesus's glory at his ascension and return and not with his resurrection. Outside the canonical Scriptures, the Apocalypse of Peter also provides an early interpretation linking light with Jesus's return. Jesus says, "I will come in my glory shining seven times brighter than the sun. I will come in my glory with all my holy angels" (1:7). He speaks of how he will "come on an eternal, bright cloud and the angels of God who are with me will sit on the throne of my glory" (6:1). Later, in the transfiguration scene, the disciples ask Jesus to reveal to them one of their righteous brothers who has departed out of the world. "Suddenly two men appeared standing in front of the Lord, at whom we were not able to look. For a ray like the sun was coming from their face and their clothing was radiant, of what sort a person's eye has never seen. Neither is a mouth able to describe nor heart express the glory that they were wearing and the beauty of their appearance. . . . Their bodies were whiter than any snow" (15:2–5). The Lord showed him the place where they lived, and "the inhabitants of that place were clothed in the clothes of radiant angels" (16:3) (Eric J. Beck, *Justice and Mercy in the Apocalypse of Peter: A New Translation and Analysis of the Purpose of the Text*, WUNT 2/427 [Tübingen: Mohr Siebeck, 2019], 66–73). Overall, it is clear that the transfiguration is a picture of the *parousia* glory.

Similarly, the Pistis Sophia, a Coptic and Gnostic writing, describes the transfiguration as almost a combination of the transfiguration story and the ascension story. It says that on the day

Christ's return. Peter says that there will come a time when people ask, "Where is his 'coming' [*parousias*] that he promised?" (2 Pet. 3:4). In response, Peter directs their attention to the Mount of Transfiguration. Peter has made known to them "the power and *coming* [*parousian*]" of the Lord Jesus Christ as an eyewitness to it (2 Pet. 1:16). They will do well to pay attention to his account of the event "until the day dawns and the morning star rises" in their hearts (1:19). Peter is certain of the last day because he was with Jesus on Tabor. The transfiguration guarantees the *parousia*.

All of this might imply that Jesus's full glory is still partly hidden in his resurrection. It only truly shines forth as he ascends, and then again in his return to the earth. The imagery of light, shining garments, a cloud, and the connection to the coming of the Son of Man points to the glory of Jesus in his ascension and on his return.

However, the transfiguration is also different from the ascension and Jesus's return. It is a proleptic apocalypse. In the ascension, Jesus is enthroned and exalted as the Son of Man, but in the transfiguration he is not. The ascension is the *coronation* of Jesus, while the transfiguration is a *preview* of his future exaltation. In more modern terms, the transfiguration is like election day, when we learn the results; the ascension is like inauguration day, when the king is installed.[31]

Jesus's transfiguration must also be distinguished from his return. When Jesus returns, he comes to complete the work he began. The transfiguration is a *proleptic vision* of this future event. While we can associate the ascension and return of Christ with the transfiguration, they should also be distinguished. One is an appetizer; the others are the main entrée.

The New Creation

Though we have already spoken of Jesus's return, we must also relate the transfiguration to new creation. In short, the transfiguration previews the metamorphosis of all things, just as Jesus's clothes shine as a symbol of all creation taking in the light of God.

All common things will acquire a brightness. All human faces in Christ will be transfigured, while those outside of Christ will experience only gloom and

---

of ascension, "there came forth after it a great *power* of light, giving a very great light, and there was no measure to its accompanying light, *for* it came forth from the Light of Lights. . . . Now it happened when the light-power had come down upon Jesus, it gradually surrounded him completely. Then Jesus rose *or* ascended to the height, giving light exceedingly, with a light to which there was no measure." Alexander Schmidt, ed., *Pistis Sophia*, Nag Hammadi Studies 9 (Leiden: Brill, 1978), 9–13.

31. Thanks to Quinn Mosier for this analogy given in private correspondence.

darkness. The glory to come can be looked at in three respects: the glory of God, the glory of God's people, and the glory of the new creation. The transfiguration foreshadows all three.

First, and most fundamentally, the transfiguration is a preview of the glory of God to be seen in Christ. Chrysostom notes that on the last day, we will see Christ, not in the same way his disciples saw him on the mountain but in an even more glorious way.[32] We will see him not only with Moses and Elijah but with an army of angels, with archangels, with cherubim, and with countless multitudes. Revelation 21:22–24 clearly speaks of this glory to come when Christ installs his kingdom: "I did not see a temple in it, because the Lord God the Almighty and the Lamb are its temple. The city does not need the sun or the moon to shine on it, because the glory of God illuminates it, and its lamp is the Lamb. The nations will walk by its light, and the kings of the earth will bring their glory into it." No temple is needed in the new creation because the Father, Son, and Spirit are present. Eternal sunlight will be reality. Jesus's glory revealed in the transfiguration signifies that he is the presence of God—the radiance of his glory. The new city does not even need the sun or moon because the glory of the Father and of the Son brighten it. Now the face of the Lord truly shines on his people (Num. 6:24–26).

Second, the transfiguration reveals that God's people will be glorified. Many Old Testament texts predict that one day the church will be glorified. Daniel says that those who are wise shall shine "like the bright expanse of the heavens" and "like the stars forever" (Dan. 12:3).[33] The prophet Isaiah calls God's people to arise and shine, for their light has come, and the glory of God has risen upon them (Isa. 60:1). Psalm 34:5 says those who look at the Lord have radiant faces and shall never be ashamed.

Paul takes up this theme at various places. He affirms that the new bodies that believers receive have a certain splendor or glory (1 Cor. 15:40–44). He says that Jesus "will transform the body of our humble condition into the likeness of his glorious body" (Phil. 3:21). "When Christ appears," we will also "appear with him in glory" (Col. 3:4). In the new creation, the heavenly body will bear the light as it looks to the light. Jesus's transfiguration previews our transfiguration.

Third, the transfiguration signifies how God's creation will be glorified. All creation reaches toward the light—every blade of grass and every flower. Paul asserts that creation longs for "the revealing of the sons of God." At that point, "creation itself will also be set free from the bondage to decay into *the glorious freedom of God's children*" (Rom. 8:19–21). Note that creation will obtain glory!

---

32. Chrysostom, "Homily 56 on Matthew" (Daley, 79).
33. Chrysostom, "Homily 56 on Matthew" (Daley, 80).

Revelation provides more details on this glory. The new Jerusalem, as seen by John, was

> arrayed with God's glory. Her radiance was like a precious jewel, like a jasper stone, clear as crystal. . . . The building material of its wall was jasper, and the city was pure gold clear as glass. The foundations of the city wall were adorned with every kind of jewel: the first foundation is jasper, the second sapphire, the third chalcedony, the four emerald, the fifth sardonyx, the sixth carnelian, the seventh chrysolite, the eighth beryl, the ninth topaz, the tenth chrysoprase, the eleventh jacinth, the twelfth amethyst. The twelve gates are twelve pearls. . . . The main street of the city was pure gold, transparent as glass. (21:11, 18–21)

Readers may wonder why the author spends so much time on the kinds of jewels the city is made from. In the light of the transfiguration, this scene communicates the glory and brightness of the city. Darkness will have no place. Light will fill the city. The transfiguration is a picture of the metamorphosis to come for all of God's handiwork.

CONCLUSION

The transfiguration is a well deep beyond imagining. When we think we have hit rock bottom, a new spring appears. When we think we have exhausted the meaning of the passage, a new path opens. When we think we have understood the implications, a new mystery arises. Part of the glory of the transfiguration is seen when we correlate it to other events in Christ's life.

Neglecting the transfiguration puts us in danger of distorting the Christian faith. It has a complementary function for our theology, pairing biblical theology with systematic theology, shame with glory, the means with the end, mystery with revelation, and heavenly with earthly. Most importantly, it reminds us that we should interpret all of Christ's life through a dual lens. He is the messianic Son who has been made like us and who will rescue us as our true Adam. However, he is also unlike us. His bright clothes, the holy mountain, and the declaration of sonship reveal that he is also the eternal Son.

Conclusion

Restoring the Transfiguration

> When [Christ] appears, we will be like him because we will see
> him as he is.
>
> −1 John 3:2

The light of the transfiguration has been swallowed in the shadow of modern scholarship. When we think of Jesus's life, we often think of his birth, life, death, resurrection, and return. But we sometimes forget to zoom in on his life, and particularly this glorious moment.[1]

We struggle to know what to do with the transfiguration because it sits "out of place" in the biblical storyline. It feels like an actor who has forgotten his cue and prematurely bursts onto stage. As one author writes, it looks "at first glance like a gratuitous interlude in the gospel narrative."[2]

However, the transfiguration is carefully located in Jesus's ministry. It is a great hinge of Jesus's life and ministry. Jesus's time in Galilee is ending, his mission to Jerusalem is about to begin. The transfiguration straddles this fault line. In this way, the transfiguration introduces us to a new phase of Jesus's ministry: his suffering. Yet the new phase of Jesus's ministry commences by fronting his

---

1. Kevin Vanhoozer says, "The transfiguration is a mini-summa that recalls God's presence in the history of Israel and anticipates the consummation of the covenant: the glory of God's presence in his people and all creation. As such, it provides program notes as it were for understanding the whole narrative sweep of Scripture." Kevin J. Vanhoozer, "Ascending the Mountain, Singing the Rock: Biblical Interpretation Earthed, Typed, and Transfigured," *MT* 28, no. 4 (2012): 794.
2. John Gatta, *The Transfiguration of Christ and Creation* (Eugene, OR: Wipf & Stock, 2011), xv.

glory. Brian Daley calls it "the interpretive link between the beginning of Jesus' mission, at his baptism in the Jordan, and the climax of that mission on Calvary."[3]

The transfiguration is concomitant to the cross. Here we see that the living and the dead are one in Christ, the old and new covenant are inseparable, the suffering and glory of Christ are united, the age to come is already present in Jesus, our metamorphosis is guaranteed, and God's final word is found in his Son. Here the diverse elements of the Scriptures meet. It is an integrative symbol, with images and words, darkness and light, heaven and earth, new and old luminaries, and revelation and mystery. It stands as a dogma among dogmas.

Forgetfulness of the transfiguration might lead to distortions of the truth. We might separate the old from the new, the shame of Jesus from his honor, the human nature from Jesus's divine nature, the persons of the Trinity from each other, the harmony of heaven from the disunity of earth, the mystery of God from the revelation of God. The transfiguration protests such distortions.[4]

In seeking to revive interest in the transfiguration in the Western tradition, my thesis has been that the transfiguration reveals Jesus's double sonship. It is both an epiphany (because Jesus is God) and an apotheosis (because Jesus is man).[5] God does not merely *bestow* Jesus's identity; he *reveals* Jesus's full identity. It is a vision both of what is and of what is to be. The narrative gives hope to the troubled disciples by means of revelation. The suffering of their Messiah will lead to glory.

The most controversial piece of this argument is that Jesus is a preexistent figure. Not many modern interpreters see preexistence in the Synoptic Gospels. But I think they have blinders on. They haven't given the transfiguration a fair shake.

Maybe you think I have pushed my argument too far. Perhaps the white clothes, shining face, mountaintop setting, bright cloud, and heavenly voice point to Jesus as only God's messenger and human king. However, if we press deeper into these images, their truth is unlocked. A solitary detail from the narrative might not persuade. My argument pertains to the coalition of these features.

---

3. Brian Daley, introduction to *Light on the Mountain: Greek Patristic and Byzantine Homilies on the Transfiguration of the Lord*, trans. Brian Daley, Popular Patristics 48 (New York: St. Vladimir's Seminary Press, 2013), 12.

4. This is a reworking of Ramsey's eloquent summary. Arthur Michael Ramsey, *The Glory of God and the Transfiguration of Christ* (Eugene, OR: Wipf & Stock, 2009), 144.

5. One curious counterargument to my proposal is that there isn't an explicit moment of recognition where the disciples declare that Jesus is a divine being. However, we should distinguish between their understanding of the event on the mountain and their understanding of the event after Jesus was raised and ascended.

Additionally, if we begin by trusting that the early church has something to teach us in their articulation of hermeneutics, trinitarian theology, and Christology, then the pieces fall into place. The four senses, Nicaea, and Chalcedon are wise guides to interpreting the transfiguration. The fourfold method allows readers to break free from the "literal" chains that imprison interpreters. Our trinitarian grammar reminds us that God is light in himself. And Chalcedon asserts that Jesus is doubly begotten. It is comforting to know that the Christian tradition stands behind the interpretation offered here. It seems that we would need something more forceful than minor detractors to overturn the received interpretation of this event.

A Brief Biblical Theology of the Transfiguration

Though I have attempted to connect the dots from Genesis to Revelation throughout this book, it is useful to briefly summarize a biblical theology of the transfiguration.

The transfiguration story begins where all stories do: with Adam and Eve in the garden. Adam and Eve are made in God's image and likeness on God's mountain (Gen. 1:28). They are icons, or idols, of God. Though we typically view idols negatively, the sense from Genesis is that humanity has the Spirit of God breathed into it, indicating its participation in the divine. Adam and Eve's vocation is to mirror and represent Yahweh. This is why Jewish literature outside of the Bible speaks of Adam and Eve having glory in the garden and why Paul speaks of sin as having "exchanged the glory of . . . God" (Rom. 1:23). The fall was therefore a descent from glory. Paul speaks of it in terms of having fallen "short of the glory of God" (3:23). Darkness ensues as humanity flees from its purpose.

Moses's story previews the restoration of this "image." He ascends the mountain of God, enters the glory cloud, and peers into heaven, seeing that the garden was a copy of the heavens. Moses is instructed to build another copy on the earth so that others might enter God's presence. The result of him being with God is that his face now shines (Exod. 34:29).

In 2 Corinthians, Paul employs Moses as a prototype. Paul was not shy about using the verb *metamorphoō* to describe our spiritual pilgrimage to glory (Rom. 12:2; 2 Cor. 3:18). Gregory of Nyssa mimics Paul and presents Moses as an example of seeking after God in his book *Life of Moses*. Moses is an archetype for those who seek God's face. His life represents spiritual stages as he seeks God's glory.

Moses first pursues solitude in the desert, where he sees divine light in the burning bush. Next comes Moses's renunciation (*purgation*) of his past and his seeking of a new life in the wilderness. Moses then communes with God in fire and a cloud of darkness on Mount Sinai. He is *illumined*. His face shines as he comes down the mountain, demonstrating the weight of this moment. Moses is still not satisfied. The greater degree of glory awakens him. He wants more. He desires *union*.[6] This union is not satisfied until he sees Jesus.

Israel's priests reenact Moses's ascent up Sinai as they meet with God in the temple and then come out of God's dwelling on earth, blessing God's people with the shining presence of God's face (Num. 6:24–26). However, Israel is not able to live up to their vocation of being God's light to the nations. Therefore, God sends his only begotten Son as the light of the world (John 1). The Spirit rests on him, and he acts in the way that God has purposed for humanity all along. Yahweh will fix what has gone wrong. The disciples get a preview of this restoration on Mount Tabor. Jesus ascends the mountain, his face shines, his clothes turn dazzlingly white, and the glory cloud appears. Jesus is the true image of God (Col. 1:18).

The promise for the redeemed is that those who participate in Christ will also be changed. As Ephrem the Syrian said, "Christ came to find Adam who had gone astray. He came to return him to Eden in the garment of light. . . . Blessed is He who had pity on Adam's leaves and sent a robe of glory to cover his naked state."[7] Paul says that we all now have unveiled faces like Moses and are being transformed into the same image from glory to glory (2 Cor. 3:18). However, that transformation will only occur in full on the last day. At that time, our earthly bodies will be made new and become heavenly bodies. We will be raised in glory (1 Cor. 15:40–43).

This glory is explicated in the rest of the New Testament. Paul says that God will transform our lowly bodies to be like his glorious body (Phil. 3:20–21). He asserts that when Christ appears, we will also appear with him in glory (Col. 3:4). John says that when Jesus appears, we shall be like him, for we shall see him as he is (1 John 3:2). And Peter confirms that he will be a partaker of the glory to be revealed (1 Pet. 5:1).

Yet this will take place only through suffering. The transfiguration's larger context is the looming cross. In Romans 8:18–25, Paul follows this "suffering

---

6. Gregory puts it this way: "Although lifted up through such lofty experiences, he is still unsatisfied in his desire for more. He still thirsts for that with which he constantly filled himself to capacity, and he asks to attain as if he had never partaken, beseeching God to appear to him, not according to his capacity to partake, but according to God's true being. . . . [He] longs to be filled with the very stamp of the archetype." Gregory of Nyssa, *The Life of Moses*, trans. Abraham J. Malherbe and Everett Ferguson (New York: HarperCollins, 2006), 104.

7. St. Ephrem, *Virginity* 16.9 and *Fast* 3.2, in Sebastian Brock, *The Luminous Eye: The Spiritual World Vision of Saint Ephrem the Syrian*, Cistercian Studies 124 (Kalamazoo, MI: Liturgical Press, 1992), 87–88.

then glory" pattern when he speaks of how the sufferings of this present time are not worth comparing to the glory that is to come. As Desmond Tutu writes, "The principle of transfiguration says nothing, no one and no situation, is 'untransfigurable,' that the whole of creation, nature, waits expectantly for its transfiguration, when it will be released from its bondage and share in the glorious liberty of the children of God, when it will not be just dry inert matter but will be translucent with divine glory."[8] When the Lord returns, we will wear a crown of righteousness (2 Tim. 4:8). The shining mountain is not only an event to study; it transfigures us as we behold the glorious Son and wait for his return.

Even all of creation waits for the revealing of the children of God when they will obtain the "the glorious freedom of God's children" (Rom. 8:21). We groan while we wait for the redemption of our bodies (8:23; 2 Cor. 4:17). In the new heavens and new earth, God's presence in the Son and through the Spirit will dwell with us on his mountain. Jesus's divine rays will suffuse all creation. His transfiguration is not only about his transformation; it is about our transformation and the transfiguration of the cosmos. The earth will have no need for the sun or moon to shine, for the glory of God and the lamp of the Lamb will be its light. We will shine as the stars in the sky (Dan. 12:3; Matt. 13:43). At that time, the nations will walk by his light, and the kings will bring their glory to God's city (Rev. 21:23–24). We still await that day, but we wait for it with hope.

8. Desmond Tutu, *God Has a Dream: A Vision of Hope for Our Time* (New York: Doubleday, 2004), 3.

Light from Light

While we should be nervous about using metaphors to help explain how God is one in three, the fathers (and later the confessions) were not hesitant to employ the metaphor of light to explain both the unity and the distinction of the three persons.[1] Gregory of Nazianzus affirms the following about the Father, Son, and Spirit all being light:

> The Father was the True Light that enlightens every man coming into the world. The Son was the True Light which lighteneth every man coming into the world. The Other Comforter was the True Light which lighteneth every man coming into the world. Was and Was and Was, but Was One Thing. Light thrice repeated; but One Light and One God. . . . And now we have both seen and proclaim concisely and simply the doctrine of God the Trinity, comprehending out of Light (the Father), Light (the Son), in Light (the Holy Ghost).[2]

Athanasius uses light to buttress his claim that the Son is of the same essence (*homoousion*) as the Father: "He [the Son] is the Same as God. . . . For the radiance also is light, not second to the sun, nor a different light, nor from

---

1. John of Damascus speaks of the relationship between the Father, Son, and Spirit as the relationship between the sun, a ray, and radiance. John of Damascus, *Exposition of the Orthodox Faith* 1.8 (NPNF² 9:11). Yet John is also quick to say, "It is impossible to find in creation an image that exactly reflects the mode of the Holy Trinity as it is in itself." *On the Orthodox Faith*, trans. Norman Russell (Yonkers: St. Vladimir's Seminary Press, 2022), 77.
2. Gregory of Nazianzus, Oration 31.3 (NPNF² 7:318).

participation of it, but a whole and proper offspring of it. And such an offspring is necessarily one light; and no one would say they are two lights."[3]

The Nicene Creed confessed that Jesus the Son was "Light from Light," in part, because of the transfiguration. In the transfiguration, we see that God has revealed himself as light and that he reveals himself as Father, Son, and Spirit. However, the question remains as to what precisely the disciples see of God in the transfiguration. Related to it is the question of what we will see in the beatific vision.

A paradox exists in the Scriptures. The Old Testament and the New Testament affirm both the invisibility and the incomprehensibility of God, on the one hand. On the other hand, they affirm the revelation of God in the Son and Spirit. Moses couldn't see God, but he met with him face to face. Paul affirms that God "is immortal" and dwells "in unapproachable light, whom no one *has seen or can see*" (1 Tim. 6:16). But he also affirms that Jesus is "the image of the invisible God" (Col. 1:15).[4]

Therefore, we return to our question: What do the disciples see of God in the transfiguration, and how does this relate to the beatific vision? A long debate swirls around this question, and the East and West differ in how they answer it. The West follows Augustine and Aquinas, who affirm a certain metaphysic of divine essence in relation to simplicity, while the East tends toward a more apophatic theology.

The East followed the Cappadocian fathers, among whom Gregory of Nyssa is illustrative, and distinguished between the revelation of God's *essence* and his *energies*.[5] The East essentially says:

---

3. Athanasius, *Against the Arians* 3.13 (*NPNF*[2] 4:395).

4. This plays into the Orthodox position on icons. The Father is unrepresentable because he did not become incarnate. However, the Son is representable because he was incarnate. In displaying Jesus, the Orthodox didn't seek to display the two natures of Christ. They represented his person, who unites two natures without confusion or division. They affirm that we only have one way of knowing the Trinity: through the Son. Leonid Ouspensky, *Theology of Icon*, trans. Anthony Gythiel (Crestwood, NY: St. Vladimir's Seminary Press, 1992), 1:153–54.

5. David Bradshaw asserts, "The distinction of *ousia* and *energeia*, essence and energy, has long been recognized as the most important philosophical tenent distinguishing eastern Christian thought from its western counterpart" (Bradshaw, *Aristotle East and West: Metaphysics and the Division of Christendom* [Cambridge: Cambridge University Press, 2007], xi). Some of the differences between the East and West boil down to how they define simplicity. The West views simplicity as God's essence being identical to his attributes. The East has a softer version of divine simplicity.

In addition to the Cappadocians and Palamas, St. Dionysius the Areopagite, John of Damascus, St. Maximus the Confessor, and Cyril of Alexandria distinguished between essence and energies. Bradshaw writes that the distinction between essence and energies is best described as the distinction between an agent and that agent's activity. In the case of God, the *energeiai* are diverse. Some are eternal and others are temporal; some are contingent and others necessary. Bradshaw, "Essence

God cannot be seen according to his essence, being, or nature (*kat ousian*). God can be seen in his energies, operations, or workings (*kat energeian*).

Gregory of Nyssa puts it this way: "He who is by nature invisible becomes visible in his operations."[6] Gregory Palamas, who wrote about a millennium after the Cappadocians, solidified this distinction, comparing God's essence to the sun and his energies to the rays of light.[7] We can only see God in creation, and he remains invisible because he transcends the created order.

Cyril affirms this principle and speaks of the vision of God in negative terms. Only the Son and Holy Spirit have a pure vision of the nature of the Father. Only the Son sees the Father, and only the Spirit searches the depths of God.[8] The point is *not* that when we see God's energies, we don't see God. The opposite is the case. Humans truly relate to God through his operations. God's energies are not simply divine activity *ad extra* but God himself as creatures see him.

Aquinas and the Western tradition argue that there are problems with this view. If God is simple, if he is pure act, then we can't draw a sharp distinction between God's essence and God's energies. Augustine affirms that God simply *is* the divine essence; therefore, if he is to be seen, he must be seen in his essence. Aquinas, following Augustine, holds that "everything which is not the divine essence is a creature." If this is the case, there is no room for divine energies that are not identical to the divine essence.[9]

Aquinas affirms that the created intellect ought to be able to see the essence of God; otherwise, the natural desire for God's essence would remain void.[10] However, he is quick to state that seeing God is not the same as fully comprehending him.

---

and Energies: What Kind of Distinction?," *Analogia* 6 (2019): 35. A reference to God's "energies" or "operations" can be found in texts like Eph. 1:11, 19–20; 3:7; 4:16; Phil. 2:12–13; Col. 1:29; 2:12.

6. Gregory Palamas, *The Saving Work of Christ: Sermons by Saint Gregory Palamas*, ed. Christopher Veniamin (Waymart, PA: Mount Thabor, 2008), 55; Hans Boersma, *Seeing God: The Beatific Vision in Christian Tradition* (Grand Rapids: Eerdmans, 2018), 80. Augustine (*On the Trinity* 2.35 [*NPNF*¹ 3:54]) likewise states, "For the nature itself, or substance, or essence, or by whatever other name that very thing, which is God, whatever it be, is to be called, cannot be seen corporeally: but we must believe that by means of the creature made subject to Him, not only the Son, or the Holy Spirit, but also the Father, may have given intimations of Himself to mortal senses by a corporeal form or likeness." Saint Anastasius (*The Guide* 8 [PG 89:132]) accuses his adversaries of confusing the "nature" and the "*prosōpon*" in God. The second term signifies God's person, but even his person does not reveal his essence. See Vladimir Lossky, *The Vision of God* (Crestwood, NY: St. Vladimir's Seminary Press, 2013), 137.

7. Gregory Palamas, *Gregory Palamas: The Triads*, trans. Nicholas Gendle (New York: Paulist Press, 1982), 57, 108.

8. Lossky, *Vision of God*, 92.

9. Aquinas, *Summa Theologiae*, Pt. I, Q. 28; see also Bradshaw, *Aristotle East and West*, 165.

10. Aquinas, *Summa Theologiae*, Pt. I, Q. 12, art. 7, ad 2.

The Western cautions are worthwhile considerations. However, Palamas, and even more so the Cappadocians, are careful not to abandon simplicity, even if they have a slightly different conception of it. The energies are not separate from, independent of, or simply activities of God. The essence and energies have ontological identity.[11] They are both God himself. The energies are simply not a full revelation of God since God is transcendent and cannot be known in full.[12] John Meyendorff, in his introduction to Palamas's *Triads*, states that Gregory's distinction between "essence" and "energy" "is nothing but a way of saying that the transcendent God remains transcendent, as He also communicates Himself to humanity."[13]

The transfiguration has something to say with respect to this debate, even if it won't necessarily reconcile the two schools. Three affirmations should be balanced together, all in relation to the three persons.

First, a certain apophaticism exists in the transfiguration. Several symbols point to a theology of negation. The presence of the cloud, Jesus's shining face, and only the audio (not a visual) of the Father preserves the incomprehensibility and invisibility of God. Calvin notes that it deserves our attention that the *voice* of God was heard from the *cloud*. Neither a body nor a face was seen. "Let us therefore remember the warning which Moses gives us, that God has no visible shape, lest we deceive ourselves by imagining that He resembled a man (Deut.

11. Palamas asserts that although the divine energies are "realities," they are not self-subsistent beings. They are "enhypostatic" in that they permanently exist only in the hypostasis of another (Gregory Palamas, *Triads* 2.3.6; 3.1.9). Vladimir Lossky, in his book overviewing Eastern theology (*The Mystical Theology of the Eastern Church* [Crestwood, NY: St. Vladimir's Seminary Press, 1997], 79, 88), asserts that Orthodox theology does not admit any kind of "composition" in God. The energies are not separate from the Trinity. However, it is confusing when Lossky states that God's energies hold a middle place between God's being in himself and his work in the economy (82).

12. Basil states, "The *energeiai* are various, and the essence simple, but we say that we know our God from His *energeiai*, but do not undertake to approach near to His essence. His *energeiai* come down to us, but His essence remains beyond our reach" (Epistle 234.1 [*NPNF²* 8:274]). Bradshaw summarizes the Cappadocians' view in this way: "The Cappadocians accept from the philosophical tradition the proposition that God is intrinsically active, so that the divine *energeia* can in some sense be identified with God Himself. But they reject the identification of the divine *energeia* with self-knowing. For them the *energeiai* at issue are decidedly other-directed, consisting both in specific acts, such as the creation and oversight of the world, and in more generalized modes of acting (or, as we would say, characteristics displayed in acting), such as divine wisdom, power, and goodness. Because of this difference they can no longer accept the identification of God's *ousia* and *energeia*." Bradshaw, *Aristotle East and West*, 170.

13. John Meyendorff, introduction to Gregory Palamas, *Triads*, 20. D. Glenn Butner Jr. (*Trinitarian Dogmatics: Exploring the Grammar of the Christian Doctrine of God* [Grand Rapids: Baker Academic, 2022], 82) says we can affirm a distinction between essence and energies while affirming divine simplicity all without exhaustive explanation. He cites Marcus Plested, who asserts that the energies are the essence revealed, thereby making it more of a virtual distinction.

14:15)."[14] Additionally, Maximus the Confessor notes that Christ's shining face illustrates the "characteristic hiddenness" of his being. It was too bright for the disciples.[15] God certainly dwells in unapproachable light and therefore requires a theology of negation.

However, second, in the same breath, we must recognize that the transfiguration is mainly a scene of light, of revelation. The Father is also revealed *through* the Son since they are one. The disciples are able to see the "Father of lights" through the Son since the Son has taken on flesh (James 1:17). In John 14, Philip asks Jesus to show the Father to the Twelve. Jesus replies, "The one who has seen me has seen the Father. How can you say, 'Show us the Father'?" (John 14:9). To behold the luminous face of Jesus is to behold the face of the Father. Jesus continues to speak about how he is in the Father and the Father is in him. Maybe the Eastern tradition has not stressed this answer enough in preserving the invisibility of God.[16] As Vidu states, the beatific vision is "not only *instrumentally* enabled by Christ, in the sense of his redemptive work, but . . . Christ continues to be *materially* part of the very content of that vision."[17]

Third, we must not neglect the Holy Spirit in the vision of God. The Father is revealed *through* the Son and *in* the Spirit. The Spirit both reveals and conceals. The cloud covers the disciples, and the voice speaks from heaven about the Son. This cloud conceals and discloses. It is a cloud of knowing and unknowing.

Whether we should still say that the essence of God is hidden is a difficult question. If the Son is of the same essence of God the Father, then didn't the disciples see the essence of God? However, at the same time, we must respect the incomprehensibility and limitlessness of God that the East emphasizes while also heeding the warnings of the West against a deviation from simplicity. The transfiguration affirms both real sight and real transcendence. I personally find the energies and essence distinction helpful for wading through the paradox of God's invisibility and revelation.

In sum, in seeing the face of Jesus in the transfiguration by the Holy Spirit, the disciples see God. They see the radiance of the glory of God (Heb. 1:3). They see the light of the gospel that displays the glory of Christ (2 Cor. 4:4). Christ is the image of the *invisible God* (Col. 1:15). Yet at the same time, the

14. John Calvin, *Commentary on a Harmony of the Evangelists, Matthew, Mark, and Luke*, trans. William Pringle, vol. 2 (Grand Rapids: Eerdmans, 1949), 313.

15. Maximus the Confessor, *Questions and Doubts* 191.47–48.

16. Though the light of the transfiguration might indicate the "essence" of God condescending to human flesh. John of Damascus, along with a few other fathers, associates the light of God with his energies. "The divine irradiation and *energeia* is one, simple, and undivided, beneficently diversified in divisible things, dispensing to all of them the components of their proper nature while remaining simple." John of Damascus, *An Exposition of the Orthodox Faith* 1.14 (NPNF² 9:17).

17. Adonis Vidu, *The Divine Missions: An Introduction* (Eugene, OR: Cascade Books, 2021), 100.

invisibility of God is not compromised as a bright cloud covers the disciples. God, by nature, is invisible.[18] When Paul writes to Timothy that the eternal and immortal God is invisible, he is not only speaking of the Father but of the Son and the Spirit (1 Tim. 1:17).

John Calvin puts it this way: "Because God's majesty, which is far removed from us, would be like a secret and hidden spring, He has revealed Himself in Christ. And so we have an open fountain at hand to draw from. The words mean that God did not want to have the life hidden and as it were buried within Himself, and therefore He transfused it into His Son that it might flow to us."[19]

May the light of the Son flow through us.

18. Augustine (*De Trinitate* 3.26) notes that even when God appeared in visible or audible fashion, it was by means of his creation and not in his own proper substance.

19. John Calvin, *The Gospel according to St. John, 1–10*, trans. T. H. L. Parker, Calvin's Commentaries (Grand Rapids: Eerdmans, 1995), 131. John Owen puts it this way: "In his incarnation, the Son was made the representative image of God unto us—as he was, in his person, the essential image of the Father, by eternal generation. The invisible God—Whose nature and divine excellencies our understandings can make no approach unto—does in him represent, exhibit, or make present unto our faith and spiritual sense, both himself and all the glorious excellencies of his nature." John Owen, *The Works of John Owen*, ed. William H. Goold, vol. 1, *The Glory of Christ* (Edinburgh: Banner of Truth, 1965), 72.

A Transfiguration Bibliography

Books and Dissertations

Andreopoulos, Andreas. *Metamorphosis: The Transfiguration in Byzantine Theology and Iconography*. Crestwood, NY: St. Vladimir's Seminary Press, 2005.

———. *This Is My Beloved Son: The Transfiguration of Christ*. Brewster, MA: Paraclete, 2012.

Anthony, Peter. *Patristic Perspectives on Luke's Transfiguration: Interpreting Vision*. London: Bloomsbury T&T Clark, 2022.

Baldacci, P. R. "The Significance of the Transfiguration Narrative in the Gospel of Luke: A Redactional Investigation." PhD diss., Marquette University, 1974.

Baltensweiler, H. *Die Verklärung Jesu: Historisches Ereignis und synoptische Berichte*. Zurich: Zwingli, 1959.

Belleville, Linda. *Reflections of Glory: Paul's Polemical Use of the Moses-Doxa Tradition in 2 Corinthians 3.1–18*. London: Bloomsbury Academic, 2015.

Best, Thomas F. "Transfiguration and Discipleship in Matthew." PhD diss., Graduate Theological Union, 1974.

Blinzler, J. *Die neutestamentlichen Berichte über die Verklärung Jesu*. Münster: Aschendorff, 1937.

Blowers, Paul M. *Maximus the Confessor: Jesus Christ and the Transfiguration of the World*. Oxford: Oxford University Press, 2016.

Boobyer, G. H. *St. Mark and the Transfiguration Story*. Edinburgh: T&T Clark, 1942.

Thanks to Thomas Best, who first published his "The Transfiguration: A Select Bibliography" with *JETS* (1981). I also don't claim that this covers everything written on the transfiguration. There are many sources I'm sure I missed. However, this should be a good starting point for those wishing to study this event in more detail.

Brandt, Pierre-Yves. *L'identité de Jésus et l'identité de son disciple: Le récit de la transfiguration comme clef de Lecture de l'Évangile de Marc*. Novum Testamentum et Orbis Antiquus 50. Fribourg, Switzerland: Editions Universitaires, 2002.

Canty, Aaron. *Light and Glory: The Transfiguration of Christ in Early Franciscan and Dominican Theology*. Washington, DC: Catholic University of America Press, 2010.

Dabrowski, E. *La transfiguration de Jésus*. Edition française augmentée. Rome: Pontifical Biblical Institute, 1939.

Daley, Brian E., trans. *Light on the Mountain: Greek Patristic and Byzantine Homilies on the Transfiguration of the Lord*. Popular Patristics 48. New York: St. Vladimir's Seminary Press, 2013.

Daniel, F. H. "The Transfiguration (Mk 9:2–13 and Parallels): A Redaction-Critical and Traditio-Historical Study." PhD diss., Vanderbilt University, 1976.

Duplantier, J. P. "Les récits synoptiques de la Transfiguration: Étude sur la composition et le 'milieu' littéraire de Mc; 9,2–8; Mt 17, 1–9; Lc 9, 28–36." PhD diss., University of Strasbourg, 1970.

Gatta, John. *The Transfiguration of Christ and Creation*. Eugene, OR: Wipf & Stock, 2011.

Gause, R. H. "The Lukan Transfiguration Account Luke 9:27–36: Luke's Pre-Crucifixion Presentation of the Exalted Lord in the Story of the Kingdom of God." PhD diss., Emory University, 1975.

Habra, G. *La Transfiguration selon les Pères grecs*. Paris: Editions S. O. S., 1973.

Hay, Andrew R. *God's Shining Forth: A Trinitarian Theology of Divine Light*. Eugene, OR: Wipf & Stock, 2017.

Hayes, Cory. "Deus in Se et Deus pro Nobis: The Transfiguration in the Theology of Gregory Palamas and Its Importance for Catholic Theology." PhD diss., Duquesne University, 2015.

Heil, John Paul. *The Transfiguration of Jesus: Narrative Meaning and Function of Mark 9:2–8, Matt 17:1–8 and Luke 9:28–36*. AnBib 144. Rome: Pontifical Biblical Institute, 2000.

Höller, J. *Die Verklärung Jesu: Eine Auslegung der neutestamentlichen Berichte*. Freiburg: Herder, 1937.

Horstmann, M. *Studien zur markinischen Christologie*. 2nd ed. Neutestamentliche Abhandlungen 6. Münster: Aschendorff, 1969.

Koskela, Douglas M. *The Radiance of God: Christian Doctrine through the Image of Divine Light*. Eugene, OR: Cascade Books, 2021.

Lange, J. *Das Erscheinen des Auferstandenen im Evangelium nach Matthäus*. Forschung Zur Bibel 11. Würzburg: Echter, 1973.

Lee, Simon. *Jesus' Transfiguration and the Believers' Transformation: A Study of the Transfiguration and Its Development in Early Christian Writings*. Tübingen: Mohr Siebeck, 2009.

Lossky, Vladimir. *The Mystical Theology of the Eastern Church*. Crestwood, NY: St. Vladimir's Seminary Press, 1997.

———. *The Vision of God*. Crestwood, NY: St. Vladimir's Seminary Press, 2013.

Mantzaridis, Georgios I. *The Deification of Man: St. Gregory Palamas and the Orthodox Tradition*. Translated by Liadain Sherrard. New York: St. Vladimir's Seminary Press, 1997.

McFarland, Ian A. *The Word Made Flesh: A Theology of the Incarnation*. Louisville: Westminster John Knox, 2019.

McGuckin, John A. *The Transfiguration of Christ in Scripture and Tradition*. Lewiston, NY: Mellen, 1987.

Moses, A. D. A. *Matthew's Transfiguration Story and Jewish-Christian Controversy*. LNTS 122. Sheffield: Bloomsbury Academic, 1996.

Nellas, Panayiotis. *Deification in Christ: Orthodox Perspectives on the Nature of the Human Person*. Crestwood, NY: St. Vladimir's Seminary Press, 1987.

Nes, Solrunn. *The Uncreated Light: An Iconographical Study of the Transfiguration in the Eastern Church*. Grand Rapids: Eerdmans, 2007.

Ouspensky, Leonid. *Theology of Icon*. Translated by Anthony Gythiel. Vol. 1. Crestwood, NY: St. Vladimir's Seminary Press, 1992.

Perry, John Michael. *Exploring the Transfiguration Story*. Kansas City: Sheed and Ward, 1993.

Plume, Thomas, ed. *A Century of Sermons upon Several Remarkable Subjects by the Right Reverend Father in God John Hackett, Late Lord Bishop of Lichfield and Coventry*. London: Robert Scott, 1675.

Pricop, Cosmin. *Die Verwandlung Jesu Christi*. WUNT 2/422. Tübingen: Mohr Siebeck, 2016.

Ramsey, Arthur Michael. *The Glory of God and the Transfiguration of Christ*. Eugene, OR: Wipf & Stock, 2009.

Reid, Barbara E. *The Transfiguration: A Source- and Redaction-Critical Study of Luke 9:28–36*. Paris: J. Gabalda, 1993.

Schönborn, Christopher. *God's Human Face: The Christ-Icon*. Translated by Lothar Krauth. San Francisco: Ignatius, 1994.

Trites, Allison. *The Transfiguration of Christ: A Hinge of Holy History*. Hantsport, Nova Scotia: Lancelot, 1994.

Van Dussen, D. Gregory. *Transfiguration and Hope: A Conversation across Time and Space*. Eugene, OR: Wipf & Stock, 2018.

Wenkel, David H. *Shining Like the Sun: A Biblical Theology of Meeting God Face to Face*. Wooster, OH: Weaver Book Company, 2016.

Wilson, Andrew P. *Transfigured: A Derridean Re-Reading of the Markan Transfiguration*. LNTS 319. New York: Boomsbury T&T Clark, 2007.

Wypadlo, Adrian. *Die Verklärung Jesu nach dem Markusevangelium*. WUNT 308. Tübingen: Mohr Siebeck, 2013.

Articles

Agua Pérez, Agustín del. "The Narrative of the Transfiguration as a Derashic Scenifica-
tion of a Faith Confession (Mark 9:2–8 Par)." *NTS* 39, no. 3 (July 1993): 340–54.

Aichele, George, and Richard Walsh. "Metamorphosis, Transfiguration, and the Body."
BibInt 19, no. 3 (2011): 253–75.

Ashton, John. "The Johannine Son of Man: A New Proposal." *NTS* 57, no. 4 (October
2011): 508–29.

Bacon, B. W. "The Transfiguration Story." *AJT* 6 (1902): 236–65.

Badcock, F. J. "The Transfiguration." *JTS* 22 (1920–21): 321–26.

Bernardin, Joseph Buchanan. "The Transfiguration." *JBL* 52, nos. 2–3 (1933): 181–89.

Best, Thomas F. "The Transfiguration: A Select Bibliography." *JETS* 24, no. 2 (June
1981): 157–61.

Bradshaw, David. "Essence and Energies: What Kind of Distinction?" *Analogia* 6 (2019):
5–35.

Bucur, Bogdan G. "Matt 17:1–9 as a Vision of a Vision: A Neglected Strand in the Patristic
Reception of the Transfiguration Account." *Neotestamentica* 44, no. 1 (2010): 15–30.

Burkett, Dilbert. "The Transfiguration of Jesus (Mark 9:2–8): Epiphany or Apotheosis?"
JBL 138, no. 2 (2019): 413–32.

Byassee, Jason. "A Transfiguring God." *ProEccl* 26, no. 2 (2017): 150–58.

Caird, G. B. "Expository Problems: The Transfiguration." *ET* 67, no. 10 (1956): 291–94.

———. "The Transfiguration." *ET* 67 (1955): 291–94.

Carlston, Charles Edwin. "Transfiguration and Resurrection." *JBL* 80, no. 3 (September
1961): 233–40.

Chamberas, Peter A. "Transfiguration of Christ: A Study in the Patristic Exegesis of
Scripture." *St. Vladimir's Theological Quarterly* 14, nos. 1–2 (1970): 48–65.

Collins, Adela Yarbro. "Mark and His Readers: The Son of God among Greeks and
Romans." *HTR* 93, no. 2 (April 2000): 85–100.

Coune, M. "Radieuse Transfiguration, Mt 17,1–9; Mc 9,2–10; Lc 9,28–36." *Assemblées
du Seigneur* 15 (1973): 44–84.

———. "La Transfiguration dans l'exégèse des sept premiers siècles." *Assemblées du
Seigneur* 28 (1962): 64–80.

Currie, S. D. "Isaiah 63:9 and the Transfiguration in Mark." *Austin Seminary Bulletin*
82 (1966): 7–34.

Dabeck, P. "Siehe, es erschienen Moses und Elias." *Bib* 23 (1942): 175–89.

Davies, Jamie. "Apocalyptic Topography in Mark's Gospel: Theophany and Divine Invisibility at Sinai, Horeb, and the Mount of Transfiguration." *JTI* 14, no. 1 (June 15,
2020): 140–48.

Davies, John G. "Prefigurement of the Ascension in the Third Gospel." *JTS* 6, no. 2
(1955): 229–33.

Denis, A. M. "Une théologie de la Redemption: La Transfiguration chez saint Marc." *Vie Spirituelle* 41 (1959): 136–49.

Domeris, William. "Reading the Markan Transfiguration (Mark 9:1–9) in the Light of Jesus' Scattering of the Tyrian Baal Coins." *Conspectus* 26 (September 2018): 46–60.

Feník, Juraj, and Róbert Lapko. "Jesus's Inverse Transfiguration in John 13." *Neotestamentica* 55, no. 2 (2021): 347–64.

Feuillet, A. "Les perspectives propres a chaque évangéliste dans les récits de la Transfiguration." *Bib* 39 (1958): 281–301.

Foster, Paul. "Polymorphic Christology: Its Origins and Development in Early Christianity." *JTS* 58, no. 1 (April 2007): 66–99.

Fuchs, A. "Die Verklärungserzählung des Markus-Evangeliums in der sicht moderner Exégèse." *Theologisch-Praktische Quartalschrift* 125 (1977): 29–37.

Gatta, John. "The Transfiguration of Christ and Cosmos: A Focal Point of Literary Imagination." *Sewanee Theological Review* 49, no. 4 (2006): 484–506.

Gennarini, S. "Le principali interpretazioni postliberali della pericope della transfigurazione di Gesu." *Rivista di Storia e Letteratura Religiosa* 8 (1972): 80–132.

Gerber, W. "Die Metamorphose Jesu, Mark. 9,2f. Par." *TZ* 23 (1967): 385–95.

Giambrone, Joseph Anthony. "'Why Do the Scribes Say' (Mark 9:11): Scribal Expectations of an Eschatological High Priest and the Interpretation of Jesus' Transfiguration." *RB* 128, no. 2 (2021): 201–35.

Gregory Palamas. "The Light of the Transfiguration." *Orthodox Tradition* 31, no. 1 (2014): 55.

Guijarro Oporto, Santiago. "The Transfiguration of Jesus and the Easter Visions." *BTB* 47, no. 2 (2017): 95–99.

Harrison, Everett Falconer. "The Transfiguration." *BibSac* 93, no. 371 (July 1936): 315–23.

Hart, Aidan. "Transfiguration and the Marriage of Form and Light in Icons and Church Architecture." *The Pemptousia Journal for Theological Studies* 14 (2021): 39–61.

Holzmeister, V. "Einzeluntersuchungen über das Geheimnis der Verklärung Christi." *Bib* 21 (1940): 200–210.

Johnson, S. Lewis. "Transfiguration of Christ." *BibSac* 124, no. 494 (April 1967): 133–43.

Juncker, Günther. "Christ as Angel: The Reclamation of a Primitive Title." *TJ* 15, no. 2 (1994): 221–50.

Kennedy, H. A. A. "The Purpose of the Transfiguration." *JTS* 4, no. 16 (1903): 543–47.

Kenny, Anthony. "The Transfiguration and the Agony in the Garden." *CBQ* 19 (1957): 444–52.

Kibbe, Michael H. "Light That Conquers the Darkness: Oscar Romero on the Transfiguration of Jesus." *Theology Today* 75, no. 4 (January 2019): 447–57.

Larsen, Kevin W. "A Focused Christological Reading of Mark 8:22–9:13." *TJ* 26, no. 1 (2005): 33–46.

Lee, Dorothy A. "On the Holy Mountain: The Transfiguration in Scripture and Theology." *Colloquium* 36, no. 2 (November 2004): 143–59.

Lohmeyer, E., and W. Schmauch. "Die Verklärung Jesu nach dem Markus-Evangelium." *ZNW* 21 (1922): 185–215.

Lose, David J. "What Does This Mean? A Four-Part Exercise in Reading Mark 9:2–9 (Transfiguration)." *Word & World* 23, no. 1 (2003): 85–93.

Louth, Andrew. "Reflections on Brian Daley's God Visible." *ProEccl* 28, no. 4 (2019): 370–77.

Madsen, Thorvald B. "Listen to Him: The Exhortation of Matthew 17:5 in the Context of the Transfiguration Narrative." *Midwestern Journal of Theology* 15, no. 2 (2016): 119–30.

Maier, Walter A. "The Divine Presence within the Cloud." *CTQ* 79, nos. 1–2 (January 2015): 79–102.

Manoussakis, John Panteleimon. "Theophany and Indication: Reconciling Augustinian and Palamite Aesthetics." *MT* 26, no. 1 (January 2010): 76–89.

Maronde, Christopher Allan. "'You Are My Beloved Son': The Foundations of a 'Son of God' Christology in the Second Psalm." *CTQ* 85, nos. 3–4 (July 2021): 313–39.

Martin, Thomas W. "What Makes Glory Glorious? Reading Luke's Account of the Transfiguration over against Triumphalism." *JSNT* 29, no. 1 (September 2006): 3–26.

Masson, C. "La Transfiguration de Jesus." *RTP* 97 (1964): 1–14.

McCurley, F. R., Jr. "'And after Six Days' (Mk 9:2): A Semitic Literary Device." *JBL* 93 (1974): 67–81.

McGuckin, John A. "The Patristic Exegesis of the Transfiguration." *Studia Patristica* 18, no. 1 (1986): 335–41.

Milad, Corine B. "Incarnation and Transfiguration: Origen's Theology of Descent." *JTI* 12, no. 2 (2018): 200–216.

Miller, David Marvin. "Seeing the Glory, Hearing the Son: The Function of the Wilderness Theophany Narratives in Luke 9:28–36." *CBQ* 72, no. 3 (July 2010): 498–517.

Miller, Robert J. "Is There Independent Attestation for the Transfiguration in 2 Peter?" *NTS* 42, no. 4 (October 1996): 620–25.

Morado, Guillermo Juan. "La significatividad de la transfiguración de Jesús." *Revista Española de Teología* 80, no. 1 (2020): 33–60.

Moss, Candida R. "The Transfiguration: An Exercise in Markan Accommodation." *BibInt* 12, no. 1 (2004): 69–89.

Mosser, Carl. "Orthodox-Reformed Dialogue and the Ecumenical Recovery of Theosis." *Ecumenical Review* 73, no. 1 (2021): 131–51.

———. "Recovering the Reformation's Ecumenical Vision of Redemption as Deification and Beatific Vision." *Perichoresis: The Theological Journal of Emanuel University* 18, no. 1 (March 1, 2020): 3–24.

Müller, H.-P. "Die Verklärung Jesu." *ZNW* 51 (1960): 56–64.

Murphy-O'Connor, J. "The Structure of Matthew XIV–XVII." *RB* 82 (1975): 360–84.

Neyrey, J. H. "The Apologetic Use of the Transfiguration in 2 Peter 1:16–21." *CBQ* 42 (1980): 504–19.

Nicolaides, Angelo. "The Transfiguration as a Divine Mystery in Orthodoxy." *Pharos Journal of Theology* 101 (2020): 1–11.

Ortlund, Gavin. "Will We See God's Essence? A Defense of a Thomistic Account of the Beatific Vision." *SJT* 74, no. 4 (November 2021): 323–32.

Otto, Randall E. "The Fear Motivation in Peter's Offer to Build *treis skēnas.*" *WTJ* 59, no. 1 (1997): 101–12.

Paretsky, Albert. "The Transfiguration of Christ: Its Eschatological and Christological Dimensions." *New Blackfriars* 72, no. 851 (July 1991): 313–24.

Pedersen, S. "Die Proklamation Jesu als des eschatologischen Offenbarungsträgers." *NovT* 17 (1975): 241–65.

Penner, James A. "Revelation and Discipleship in Matthew's Transfiguration Account." *BibSac* 152, no. 606 (April 1995): 201–10.

Pfeil, Margaret R. "Oscar Romero's Theology of Transfiguration." *Theological Studies* 72, no. 1 (March 2011): 87–115.

Poirier, John C. "Jewish and Christian Tradition in the Transfiguration." *RB* 111, no. 4 (October 2004): 516–30.

Reid, Barbara E. "Voices and Angels: What Were They Talking about at the Transfiguration? A Redaction-Critical Study of Luke 9:28–36." *Biblical Research* 34 (1989): 19–31.

Roberts, Alastair. "Transfigured Hermeneutics—Introduction." *Reformation21* (blog). December 9, 2015. https://www.reformation21.org/blogs/transfigured-hermeneutics-intr-1.php.

———. "Transfigured Hermeneutics—Transfiguration and Exegesis." *Reformation21* (blog). December 18, 2015. https://www.reformation21.org/blogs/transfigured-hermeneutics-tran.php.

———. "Transfigured Hermeneutics 3: Transfiguration as Theophany." *Reformation21* (blog). January 13, 2016. https://www.reformation21.org/blogs/transfigured-hermeneutics-3-tr.php.

———. "Transfigured Hermeneutics 4—Jesus as God's Glory Face in John's Gospel." *Reformation21* (blog). February 1, 2016. https://www.reformation21.org/blogs/transfigured-hermeneutics-4-je.php.

———. "The High Priest and the New Temple: Transfigured Hermeneutics 5." *Reformation21* (blog). February 26, 2016. https://www.reformation21.org/blogs/the-high-priest-and-the-new-te.php.

———. "The Climactic Word: Transfigured Hermeneutics 6." *Reformation21* (blog). March 16, 2016. https://www.reformation21.org/blogs/the-climactic-word.php.

Schmithals. "Die Markusschluss, die Verklärungsgeschichte und die Aussendung der Zwölf." *ZTK* 69 (1972): 379–411.

Spitta, D. F. "Die evangelische Geschichte von der Verklärung Jesu." *ZWT* 53 (1911): 97–167.

Steenberg, Irenaeus Archimandrite. "Two-Natured Man: An Anthropology of Transfiguration." *ProEccl* 14, no. 4 (2005): 413–32.

Stein, Robert H. "Is the Transfiguration (Mark 9:2–8) a Misplaced Resurrection-Account?" *JBL* 95, no. 1 (March 1976): 79–96.

Stevenson, Kenneth W. "From Hilary of Poitiers to Peter of Blois: A Transfiguration Journey of Biblical Interpretation." *SJT* 61, no. 3 (2008): 288–306.

———. "From Origen to Palamas: Greek Expositions of the Transfiguration." *Bollettino Della Badia Greca Di Grottaferrata* (Tertia Seria) 4 (2007): 197–212.

———. "'Rooted in Detachment': Transfiguration as Narrative, Worship and Community of Faith." *Ecclesiology* 1, no. 3 (2005): 13–26.

Tanev, Stoyan. "Created and Uncreated Light in Augustine and Gregory Palamas: The Problem of Legitimacy in Attempts for Theological Reconciliation." *Analogia* 4, no. 3 (2017): 81–113.

Tàrrech, Armand Puig I. "The Glory on the Mountain: The Episode of the Transfiguration of Jesus." *NTS* 58 (2012): 151–72.

Thrall, Margaret Eleanor. "Elijah and Moses in Mark's Account of the Transfiguration." *NTS* 16, no. 4 (July 1970): 305–17.

Torrance, T. F. "The Transfiguration of Jesus." *EQ* 14, no. 3 (n.d.): 214–29.

Toulis, Petros. "Theophanes of Nicea's Five Orations on the Light of Tabor: Palamite or Thomistic Influence on His Theology?" *Greek Orthodox Theological Review* 55, nos. 1–4 (2010): 243–50.

Tremel, B. "Des récits apocalyptiques: Baptême et Transfiguration." *Lumen Victae* 23 (1974): 70–83.

Trites, Allison. "The Transfiguration of Jesus: The Gospel in Microcosm." *EQ* 51, no. 2 (1979): 67–79.

Vanhoozer, Kevin J. "Ascending the Mountain, Singing the Rock: Biblical Interpretation Earthed, Typed, and Transfigured." *MT* 28, no. 4 (October 2012): 781–803.

Wenham, David, and A. D. A. Moses. "'There Are Some Standing Here . . .': Did They Become the 'Reputed Pillars' of the Jerusalem Church? Some Reflections on Mark 9:1, Galatians 2:9 and the Transfiguration." *NovT* 36, no. 2 (April 1994): 146–63.

Wessner, Mark D. "Toward a Literary Understanding of 'Face to Face' (פָּנִים אֶל־פָּנִים) in Genesis 32:23–32." *ResQ* 42, no. 3 (2000): 169–77.

———. "Toward a Literary Understanding of Moses and the Lord 'Face to Face' (פָּנִים אֶל־פָּנִים) in Exodus 33:7–11." *ResQ* 44, no. 2 (2002): 109–16.

Williams, Stephen N. "The Transfiguration of Jesus Christ Part 1." *Themelios* 28, no. 1 (2002): 13–25.

———. "The Transfiguration of Jesus Christ Part 2: Approaching Sonship." *Themelios* 28, no. 2 (2003): 16–27.

Wilson, Ian Douglas. "'Face to Face' with God: Another Look." *ResQ* 51, no. 2 (2009): 107–14.

Wright, William M. "The Literal Sense of Scripture according to Henri de Lubac: Insights from Patristic Exegesis of the Transfiguration." *MT* 28, no. 2 (April 2012): 252–77.

Yeago, David. "The New Testament and the Nicene Dogma: A Contribution to the Recovery of Theological Exegesis." *ProEccl* 3, no. 2 (1994): 152–64.

Ziesler, John A. "Transfiguration Story and the Markan Soteriology." *ET* 81, no. 9 (June 1970): 263–68.

Historical Resources

Aquinas, Thomas. *Catena Aurea: Commentary on the Four Gospels.* Vol. 3, part 1, *St. Luke.* Oxford: John Henry Parker, 1874: 318–26.

———. *Catena Aurea: Commentary on the Four Gospels.* Vol. 1, part 3, *The Gospel of St. Matthew.* Oxford: John Henry Parker, 1841: 559–609.

———. *Summa Theologiae.* Vol. 53, *The Life of Christ.* Translated by Samuel Parsons and Albert Pinheiro. Cambridge: Cambridge University Press, 2006: 53, 149–63.

Augustine. "The Harmony of the Gospels." Edited by Philip Schaff. *NPNF[1]* 6:154–55.

———. Sermons 28 and 29. In *Sermons on Selected Lessons of the New Testament.* Edited by Philip Schaff. *NPNF[1]* 6:347–49.

Calvin, John. *Commentary on a Harmony of the Evangelists, Matthew, Mark, and Luke.* Vol. 2. Translated by William Pringle. Edinburgh: Calvin Translation Society, 1845: 307–19.

Chrysostom, John. "Two Homilies on Eutropius." Edited by P. Schaff. *NPNF[1]* 9:258.

Confessor, Maximos the. *On Difficulties in the Church Fathers: The Ambigua.* Translated by Nicholas Constas. Cambridge, MA: Harvard University Press, 2014: 191–203, 267–77.

Cyril of Alexandria. Sermon 51. In *A Commentary upon the Gospel according to St. Luke.* Vol. 1. Translated by R. Payne Smith. Oxford: Oxford University Press, 1859: 226–30.

Daley, Brian, trans. *Light on the Mountain: Greek Patristic and Byzantine Homilies on the Transfiguration of the Lord.* Popular Patristics 48. New York: St. Vladimir's Seminary Press, 2013.

Edwards, Jonathan. "A Divine and Supernatural Light, Immediately Imparted to the Soul by the Spirit of God, Shown to Be Both a Scriptural, and Rational Doctrine (1734)." In *The Sermons of Jonathan Edwards: A Reader.* Edited by Wilson H. Kimnach, Kenneth P. Minkema, and Douglas A. Sweeney. New Haven: Yale University Press, 2017: 121–40.

Gregory of Nyssa. *Gregory of Nyssa: The Life of Moses.* Translated by Abraham Malherbe and Everett Ferguson. New York: Paulist Press, 1978.

Gregory Palamas. *Gregory Palamas: The Triads*. Translated by Nicholas Gendle. New York: Paulist Press, 1982: 31–40, 71–92.

———. *Saint Gregory Palamas: The Homilies*. Edited by Christopher Veniamin. Waymart, PA: Mount Thabor, 2009: 266–81.

———. *The Saving Work of Christ: Sermons by Saint Gregory Palamas*. Edited by Christopher Veniamin. Waymart, PA: Mount Thabor, 2008: 39–56.

Kreitzer, Beth, ed. *Luke*. Reformation Commentary on Scripture: New Testament 3. Downers Grove, IL: IVP Academic, 2015: 381–88.

Lee, Jason K., and William M. Marsh, eds. *Matthew*. Reformation Commentary on Scripture: New Testament 1. Downers Grove, IL: IVP Academic, 2021: 222–23.

Luther, Martin. *Annotations on Matthew 1–18*. Edited by Christopher Boyd Brown. Vol. 67 of *Luther's Works*. St. Louis: Concordia, 2015: 307–22.

———. *D. Martin Luthers Evangelien-Auslegung*. Vol. 2. Edited by Erwin Mühlhaupt. Göttingen: Vandenhoeck & Ruprecht, 1939: 573–79.

Maximos the Confessor. *On Difficulties in the Church Fathers*. Vol. 1, *The Ambigua*. Translated by Nicholas Constas. Cambridge, MA: Harvard University Press, 2014: 191–203, 267–77.

Owen, John. *The Works of John Owen*. Edited by William H. Goold. Vol. 1, *The Glory of Christ*. Edinburgh: Banner of Truth, 1965: 315–16, 322, 383–84.

Polemis, I. D. *Theophanes of Nicaea: His Life and Works*. Oxford: Oxford University Press, 1991: 71–112.

Chapters or Sections in a Book

Allison, Dale. *The New Moses: A Matthean Typology*. Eugene, OR: Wipf & Stock, 2013: 243–48.

Anatolios, Khaled. *Deification through the Cross: An Eastern Christian Theology of Salvation*. Grand Rapids: Eerdmans, 2022: 150–51, 157.

Barton, Stephen C. "The Transfiguration of Christ according to Mark and Matthew: Christology and Anthropology." In *Auferstehung—Resurrection: The Fourth Durham-Tübingen Research Symposium; Resurrection, Transfiguration and Exaltation in Old Testament, Ancient Judaism and Early Christianity*. WUNT 135. Tübingen: Mohr Siebeck, 2001: 231–46.

Bauckham, Richard. *Jesus and the God of Israel: God Crucified, and Other Studies on the New Testament's Christology of Divine Identity*. Grand Rapids: Eerdmans, 2008: 263–65.

———. "The Throne of God and the Worship of Jesus." In *The Jewish Roots of Christological Monotheism*, edited by Carey C. Newman, James R. Davila, and Gladys S. Lewis. Leiden: Brill, 1999: 43–69.

———. *Who Is God? Key Moments of Biblical Revelation*. Grand Rapids: Baker Academic, 2020: 99–103.

Bertram, G. "Die Himmelfahrt Jesu von Kreuz und der Glaube an seine AufBest." In *Festgabe für Adolf Deissmann*, 187–217. Tübingen: Mohr, 1927.

Bird, Michael F. *Jesus the Eternal Son: Answering Adoptionist Christology*. Grand Rapids: Eerdmans, 2017: 97–103.

Blackwell, Ben C. *Christosis: Engaging Paul's Soteriology with His Patristic Interpreters*. Grand Rapids: Eerdmans, 2016: 103–10.

Boersma, Hans. *Seeing God: The Beatific Vision in Christian Tradition*. Grand Rapids: Eerdmans, 2022: 129–42, 149–50.

Bultmann, R. *History of the Synoptic Tradition*. Translated by John Marsh. New York: Harper & Row, 1968: 259–61, 309, 432–33.

Burkill, T. A. *Mysterious Revelation*. Ithaca, NY: Cornell University Press, 1963: 156–64, 180–82.

Cope, O. L. *Matthew: A Scribe Trained for the Kingdom of Heaven*. Catholic Biblical Quarterly Monograph Series 5. Washington, DC: Catholic Biblical Association, 1976: 99–102.

Crowe, Brandon D. *The Last Adam: A Theology of the Obedient Life of Jesus in the Gospels*. Grand Rapids: Baker Academic, 2017: 48–50.

Davies, W. D. *The Setting of the Sermon on the Mount*. Cambridge: Cambridge University Press, 1964: 50–56, 99.

Deutsch, Celia. "The Transfiguration: Vision and Social Setting in Matthew's Gospel (Matthew 17:1–9)." In *Putting Body and Soul Together: Essays in Honor of Robin Scroggs*, edited by Virginia Wiles, Alexandra Brown, and Graydon F. Snyder. Valley Forge, PA: Trinity Press International, 1997: 124–37.

Dibelius, M. *From Tradition to Gospel*. New York: Scribner's, 1934: 267–75.

Dodd, C. H. "The Appearances of the Risen Christ: An Essay in Form-Criticism of the Gospels." In *Studies in the Gospels: Essays in Memory of R. H. Lightfoot*, edited by D. E. Nineham. Oxford: Blackwell, 1955: 9–35.

Dunn, James. *Christology in the Making: A New Testament Inquiry into the Origins of the Doctrine of the Incarnation*. Philadelphia: Westminster, 1980: 46–47, 89.

Fletcher-Louis, Crispin. "The Revelation of the Sacral Son of Man: The Genre, History of Religions Context and the Meaning of the Transfiguration." In *Auferstehung—Resurrection: The Fourth Durham-Tübingen Research Symposium; Resurrection, Transfiguration and Exaltation in Old Testament, Ancient Judaism and Early Christianity*. WUNT 135. Tübingen: Mohr Siebeck, 2001: 247–98.

Gathercole, Simon J. *The Gospel and the Gospels: Christian Proclamation and Early Jesus Books*. Grand Rapids: Eerdmans, 2022: 87, 136, 311, 322–23, 346–48, 357–58, 440.

———. *The Preexistent Son: Recovering the Christologies of Matthew, Mark, and Luke*. Grand Rapids: Eerdmans, 2006: 46–50.

Green, Joel. "Transfiguration." In *Dictionary of Jesus and the Gospels*, edited by Joel Green. 2nd ed. Downers Grove, IL: IVP Academic, 2013: 966–72.

Hamerton-Kelly, R. G. *Pre-existence, Wisdom, and the Son of Man: A Study of the Idea of Pre-Existence in the New Testament.* Cambridge: Cambridge University Press, 1973: 53–55.

Harrelson, W. "The Celebration of the Feast of Booths according to Zechariah 14:16–21." In *Religions in Antiquity,* edited by J. Neusner. Leiden: Brill, 1968: 86–96.

Hart, David Bentley. Foreword to *The Uncreated Light: An Iconographical Study of the Transfiguration in the Eastern Church,* by Solrunn Nes. Grand Rapids: Eerdmans, 2007: xiii–xv.

Hilhorst, Anthony. "The Mountain of Transfiguration in the New Testament and in Later Tradition." In *The Land of Israel in Bible, History, and Theology: Studies in Honour of Ed Noort,* edited by Jacques van Ruiten and J. Cornelis de Vos. Vetus Testamentum, Supplements 124. Leiden: Brill, 2009: 317–38.

Hooker, Morna. "'What Doest Thou Here, Elijah?' A Look at St Mark's Account of the Transfiguration." In *The Glory of Christ in the New Testament: Studies in Christology,* edited by L. D. Hurst and N. T. Wright. Oxford: Clarendon, 1987: 59–70.

Huizenga, Leroy. *The New Isaac: Tradition and Intertextuality in the Gospel of Matthew.* Leiden: Brill, 2012: 209–35.

Kee, H. C. "The Transfiguration in Mark: Epiphany or Apocalyptic Vision?" In *Understanding the Sacred Text: Essays in Honor of Morton S. Enslin on the Hebrew Bible and Christian Beginnings,* edited by John Reumann. Valley Forge, PA: Judson, 1972: 135–52.

King, Jonathan. *The Beauty of the Lord: Theology as Aesthetics.* Bellingham, WA: Lexham, 2018: 192–211.

Kirk, J. R. Daniel. *A Man Attested by God: The Human Jesus of the Synoptic Gospels.* Grand Rapids: Eerdmans, 2016: 191–99.

Kooy, Vernon H. "The Transfiguration Motif in the Gospel of John." In *Saved by Hope: Essays in Honor of Richard C Oudersluys,* edited by James I. Cook. Grand Rapids: Eerdmans, 1978: 64–78.

Lee, Dorothy A. "Transfiguration and the Gospel of John." In *In Many and Diverse Ways: In Honor of Jacques Dupuis,* edited by Daniel Kendall and Gerald O'Collins. Maryknoll, NY: Orbis Books, 2003: 158–69.

Leon-Dufour, X. "La Transfiguration de Jésus." In *Études d'Évangile.* Paris: Éditions du Seuil, 1965: 83–122.

Liefeld, W. L. "Theological Motifs in the Transfiguration Narrative." In *New Dimensions in New Testament Study,* edited by R. N. Longenecker and M. C. Tenney. Grand Rapids: Zondervan, 1974: 162–79.

———. "Transfiguration." In *Dictionary of Jesus and the Gospels,* edited by Joel Green. Downers Grove, IL: IVP Academic, 1992: 834–41.

Louth, Andrew. "From Doctrine of Christ to Icon of Christ: St. Maximus the Confessor on the Transfiguration of Christ." In *In the Shadow of the Incarnation: Essays on Jesus*

Christ in the Early Church in Honor of Brian E. Daley, S.J., edited by Peter W. Martens. Notre Dame, IN: University of Notre Dame Press, 2008: 260–75.

Manoussakis, John Panteleimon. *For the Unity of All: Contributions to the Theological Dialogue between East and West.* Eugene, OR: Cascade Books, 2015: 51–68.

McFarland, Ian A. *The Word Made Flesh: A Theology of the Incarnation.* Louisville: Westminster John Knox, 2019: 41, 93, 103, 120, 218, 246–49.

Moulton, W. J. "The Significance of the Transfiguration." In *Biblical and Semitic Studies: Critical and Historical Essays by the Members of the Semitic and Biblical Faculty of Yale University.* New York: Scribner's, 1901: 159–210.

Nogueira, Paulo. "Visionary Elements in the Transfiguration Narrative." In *Apocalyptic in History and Tradition*, edited by Christopher Rowland and John Barton. London: Sheffield Academic, 2003: 142–50.

Orlov, Andrei. *The Glory of the Invisible God: Two Powers in Heaven Traditions and Early Christology.* London: Bloomsbury T&T Clark, 2021: 83–144.

Ortlund, Gavin. *Theological Retrieval for Evangelicals: Why We Need Our Past to Have a Future.* Grand Rapids: Crossway, 2019: 171–74.

Potter, Jonathan. "Naked Divinity: The Transfiguration Transformed in the Acts of John." In *Jesus and Mary Reimagined in Early Christian Literature*, edited by Vernon K. Robbins and Jonathan M. Potter. Atlanta: SBL Press, 2015: 181–222.

Stein, Robert H. *Jesus the Messiah: A Survey of the Life of Christ.* Downers Grove, IL: IVP Academic, 1996: 167–76.

Stevenson, Kenneth W. "'In All Supernatural Works, We Rather Draw Back Than Help On': The Seven Transfiguration Sermons of John Hacket (1592–1670)." In *Exchanges of Grace: Essays in Honour of Ann Loades*, edited by Natalie K. Watson and Stephen Burns. London: SCM, 2008: 66–77.

Torrance, T. F. "A Theology of Light: A University Sermon." In *The Christian Frame of Mind: Reason, Order, and Openness in Theology and Natural Science.* Colorado Springs: Helmers & Howard, 1989: 154–55.

Trites, Allison. "The Transfiguration in the Theology of Luke: Some Redactional Links." In *The Glory of Christ in the New Testament: Studies in Christology*, edited by L. D. Hurst and N. T. Wright. Oxford: Clarendon, 1987: 71–82.

Urbano, Arthur. "Jesus's Dazzling Garments: Origen's Exegesis of the Transfiguration in the Commentary on Matthew." In *The Garb of Being: Embodiment and the Pursuit of Holiness in Late Ancient Christianity*, edited by Georgia Frank, Susan R. Holman, and Andrew S. Jacobs. New York: Fordham University Press, 2020: 35–56.

Wainwright, Geoffrey. "The Transfiguration of Jesus in Wesleyan Exegesis and Application." In *Orthodox and Wesleyan Scriptural Understanding and Practice*, edited by S. T. Kimbrough. Crestwood, NY: St. Vladimir's Seminary Press, 2005: 321–33.

Weinandy, Thomas G. *Jesus Becoming Jesus: A Theological Interpretation of the Synoptic Gospels.* Washington, DC: Catholic University of America Press, 2018: 227–42.

Systematic Theologies

Akin, Daniel L., ed. *A Theology for the Church*. Nashville: B&H Academic, 2007: 518–19.

Ames, William. *The Marrow of Theology*. Translated by John D. Eusden. Durham, NC: Labyrinth, 1983: 141, 214.

Barth, Karl. *Church Dogmatics*. Vol. III/2, *The Doctrine of Creation*, translated by Harold Knight, G. W. Bromiley, J. K. S. Reid, and R. H. Fuller. Edinburgh: T&T Clark, 1960: 478–85.

Bavinck, Herman. *Reformed Dogmatics*. Vol. 3, *Sin and Salvation in Christ*, edited by John Bolt, translated by John Vriend. Grand Rapids: Baker Academic, 2006: 250–53.

Erickson, Millard. *Christian Theology*. 3rd ed. Grand Rapids: Baker Academic, 2013: 1132.

Frame, John M. *Systematic Theology: An Introduction to Christian Belief*. Phillipsburg, NJ: P&R, 2013: 391, 394, 1076.

Horton, Michael. *The Christian Faith: A Systematic Theology for Pilgrims on the Way*. Grand Rapids: Zondervan Academic, 2011: 329, 334.

Jones, Mark. *Knowing Christ*. Edinburgh: Banner of Truth, 2015: 127–34.

Pannenberg, Wolfhart. *Systematic Theology*. Vol. 3. Grand Rapids: Eerdmans, 1997: 606, 622–26, 636.

Reymond, Robert L. *A New Systematic Theology of the Christian Faith*. 2nd ed. Nashville: Nelson, 1998: 559–64.

Sonderegger, Katherine. *The Doctrine of God*. Vol. 1 of *Systematic Theology*. Minneapolis: Fortress, 2015: 433–40.

Tillich, Paul. *Systematic Theology: Existence and the Christ*. Vol. 2. Chicago: University of Chicago Press, 1957: 160–65.

Name Index

Scripture Index